# THE STREETCARS
## OF
# NEW ORLEANS

*Courtesy N.O.P.S.I.*

# THE STREETCARS
## OF
# NEW ORLEANS

By
Louis C. Hennick
E. Harper Charlton

**JACKSON SQUARE PRESS**
Gretna 2005

Printed in the United States of America
Published by Jackson Square Press
1000 Burmaster Street, Gretna, Louisiana 70053

# TABLE OF CONTENTS

# ACKNOWLEDGMENTS

Compilation of this volume was no less easy than the first volume, although the outline and much of the data had been accomplished by the publication of E. Harper Charlton's "Street Railways of New Orleans" in 1955. Many of the dates in the earlier work had to be verified, and many necessary dates not appearing in that work had to be painstakingly researched. There were, regrettably, some errors in "Street Railways of New Orleans" that this volume rectifies. Also, there is a wealth of totally new data appearing in this volume. Most of the photos are different ones from those that appeared in Charlton's 1955 work. Practically a new book had to be written and constructed — but the foundation had been securely laid in 1955.

Again, illness in the family and other problems curtailed Charlton's research activities. Most of the "leg work" and research was done by Hennick, as well as the actual writing of pages. Photos were difficult to ferret out of the usual vague tangles which they seem to inhabit. However, the authors were fortunate in finding photos of equipment that did not appear in the 1955 book. There are much better car plans and maps this time, also.

The libraries of Centenary College, City of New Orleans, Louisiana State Museum, Louisiana State University, New York City, Philadelphia Free Library, St. Mary's Dominican College, and Tulane University provided all of the newspaper files and traction publications mentioned in the Bibliography, as well as most of the source-publications listed therein.

The City Engineering Department permitted us to use their 1925 New Orleans map, for which we are most grateful. Ordinance data from Clerk of Court and City Library.

Many difficult to obtain dates and other data important to the volume were obtained from New Orleans Public Service Inc. records. Scores of department heads and employees of the company assisted in the compilation of data. The authors shall always be most grateful for that help and regret that space does not permit listing the vast number of N.O.P.S.I. people who helped us.

Mr. Ed Gebhardt's car plans speak for themselves and greatly enhance the value of this volume. The drawings are well chosen — both ancient and modern rolling stock are represented.

Charlton, who was on the scene for much New Orleans street railway history, was the chief proofreader. Also lending much time as proofreader and researcher was Miss Rita Ann Collins. Miss Collins, Mr. Ed Gebhardt, and Mr. Otto A. Goessl helped the authors locate old photographs. Photographs in large numbers were loaned by N.O.P.S.I. and also by several photographers whose names appear elsewhere. To these people the authors are specially grateful.

Gathering photographs and historical data requires the assistance of many people; the authors owe special thanks to Mr. Francis P. Burns, Mr. Boyd Cruise, Mr. Charles "Pie" DuFour, Mr. John F. Gibbons, Jr., Mrs. H. F. Reynick, and Mrs. J. F. Scott.

Locomotive data for the really old engines was provided by Mr. R. B. Carneal. Mr. Loring F. Wilcox of the Railway & Locomotive Historical Society secured Porter and Baldwin locomotive records. Mr. Harold E. Cox provided data on the St. Louis Car. Co.

LOUIS C. HENNICK                    E. HARPER CHARLTON

# THE STREETCARS
### OF
# NEW ORLEANS

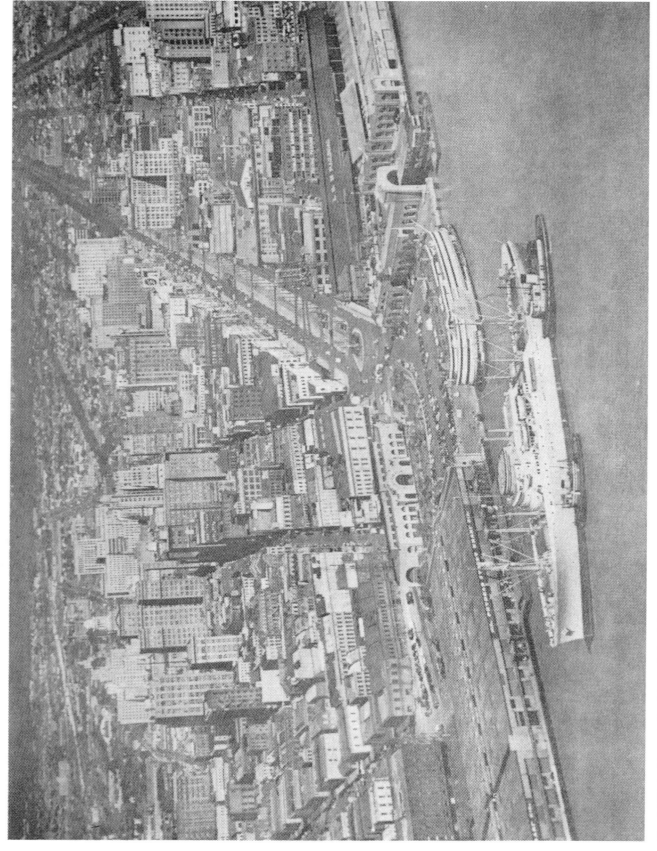

March 1953, looking out Canal towards the Lake.

Looking East—"Crescent City". Huey P. Long Bridge right foreground is 12 miles from downtown New Orleans. Photo taken about 1936.

# GENERAL HISTORY
## CHAPTER I
### INTRODUCTION

Only a tiny Indian village occupied the site of present day New Orleans when the French Nobleman Bienville explored the Mississippi River's lower portion in 1699. As Governor of the Louisiana Territory, the Frenchman returned in 1718 with an impressive band of troops, officials, and settlers seeking a new location for the territory's capitol. Where the French Quarter of New Orleans is today was Bienville's choice. The founding site was the ground now known as Jackson Square ("Place d'Arms" in the early days). The area was cleared of timber, immediately settled, and named "New Orleans" in honor of the Duc d'Orleans, Regent of France. Strategically located near the coast, on a river, and in the middle of a potentially rich resource and trade area, New Orleans was destined for fantastic growth and wealth.

Early population figures give an index for this "fantastic" growth: 1810 — 17,242; 1820 — 27,176; 1830 — 46,082; 1840 — 102,193. The city's development not only has been rapid, but also turbulent. "La Plus Belle Nouvelle Orleans" has saluted flags of France, Spain, The Confederate States, and The United States. No place in the city bears better testimony to this rapid fire change of government than does the "Vieux Carré". The term "Vieux Carré", commonly used in referring to the Franch Quarter, literally means, "Old Square". The limits of this old district, the beginnings of New Orleans and the heart of the city's charm, are the River, North Rampart Street, Esplanade, and Canal Street. French and Spanish influences that nurtured the city's culture are well stressed, but less known are the contributions of Irish, German, Italian, and other nationalities. The New Orleans "Times", a newspaper of the 1870s, used the Irish term "peelers" to designate policemen. As so with other names common to the British Isles ("van" and "float" respectively meaning closed wagon and heavy dray, for instance). Population figures published in 1867 by New Orleans' "Daily Picayune" paper are revealing: total for the city; 225,000 including 85,000 foreign, as follows: French, 25,000; Irish, 20,000; German, 20,000; Sicilian, 5,000; Italian, 5,000; Oriental, Greek, etc., 1,000; plus a figure of about 200 persons attached to the grand total, titled "Indigent". Such comprehensive illustrations defining New Orleans' cosmopolitan framework have been somewhat scarce. Is the city provincial enough to be reticent in disclosing exactly how cosmopolitan it is? Perhaps the "French" Quarter is an example. It is not entirely French. Many Spanish and even some Italian people have inhabited the Quarter. French Quarter architecture is "Latin" in nature, reflecting both Spanish and French influence.

Two wars seem to pinpoint eras in New Orleans' history and growth. After the Battle of New Orleans (1815), the last battle fought in the War of 1812, the city began expanding above Canal Street, along and

3

also out from the River. The 1820s saw much development in this area, the "American Quarter". James H. Caldwell and Samuel J. Peters, residents of the "Vieux Carré", were manifest in promoting and fostering this new Quarter. Docks, stores, banks, hotels, theaters, and homes were built in the American Quarter. The groundwork for New Orleans' commercial growth was firmly laid with the establishment of this new section.

The War Between the States caught New Orleans in the midst of an economic boom. The city had become a busy sea AND river port, comparable to the large Atlantic Coast ports of the North. Banking and financial wealth were mushrooming. The cotton and sugar trade also had been quite instrumental in nourishing New Orleans' boom. Railroads were penetrating the interior, increasing the trade and commerce of the port. The early Union capture and occupation of New Orleans checked the city's growth for several years.

Many elements have tried to dominate New Orleans. Yellow Fever, cholera, malaria, bubonic plague, and typhoid fever have disrupted the community. Hurricanes have wrought havoc. The soil is soggy and demands unique and frustrating building standards. For the city to expand, swamps and marshes must be drained. Torrential billions of mosquitoes frequently invade the city. New Orleans can be painfully cold, then suddenly become soaked in humid torpor. Yet, the city remains unvanquished.

The dominating element is WATER. The Mississippi River has made merciless onslaughts upon the city, but thanks to modern flood control techniques, the River has been curbed. Today, the city is laid out with "protection" levees (warding off water from the Mississippi River, Lake Pontchartrain and marshy lowlands) on all four sides. The serpentine bends of the Mississippi River gave New Orleans one of its more popular nicknames, "The Crescent City." The River is responsible for the growth and prosperity New Orleans enjoys. Manufacturing and industrial fabrication per se did not spark the city's rise in commerce. New Orleans was, and is, a port. The goods of the world have long flowed over ships' sides onto its wharves. Only lately have manufacturing and assembling activity enhanced the city's economic life. Well over a thousand products are now made or processed there. Long famed as a dispenser of "cotton, cane, and cocktails," New Orleans has expanded the trinity to enormous proportions.

In concluding this introduction to New Orleans, how citizens there figure and compute directions should be explained. It is essential to hold in mind that directions are reckoned with one's back to the river. That part of the city below Canal Street designates the streets starting from Canal Street as North—via North Rampart, etc. Most streets running from Canal Street on the upper or Southern section are given the prefix "SOUTH", such as South Claiborne, etc. "Back o' Town" refers to parts of the city from Rampart Street and "out" toward Lake Pontchartrain. "Over the River" is the Fifth District, Algiers. Going toward Lake Pontchartrain is "OUT". The opposite direction is "IN", to the River. Going toward the Gulf, or with the River's current, is "DOWN." Opposite direction is "UP". From approximately Jackson Avenue to a few blocks below, or "down" from, Canal Street, the River flows directly true North, then turns East, and continues to meander to the Gulf of Mexico, 110 miles below the city. A look at a New Orleans map will show West End directly North, and Southport as far West as one can go to the Southern limits of the city — UPTOWN. When one has gone to the LOWER end of the NORTH side of town, he has gone to the actual EASTERN boundary of the city. Therefore, DOWN is NORTH, and UP is SOUTH. Distinctive, fresh with surprises — a city of eternal enigma — our New Orleans!

# PRIMAL CITY TRANSPORTATION
## IN
## NEW ORLEANS

Any chronological outline of the development, operation, and decline of city transportation in New Orleans, specifically rail transportation, reaches back in time one hundred and thirty three years, to 1831. This presents a controversial situation if dogmatic rail terminology is strictly obeyed. The first railroad west of the Alleghenies, the very first in Louisiana and in New Orleans, was not strictly a "street railway", but rather, a suburban railroad. Such historic distinction embellishes the Pontchartrain Railroad Company. As early as 1825, there was discussion about building a railroad line from downtown New Orleans to the shore of Lake Pontchartrain. Talk turned to action in 1829, with the New Orleans Railroad Society formed to organize such an enterprize. An ACT of the Louisiana Legislature incorporated the Pontchartrain Railroad Company on January 20, 1830. The New Orleans "Daily Picayune" reported "the axe was driven into the first tree, March 10, 1830" as P. RR. President M. W. Hoffman and Engineer Gen. Swift commenced the task of pushing the standard gauge railroad through marshes and swamps. In one year the British-forged rails were laid. The five mile line began near the foot of Elysian Fields Avenue, at Decatur Street, and ran out Elysian Fields to the lakeside community of Milneburg. Hundreds of curious people gathered about the railroad depot at Decatur and Elysian Fields to witness the first run, on April 23rd, 1831. Locomotives ordered from Great Britain had not arrived, thus horses were pressed into service to pull the cars. Six cars, each with a horse as motive power, carried Louisiana's dignified elite on that first public railroad operation in Louisiana. The first car was alloted to Governor Andre Roman and State department heads, the second to New Orleans city authorities, the third to the crashing cymbals and sounding brass of a musical band, the fourth to Pontchartrain RR. directors, and the last two were filled with stockholders and guests. The newspaper account in the "Picayune" alluded to a sparkling celebration at Milneburg, with all parties on that first ride dining and toasting the railroad's success unto a late hour. The "Picayune" neglected to describe the well-wishers' return to town.

Pontchartrain Railroad service during horse operation was unusual. On February 13, 1832, the P. RR. announced in the Louisiana "Advertiser" that, repairs having been made to the railway, service will operate as follows: daily except Sunday, cars leave New Orleans for Milneburg at 10:00 A.M., 12:00 Noon and 4:30 P.M. Milneburg departure time the same. On Sundays, service began at 7:00 A.M. and was operated *half-hourly* until evening.

The steam locomotive made its first appearance in Louisiana on the 15th of June, 1832. The Louisiana "Advertiser" reported on this date the steam engine built by Mr. John Shields arrived from Cincinnati on the steamer " '76". This was the locomotive "Shields", unfortunately an unsuccessful machine. Later in the year, the British locomotive building firm Rothwell, Hicks & Rothwell built the locomotive "Pontchartrain" for the Pontchartrain RR. The engine (called a "steam car" in those early days) arrived in New Orleans in September and was tested for the first time on September 6th, 1832. The first official trip to Milneburg was made by the "Pontchartrain", pulling twelve cars, on September 27, 1832.

The Pontchartrain RR. Co. published a timetable in the Louisiana "Advertiser" when steam locomotives entered service, as follows: The steam train made seven trips to Milneburg, daily except Sunday, leaving New Orleans at 9:00 and 10:30 A.M., 12:00 Noon, 2:00, 3:00, 4:30, and 6:00 P.M. A horsecar made three trips, daily except Sunday, leaving New Orleans at 6:00 and 7:30 A.M. and 7:30 P.M. On Sundays there was no horsecar service, but the steam train made nine trips to Milneburg, leaving New Orleans at 7:30, 9:00, and 10:30 A.M., 12:00 Noon, and 2:00, 3:00, 4:00, 5:00, and 6:00 P.M.

Steam locomotives increased the Pontchartrain RR's hauling capacity. Great quantities of freight and many passengers were unloaded at Milneburg from Lake and coastwise vessels for the five mile rail journey to New Orleans. Vessels of light displacement no longer needed to make the lengthy trip to the mouth of the Mississippi in order to reach New Orleans.

The one way fare to Milneburg from New Orleans was 37½¢, round trip 75¢, at first. Through the years the fare was successively reduced. In the 1850s, it was cut to 25¢ one way, and further reduced to 20¢ one way (10¢ for children under 12) April 1, 1876.

Some pertinent facts in connection with the Pontchartrain RR. include the formation of the first railroad society in the United States, interesting not only for its early date (1829) but also for the fact that it succeeded. The P. RR. pioneered advances in rail technology, some successful, some not. It had the first freight loading platform. Old and New World railroads had been loading and unloading freight in the manner that wagons had been loaded — by hand and/or hand cranes. Initial heavy volume inspired Superintendent Capt. Grant to devise the freight platform, the CAR-

Pontchartrain passenger service, circa 1900. Handed down L&N locomotives and coaches were used. View is on pier at Milneburg. Engineer is father of photograph's donor. Other persons unidentified.

LEVEL type. Since the road's most powerful locomotive in 1832 equalled but 24 horses, augmenting locomotive horse-power was experimented with. At one time even *sails* were tried. The appearance of more powerful engines ended such experiments.

An amusing anecdote concerned Milneburg. The place had no police station. Rowdies at the hotels and saloons there were herded into a boxcar with barred windows that the P. RR. maintained on a siding. Each night its contents were delivered to New Orleans police downtown, at the arrival of the last train.

Actual street railway construction in New Orleans was discussed in 1833 and accomplished in 1835. On the 9th of February, 1833, the Louisiana Legislature approved the charter of New Orleans & Carrollton Railroad Company. The charter asked for a line from New Orleans to the suburb of Carrollton (a distance of approximately five miles), with two branches. One branch was built in the town of Lafayette (not to be confused with the present city of Lafayette, about 165 miles West of New Orleans on the Southern Pacific RR.) on Jackson Avenue, from Nayades (now St. Charles Avenue) to the River. The other branch was built from Baronne and Poydras, in the city proper, to Magazine Street, and up that street to La Course Street,

and in La Course to New Levee Street (now South Peters).

To clarify the picture as seen today, the various suburbs along the way will be described in terms of present street names. In 1833, the upper limit of New Orleans was near Melpomene Street, and from that point on there were various suburbs up to Carrollton (*Livaudais*, between Melpomene and Felicity; *Lafayette*, between Felicity and Toledano; *Jefferson*, between Toledano and Upperline and including the community of *Freeport*, lying on both sides of Napoleon Avenue; *Avart*, approximately between Upperline and Peters, or Jefferson, Avenue; *Rickerville*, approximately between Peters Avenue and Joseph; *Hurstville*, approximately between Joseph and Nashville Avenue; *Bloomingdale*, on both sides of State Street; *Burtheville*, just below present-day Audubon Park; *Greenville*, approximately between Moquer Avenue and Lowerline, and next was Carrollton). The suburb of Lafayette was the Parish seat of Jefferson Parish (there are no counties in Louisiana—those divisions are known as "Parishes"). Lafayette was founded in 1832, joined to New Orleans in 1852. The parish seat was then removed to Carrollton, which was in Jefferson Parish at that time. The court house, built in 1855, still stands today (see: ROUTES. St. Charles Belt Line). During the 1840s and 1850s,

Jefferson *absorbed* the various suburbs lying between it and Carrollton. The former was incorporated by New Orleans in 1870, but the latter retained its independence until 1874. The limits of New Orleans then embraced Carrollton and extended to the Upper Protection Levee (or, 17th Street Canal), where the limits are today.

On the 9th of December, 1834, the New Orleans & Carrollton R.R. Co. accepted the offer of Mr. George Baumgard for "two horses and a driver for the Magazine Street railway car at 4.50 a day" (quote from N.O. & C. RR Co. minutes). During the first week in January, 1835, the Poydras-Magazine "branch" commenced operations with cars leased from the Pontchartrain RR. Co. All lines of the New Orleans & Carrollton RR. Co. were standard gauge — 4' 8½". The Poydras-Magazine operation was the first true street railway line in New Orleans and the second in the World (the first being in New York City). On January 13, 1835, the line on Jackson Avenue began service, from Baronne and Canal, up Baronne, Delord, Nayades, and Jackson to the River. The latter line, serving the town of Lafayette, quickly earned the nickname, "The Lafayette Line". These lines' routes were entirely on streets or in streets' neutral ground, with no break in the continuity of houses. One could discern no features which made him aware of passing from one community to the next. April 1, 1835, the charter of the New Orleans & Carrollton RR. Co. was revised and printed, under the corporate name, "La Compagnie du Chemin a Coulisse de la Nouvelle-Orleans et de Carrollton". Literally translated, this means "The New Orleans & Carrollton GROOVE-road Company". The rails on the Magazine Line (possibly the Jackson Line, too — but this is not certain) were the primative strap and groove type. A flanged wheel was not necessary, as the grooved rails could accommodate a flangeless wheel.

THOSE persons who wish to take passage in the cars at any intermediate stopping points between N. Orleans and Carrollton, are particularly requested to make some motion or signal to the engineer of the locomotive previous to his arriving at that point in day-light; after dark, it is necessary, in order that the engineer may stop, that a lamp should be held out.
GEORGE MERRICK,
Chief Engineer N. O. and C. R. R.
sept 13—tf.

From *Daily Picayune* Oct. 18, 1838
It's easier today—we stand at a car stop.

The Carrollton Line (later St. Charles Line) was opened to the public with steam powered passenger trains on Saturday, September 26, 1835, at 11:00 AM. On Monday, September 28, 1835, the New Orleans "Bee" had this to say: "The railroad from the city to Carrollton on the Mississippi, distant about four and a half miles, was opened to travel on Saturday last. The route passes through a level and beautiful country; very high (Ed. note: about six feet higher than Canal Street), dry and arable land. We were very much gratified in witnessing the various improvements, and could not help hoping that next summer the forest of live oaks would be rendered fit for an agreeable ramble for our ladies and their escorts. The fare is but 25¢, while that on the Pontchartrain Railroad is 37½¢ for about the same distance; and certainly the ride to Carrollton is much more pleasant."

Travel on New Orleans & Carrollton RR's "steam cars" (passenger trains) was not cheap by today's standards. Currently, a ride on a St. Charles Line streetcar costs but a dime with the awful inflation of our times. Yet, in the 1830s when standards of living were quite different, the rail fare from Canal and Baronne up to Carrollton was 25¢ (2½ times present fare but probably FOUR times the purchasing power of today's dime). The fare from Canal and Baronne just to Jackson Ave. was 18½¢.

Horse, or mule, cars serviced the Poydras-Magazine and "Lafayette" (Jackson Avenue) Lines. The British-built locomotives "New Orleans" and "Carrollton" provided the steam train service to Carrollton. In the middle and late 1830s, steam train service on the N.O. & C. RR. Co. consisted of seven round trips to Carrollton. A schedule appearing in the New Orleans *Commercial Bulletin* gave the following times: After the 4:00 AM horsecar left Carrollton for a round trip to New Orleans, all other times were handled by steam trains. From Carrollton, trains departed for New Orleans at 8:00 and 10:00 AM, 12:00 Noon, 2:00, 4:00, 6:00, and 8:00 PM. From New Orleans, trains departed for Carrollton at 7:00, 9:00, and 11:00 AM, 1:00, 3:00, 5:00, 7:00, and 9:00 PM. Jackson Avenue mule car runs started from Canal Street at 6:00 AM and from Lafayette (town) at 6:30 AM. Service was hourly until 7:00 AM when half hour headways were maintained. The Poydras-Magazine Line had been discontinued in 1836. A new line, the La Course Street Line (see: Routes, chapter 3), was built the same year and provided identical service as that operated by the Jackson Avenue Line. Service headways on the Carrollton Line were shortened from every two hours to hourly on July 22, 1838.

An unusual mode of city transportation came into use in New Orleans in the 1840s. Passenger barges were operated out the New Canal (later New Basin Canal and now filled in) from the vicinity of Delord (now Howard Avenue) and Rampart Streets to Canal Port (near present day West End) on the Lake end. The barges were towed by mules walking along the bank of the canal. Fare charged was only 20¢, cheaper than the Pontchartrain RR. and the omnibus that operated out the New Canal Shell Road at that time. The passenger barges operated until shortly before the War Between the States, and in 1866 were revived for an unknown length of time. The passenger barge or boat is not really extinct today as a mode of city transit —

in Amsterdam, Holland, motor vessels do ply regular transit routes in some parts of the city to this day.

The American Quarter of New Orleans expanded during the 1840s. Houses began to line the countryside along the N.O. & C. RR. main line to Carrollton, with a public road on each side of the track (this was Nayades, later St. Charles Avenue). In 1848, there was enough potential business along Napoleon and Louisiana Avenues to justify branch lines, so felt the New Orleans & Carrollton RR. January 18, 1848, the N.O. & C. RR. obtained permission from the Council of the Borough of Freeport to build single track street railway lines in Napoleon and Louisiana Avenues between Nayades and the River. Both lines were put into operation on the same day, February 4, 1850. Fares were adjusted. The new mule car lines, Louisiana and Napoleon, charged 10¢ and 15¢ respectively. Fares covered a trip to downtown New Orleans, although a transfer was necessary at Nayades. Jackson Line fare was reduced to 10¢ and Carrollton Line fare cut to 15¢. Commutation tickets were sold, $8.00 per 100 for the Louisiana Line and $12.00 per 100 for the Napoleon Line.

The year 1850 saw and heard many items of railway interest in the New Orleans area besides the New Orleans & Carrollton's Louisiana and Napoleon Lines. Interest in a second railway to connect New Orleans with Lake Pontchartrain was revived. Ten years earlier, on March 25, 1840, the Louisiana Legislature had passed an act incorporating the Jefferson & Lake Pontchartrain Ry. Co. This line was projected to extend from Carrollton to Lake Pontchartrain, connecting with the N.O. & C. RR. at Carrollton for New Orleans service (SEE: Chapter 3, ROUTES, for detailed description of the J. & L.P. Ry. route). The plan lay dormant, mainly due to the absence of any potentially heavy traffic. But, 1850 was an explosion of railroad interest in New Orleans. Railroads from New Orleans to Jackson, Miss. and from New Orleans to the WEST, perhaps as far as TEXAS, were publicly urged by responsible parties. Two rail-minded groups announced intentions to build railroads to Lake Pontchartrain from New Orleans. One was the Lafayette & Pontchartrain RR. Co., organized 1850 (chartered March 12, 1852) to build a line from the town of Lafayette, from a point on the River near Jackson Avenue, out to the Lake. Although this project fell apart (even as solicitations for construction bids were advertised in New Orleans Daily "Picayune"), it aroused enough interest to move the New Orleans & Carrollton RR. to action. The N.O. & C. RR. acquired the rights to build the Jefferson & Lake Pontchartrain Railway Co. in 1850 and promptly hacked out a right of way. The J. & L. P. Ry. was built strictly according to the original plan. President G. C. Duncan of the N.O. & C. RR. AND the J. & L. P. Ry. officiated as the line's first train jolted out to Lake Pontchartrain on April 14, 1853. The new locomotive "Lake" was used for that inaugural trip.

The new railway was more similar to the suburban operation of the Pontchartrain RR. Co. than to the street railway lines. Service was steam, with through passenger trains operated from Lakeview (later called Bucktown) to Tivoli Circle via Carrollton. Lakeview was mainly a recreation spot, featuring shaded walks, a restaurant, bar, saloon, pistol gallery and a bath house. Later, after Lakeview became Bucktown, games of chance were introduced and more restaurants were built. However, Bucktown never achieved the popularity of Milneburg, and the place provided less passenger traffic than the New Orleans & Carrollton Railroad had expected.

Bucktown's eating establishments had an enjoyable atmosphere. Many were built out over the water, and some are still in existence today. Bruning's, for instance, has been known through the years as a place at which one can enjoy the wide selection of typical New Orleans dishes, with seafood predominating. Many scenes for the movie, "A Streetcar Named Desire" were shot at Bruning's.

The 1850s witnessed a flourish in New Orleans' economy. The city experienced a 44.9% increase in population between 1850 and 1860 (from 116,375 to 168,675). Two trunk line railroads were built, the New Orleans Jackson & Great Northern RR. from New Orleans to Jackson, Miss. and the New Orleans Opelousas & Great Western RR. from Algiers (across the River) to Brashear (on the Atchafalaya River). The trade of New Orleans' port increased proportionately.

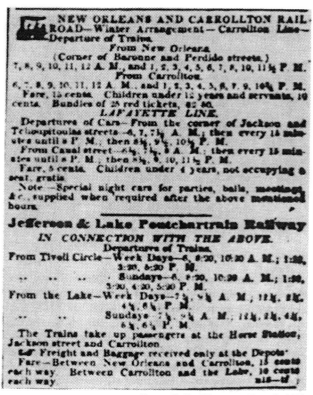

**From *Daily Picayune* Dec. 5, 1855**

*Courtesy N.O.P.S.I.*
Duckback roof sported by O.RR. mule car. Canal, Dumaine and Fair Grounds Line became Broad Line. About 1880, location unknown.

## STREET RAILWAYS COME OF AGE

Prior to 1861, street railways did not cover New Orleans with a city-wide network. In fact, in 1860, there were only four street railway routes in operation in New Orleans, all owned by the New Orleans & Carrollton RR. Co. and all running in the newer "American" Quarter of the city above Canal Street. The gap in years between the first street railway line and the city-wide system is not unusual. Such a development pattern took place in other large cities, New York City, Philadelphia, London, and Paris being good examples. Reasons for this pattern are not clear. Street railways tended at that time to be built in areas that were built up, well populated, and with a traffic potential already established. The "American" Quarter of New Orleans with its neighboring community of Lafayette certainly qualified in 1835, when the N.O. & C. RR. opened its Poydras-Magazine, and Jackson Avenue street railway lines. Yet, the older French Quarter of the city was as well suited to street railway lines. Not until 1868 was the French Quarter traversed by a street railway (Orleans RR. Co's. Bayou St. John Line). Earlier, car lines were built down streets forming that section's limits — the New Orleans City RR. Co's Rampart and Esplanade Line in 1861 and the same company's Levee and Barracks Line (on North Peters) in 1866. The scheme to build street railways as promotional devices came later, and was quite common after 1900. Land development was the usual idea (see Vol. I, page 13, last paragraph and page 14, first paragraph).

In the 1830s, 1840s, and 1850s, if one did not live in proximity to the four street railway lines of the New Orleans & Carrollton RR. Co., the omnibus was the only other form of regularly scheduled "mass transit" service available in New Orleans. New Orleans had a well developed system of horse drawn omnibus lines that have an interesting history — and an early beginning. The year omnibus lines began in New Orleans can be traced back to early 1832, or POSSIBLY late 1831. The need for better transportation caused by the location of the Pontchartrain RR's. station near the foot of Elysian Fields Avenue and the Levee Steam Cotton Press Co. on Levee Street (North Peters Street now) between Montegut and St. Ferdinand Streets brought about the city's first omnibus line. The P.RR.began service April 23, 1831, and the cotton press opened to business Feb. 1, 1832, according to the Louisiana "Advertiser". In late 1831 or early 1832, an omnibus line with small vehicles started service from Canal and Chartres Streets, down Chartres to Jackson Square, thence to Levee Street, and down that street to the cotton press, passing the railroad depot on the way. Inadequacy of the vehicles (probably due to limited carrying capacity) brought about their early replacement. An official announcement in the Louisiana "Advertiser" of December 19, 1832, gave notice that two new omnibuses built by Messrs. Carters of New York have arrived and will immediately go into service, replacing the two omnibuses that started service a while ago. The new vehicles were named "The Cotton Plant" and "The Tobacco Plant", and both were pulled by four horses. Fare was 12½¢, service offered over original route on a half hour basis, from 7:00 A.M. to 7:30 PM. The omnibuses carried letterboxes. Gentlemen were politely requested not to smoke in deference to ladies. With all the whooping about the big new omnibuses — the "Advertiser" neglected to mention who exactly owned the omnibus line!

More omnibus lines followed. May 15, 1838, Kip & Reed, Proprietors' Tchoupitoulas Line began with the bus "Columbia". Service was run hourly between Canal Street and Jackson Avenue with a 25¢ fare. Another operation starting about the same time was promoted by Mr. John Hoey. This line began at Canal and St. Charles, went up via Tivoli Circle and Dryades or South Rampart to Felicity. J. B. Slawson & Co. owned several lines, listed in Cohen's New Orleans & Lafayette Directory of 1849 as the "Rough & Ready Line of Omnibuses" with office at No. 6 Louisa. Slawson opened a grand trunk line of omnibuses on July 3, 1853—a line running from Canal and Chartres, down Chartres, and out Bienville Street and Metairie Road to the Cemeteries and the Half Way House. By 1860, according to the "Daily Picayune" of August 18, 1864, the complex of omnibus lines had become practically citywide (except for the N.O. & C. RR. Co's four street railway lines, that covered Baronne and St. Charles, Jackson, Louisiana and Napoleon Avenues). There were two omnibus lines on Tchoupitoulas, and lines on Magazine (from Canal Street to Planters' Press, opened 1839 by Kip & Reed, 12½¢ fare), Prytania, Apollo, Dryades, Esplanade, New Canal Shell Road, Bayou Road — also regular service from St. Charles Hotel to the New Orleans Jackson & Great Northern RR. depot at Clio and Solis (South Robertson), from Lafayette Square to the Mexican Gulf RR. depot at Elysian Fields and Good Children Street (now St. Claude), and from downtown New Orleans to Government Wharf.

Page XLI of A. Mygatt & Co.'s *New Orleans Business Directory,* dated 1858, lists the following omnibus lines and owners.

| | |
|---|---|
| New Basin & Apollo | Patrick Irwin |
| Common & Claiborne | J. B. Slawson |
| Mexican Gulf RR. (Station) | J. B. Slawson |
| Main St. (now Dumaine) | J. B. Slawson |
| Government Wharf | J. B. Slawson |
| Chartres | J. B. Slawson |
| Upper Shipping | J. B. Slawson |
| Magazine | Hart, Thomas & Co. |
| Camp & Prytania | Hart, Thomas & Co. |
| Tchoupitoulas | Hart, Thomas & Co. |
| Annunciation | Hart, Thomas & Co. |
| Bayou Road | Rodriguez, Binachi & Co. |

The tremendous rise in population New Orleans enjoyed during the 1850s, plus continued prosperous times and ever-expanding commerce put a terrific load upon the omnibus system. The horse drawn omnibus was an adequate city transit vehicle until increasing traffic demanded larger vehicles and closer headways. The street railway afforded the best means of solving the problems concomitant with mounting patronage. The iron wheel upon the iron rail, by reducing friction,

*Louis C. Hennick Collection*
The omnibus that operated from St. Charles Hotel to New Orleans Jackson & Great Northern RR. depot on Solis (now S. Robertson) between Clio and Calliope Streets. Print drawn circa 1854.

enabled a horse or mule to pull a heavier load, and to pull it faster than could an animal pull an omnibus across rough and uneven streets. Large cities with a mass transit problem in the 1860s were quickly discarding omnibuses in favor of the street railway. New Orleans did so between 1861-67. Were it not for the interruption by the War Between the States, the conversion no doubt would have been speedier.

Mr. J. B. Slawson, the owner of an omnibus system, made the first move toward a city-wide street railway system. On June 15, 1860, he and many constituents chartered the New Orleans City RR. Co. (the FIRST corporation to bear that name. In 1899 a SECOND corporation with that name was formed). Contractors to build the systems' six lines were Champlin & Buel and Mr. M. W. Hodgeman of St. Louis. The mule cars were built by Stephenson Car Co. of New York City. By Spring of 1861, much of the 5' 2½" gauge street railway was completed. Rolling stock was on its way by rail and water via Louisville, Ky. The outbreak of the Civil War in April caught the shipment of equipment at Louisville. The U. S. Secretary of Treasury impounded the cars. Prompt payment for the cars (no

Stephenson "bob tail" car, late 1860s, pedestal mounts and Bombay roof.

*Museum of The City of New York*

doubt in U. S. CURRENCY) loosed the Goverment's grip, and the cars proceeded to New Orleans.

Amid a gay celebration on June 1, 1861 that included unfurling a giant Confederate flag on Canal Street, the N.O.C.RR. Co's. first line, Rampart and Esplanade (later Esplanade) commenced operations. The other routes were opened in quick succession: Magazine, and Camp and Prytania (later Prytania) Lines on June 8th; Canal Line on June 15th; Rampart and Dauphine Line (later Dauphine) on July 1st; and Bayou Bridge and City Park Line a few weeks later. Each line is explained in detail, beginning with original route, in the chapter entitled "ROUTES".

Four car barns were established in 1861 that gave long years of service: Esplanade Barn at Bayou St. John; Magazine Barn at Pleasant Street; Canal Barn at White Street; and Poland Barn at Poland and St. Claude. These and other barns are taken up in detail in the chapter on "Barns and Structures".

The miracle of the New Orleans City RR. Co. was that it opened when it did. The beginning of the war nearly denied the arrival of the company's equipment. In fact, it prevented additional cars from being procured. Slawson had to improvise—some of his old idle omnibuses were placed on rail wheels and used until new cars arrived from Stephenson AFTER the war. The Confederate States formed their union on February 4, 1861. The first shot of the war was fired by Gen. P. G. T. Beauregard at Fort Sumter, S. C. the following April. More shall be seen of the General later in

connection with the New Orleans & Carrollton RR. Co. Sketchy notes are picked out of that company's minutes in keeping with the times, such as: week after week one or more directors record, "no quorum", and "the secretary of the New Orleans & Carrollton RR. lost no time in entering the service, being granted a leave of absence on April 29, 1861; he was appointed Colonel of the First Regiment of Louisiana Volunteers." Later in the year is encountered: "Brigadier Albert G. Blanchard's resignation as secretary to the Carrollton road (Ed. note—New Orleans & Carrollton RR. Co.) is accepted.

New Orleans suffered miserably during the War Between the States. A Federal invasion in the Spring of 1862 captured the city. For the rest of the war, New Orleans suffered military occupation. Business activity lessened—the city's economy faltered. In April of 1863, some railroad fares were reduced. The Jefferson & Lake Pontchartrain Ry. Co. and the Pontchartrain RR. Co. both cut their fares from 25c to 15c. The New Orleans & Carrollton RR. Co. cut its fare from Canal and Baronne to Carrollton down from 15c to ten cents, an a nickel fare was instituted from Canal and Baronne to St. Charles and Napoleon. Yet, there were service improvements. The N.O.&C. RR. Co. began on April 8, 1863 to run cars through from the stock landing at the foot of Louisiana Avenue to Canal and Baronne. An omnibus line, the "New Orleans & Carrollton Omnibus Line", was put into operation on March 6, 1863, by the Wm. Fry & Co. Service was operated from Carrollton Court House on Canal Avenue ('now South Carrollton Avenue), out Canal Avenue to Canal Street at first. In April, the line began turning off Canal Avenue into Common Street (now Tulane Avenue) and using Common to downtown New Orleans. Omnibuses ran on an hourly schedule between 6:30 A.M. and 6:30 P.M. with an 8:00 P.M. trip. Fare was 10¢, half fare for passengers under twelve years of age. Also, an intriguing little street railway managed to squeak into operation during the Federal occupation. An Act of the City of Jefferson dated October 15, 1861 put up for sale a franchise for two lines. One was up Magazine from Toledano to Joseph Street, the other up Prytania, also between Toledano and Joseph Streets. Connections were possible with New Orleans City RR. Co.'s Magazine Line at Magazine and Toledano, and the same company's Prytania Line at Prytania and Toledano. On October 30, Mr. Joseph Kaiser purchased the franchise and organized the Jefferson City RR. Co. Materials and equipment were somewhat difficult to obtain until July of 1863 when Federal Forces finished their capture of Vicksburg, placing the Mississippi River completely in their hands. Commerce again flowed — if anyone had the money. Apparently Mr. Kaiser had some capital. In February of 1863, Kaiser formally chartered the J.C. RR. Co. and began work on the Magazine Street portion late that year. However, his capital was exhausted when rails had extended up Magazine only as far as Cadiz Street. Kaiser was an apt promoter with no intention of quitting. As scarce as capital was in 1863-64, he managed financing and completed the Jefferson City RR. Co. route up Magazine (New Orleans "Daily Picayune" issues as early as October of 1865 credit the road with "service in operation"). Date service actually began is vague, but estimated to be sometime in 1864. The lightly patronized line was heavily in debt, and had failed to build the Prytania Street section according to the franchise (actually, this section—between Toledano and Joseph— was built finally in the 1880's by another company). Also, time limits for Magazine Street Line completion were not followed strictly. In 1865, the Jefferson City RR. Co. was reorganized. The new company, Magazine St. RR. Co., with Mr. Kaiser and Mr. Theodore J. Judt in charge, was likewise afflicted with poor patronage and heavy debts. Creditors wanted their investments and the City of Jefferson was anxious to prosecute the ailing street railway for failure to meets its franchise obligations. There were unpleasant accusations thrown about. One night in 1870, creditors and city officials broke into the railway's offices, carried the company safe into the street, and battered it open. Finding the safe empty did not dissuade the incensed "dignitaries" from hauling the Magazine St. RR. Co. into court. The result of this discord was a further reorganization, this time in 1873. With the financial help of Mr. George Mertz, the M. St. RR. Co. became Sixth District & Carrollton RR. Co. Still wobbly, the line was sold to Mr.

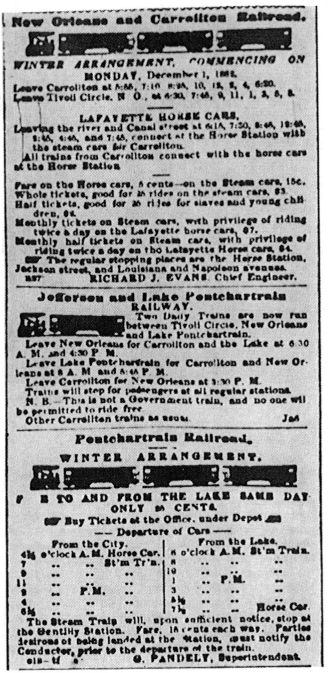

From *Daily Picayune* Feb. 4, 1863

Andre Brousseau in 1871. Company assets included ten cars, thirty mules, and almost two miles of 5' 2½" gauge line. Barns of the company were at Octavia and Magazine Streets. The corporation's troubles were solved in 1880 by selling out to a larger and financially secure street railway, the Crescent City Railroad Co.

The Crescent City RR. Co. was one of four successful wide gauge (5' 2½") street railways that sprung to life in New Orleans immediately following the Civil War. This company actually commenced operations BEFORE it was formally chartered! A strange way to do things, but there is an explanation. Rights to build the Annunciation and Tchoupitoulas Lines were *sold* by the City of New Orleans in 1866, authorized by city ordinance. Mr. David McCoard, Mr. Patrick Irwin, and associates, sponsors of the Crescent City RR. Co., bought these rights, quickly built one line (Tchoupitoulas) and started service August 10, 1866. Their company was chartered twenty days later. The following year, on February 27th, the Annunciation Line started service. In general, the Crescent City system brought street railway services to the dock, warehouse, and wholesale districts extending from downtown New Orleans, up the River to about Louisiana Avenue. Residential areas served were just "in" from the riverfront, included the well-known "Irish Channel".

Another important street railway commencing service in 1866 was the St. Charles St. RR. Co. Although the ordinance (CC 5957) for its Carondelet Line was approved March 11, 1862, the company was not organized until 1866 and the line opened July 29, 1866. First things first, the St. Charles St. RR. Co. was chartered AFTER service started, in the New Orleans "style" (September 27, 1866). Cars for the St. Charles system were built by Stephenson (New York City), shipped to New Orleans by sea transportation (The New Orleans "Daily Picayune" claimed by sailing vessels!) These were the white cars, long a strikingly familiar sight in New Orleans. The company's barns were built at 8th and Carondelet Streets, in an area then popularly called "Melpomenia".

Mr. J. H. Nicholson organized, built, and chartered the St. Charles St. RR. Co. Aside from this, he devised a method of street paving, encompassing a wooden frawework supporting an asphalt pavement. A contractor at heart, his nature was to attack the task at hand with unrelenting fervor, and keep at it until the job was finished. In November of 1866, the Rampart and Dryades Line (later Dryades) was opened, and January 23rd of the next year the Jackson RR. Depot Line (later Clio) commenced service, replacing an Omnibus line. This gave the St. Charles system three lines.

The New Orleans City RR. Co. considerably improved its plant in 1865-66. During the war, the company met a car shortage by placing old omnibus bodies upon railway wheels. These make-shift cars were replaced with new "bob-tail" type mule cars, built by Stephenson. The "bob-tail" car was characterized by having a front platform, but no rear platform (passengers entered through a door at the rear of the car). The first year for these cars was 1861. This car became the "standard" of the horse (or mule) cars. Many were built in New Orleans, some by New Orleans City RR. Co. and Crescent City RR. Co. A few cars were built for other systems (see Vol. I, page 11). The New Orleans City RR. Co. opened another line, Levee and Barracks, on May 14, 1866.

Gen. P. G. T. Beauregard and associates leased the New Orleans & Carrollton RR. Co. in May of 1866.

The General served as president for almost ten years. His first improvement was the double-tracking of Baronne Street, completed December 1, 1866. On May 30, 1867, steam locomotives were retired from the New Orleans & Carrollton and put up for sale.

After the Crescent City and the St. Charles systems, the next street railway to organize and commence service was the Canal & Claiborne Streets Railroad Co. Many of New Orleans' dignified and well known citizens financed the project, such as Mr. J. B. Slawson (past President of New Orleans City RR. Co.), Mr. E. J. Hart, Mr. J. S. Lapeyre (of the banking firm Pike, Lapeyre & Bros.), Mr. Hugh McClosky, and Gen. A. M. Labuzan. Gen. Labuzan (President of the Canal & Claiborne), and associates broke ground to start work on the new street railway October 19, 1867. Weather, even snow, made construction doubly difficult. Yet, on April 14, 1868, the Girod and Poydras Line was opened with a wine-toasted feast in company offices. The Canal and Claiborne Line (later Claiborne Line) followed one month later on May 13th.

The C. & C. Sts. RR. opened with new equipment, built by Stephenson. Gauge was the familiar 5' 2½", common to most of the street railways in the city but rather uncommon elsewhere. In every way, this system was modern and well planned. The barns at Common (now Tulane) and Rocheblave had a 308' fronting on Common Street. The barn had a paved floor (raised four feet to ward off high water), accomodated 100 cars with stalls for mules. The upper floor of the barn housed machinery for grinding and mixing feed. Canal & Claiborne even had a special mule car, numbered 1, more gaily painted and luxuriously upholstered (but similar in other respects) than the other equipment, that was used by company officers for inspection and business tours.

A less spectacular operation was the Orleans Railroad Company, organized in 1867-68 and opened (BEFORE chartering, of course) in mid-1868. Another 5' 2½" gauge mule car system, the O. RR. was organized by Mr. George Clark (elected President), Mr. Jules Boult, Geo. W. Hynson, Mr. Felix Labatut, Mr. L. E. Lemarie, Mr. B. Saloy, and Mr. D. B. Macarty. Contractors B. S. Harrison and John Bietry built the company's Canal, Dumaine and Bayou St. John Line (later Bayou St. John Line), which was opened July 4, 1868 (after "trial runs" on July 2 and 3). The Orleans Railroad Company got around to chartering its "body corporate" July 31, 1868.

Second hand equipment originated service over the Orleans RR. Co. New Orleans "Daily Picayune" issue commenting on the road's opening stated that cars were purchased from the New Orleans & Carrollton RR. Co. This was undoubtedly a typographical error, as the O.RR. Co. was 5' 2½" gauge, and the N.O.&C. RR. 4' 8½" gauge. Probably the paper meant to say N.O.C.-RR. Co. (New Orleans City RR. Co., 5' 2½" gauge) instead of "N.O.&C. RR.".

**Chemin de fer Pontchartrain.**

**ARRANGEMENT D'ÉTÉ.**

**Excursion de la ville au Lac, aller et retour, le même jour—25 cents.**

À partir du 15 avril 1871, les convois de ce chemin partiront comme suit:

| DU LAC. | | DE LA VILLE. Rue Girod. | |
|---|---|---|---|
| 5 heures du matin, | | 6 heures du matin, | |
| 6 " " | | 7 " " | |
| 7 " " | | 8 " " | |
| 8 " " | | 9 " " | |
| 9 " " | | 10 " " | |
| 10 " " | | 11 " " | |
| 11 " " | | 12 " Midi. | |
| 12 " Midi. | | 2 1|2 " Après midi. | |
| 2 1|2 " | | 3 " " | |
| 3 " " | | 4 1|2 " " | |
| 4 1|2 " " | | 5 1|2 " " | |
| 5 1|2 " " | | 6 1|2 " " | |
| 6 1|2 " " | | 7 1|2 " " | |
| 7 1|2 " " | | 8 1|2 " " | |
| 8 1|2 " " | | 9 1|2 " " | |
| 9 1|2 " " | | 10 1|2 " " | |
| Minuit | | | |

Un char à vapeur partira de la rue Girod tous les dimanches matin à 4 heures.

Un char à cheval partira de l'ancien dépôt, tous les matins à 4 heures et du Lac une heure après le dernier convoi à vapeur.

Les passagers qui désirent s'arrêter à Gentilly devront en prévenir le conducteur avant le départ du convoi.

Prix du passage jusqu'à Gentilly, 15 cents et autant pour revenir.

**THOS. O. DIMITRY,**
Assistant-Surintendant.

15 avril

From New Orleans *Bee*
This schedule shows Pontchartrain RR. operating to new station at foot of Girod Street. The French-language *Bee* lasted until 1921.

An extension of the Pontchartrain RR. Co. was opened July 19, 1868, extending to the foot of Girod Street from the terminus at Elysian Fields and Decatur. Suburban trains of the "Pontch" (later nicknamed "Smoky Mary") then offered substantially improved service, with stops at Canal Street and French Market added after the extension opened. Mr. George Pandely, the road's President, was seeing the Pontchartrain RR.'s best days. Morgan's famous Line of Steamers, such as the "Mary", "Frances", and "Louise", touched at Milneburg almost daily with U. S. Mail, tons of freight, and crowds of passengers destined for New Orleans. Lake and coastwise vessels also found the landing to be more convenient and speedier than going down to the mouth of the Mississippi and coming the 110 miles upstream to reach New Orleans. Pontchartrain RR. stock was selling at a premium, so much that people would advertise odd lots for sale in daily papers.

Not blessed with the dense passenger business or heavy freight traffic the Pontchartrain RR. enjoyed, the Jefferson & Lake Pontchartrain Ry Co. found operations to be financially impossible during the closing months of the Civil War. Service was run for the last time November 23, 1864. Salvagable rail was removed and used to upgrade worn sections of the New Orleans & Carrollton RR. Co. (which actually owned the defunct J.&L.P.). However, the Jefferson & Lake Pontchartrain Ry. Co. continued to exist "on paper", still owned right of way property, and for years held annual elections for officers. Ownership of J.&L.P. stock rested in the hands of the N.O.&C. RR. Co., following that road's changes in corporate structure through the years.

A proposition to display advertising placards in mule cars was finally adopted in New Orleans in 1868, after three years of mulling over the idea which was first presented to the city council on April 8, 1865. This is supposed to be, as far as records reveal, the first application of advertising in street cars.

Improvement of city transportation has been an unending quest, sometimes frustrating, but always fascinating. New Orleans had the LION'S share of street railway improvement experiments and patents. In 1866, the New Orleans City RR. Co. tried its "walking beam" car, a contrivance about as eccentric as could be conceived. The inventor, unfortunately, is unknown. The car was tested for some time on the Bayou Bridge and City Park Line. Propulsion of the car was achieved through the application of gear reduction and the counterbalance of the walking beam, plus a unique idea. The "motorman" turned a large wheel which set in motion, through gears, several other wheels and the walking beam on the roof, which in turn revolved a rimless wheel with spokes. Each spoke had a weight at its end, and as these spokes revolved, the weights came into contact with the ground and pushed the car. There was no compensating device to cope with changes in surface conditions or levels, and the fact that the device itself frankly played hob with the surface it encountered doomed the invention.

Pneumatic propulsion of mule cars was extensively experimented with by the Crescent City RR. Co. So promising was the invention of Mr. Charles W. Wailey that the Crescent City RR. Co. fostered a subsidiary corporation to handle the fabrication and testing of the device. July 30, 1868 the New Orleans Pneumatic Propelling Co. was chartered for that purpose. In December of 1868, a few Crescent City mule cars were fitted with 300-lb. pressure tanks (made of heavy paper, in rolls, with gum lining and steel ends) and tiny four horse power engines. The first tanks were unsuccessful, but in one year the system had been improved enough to warrant further trials. Experiments, with some cars running in regular service at sporadic intervals, extended into the 1870s. The appearance of the Ammonia, Thermo-specific, and fireless types of locomotives so interested the street railways that the pneumatic experiments were dropped.

Dr. Emile Lamm patented two types of locomotive propulsion principles, the Ammonia system (July 19, 1870) and the Thermo-specific system (April 9, 1872).

The famous walking beam car. About 1871, in front of Canal Station (Barn) at White St.

The potential worth of these inventions were weighty enough to call fourth much capital and interest, especially on the part of the New Orleans & Carrollton RR. Co. and Gen. Beauregard. For instance, the N. O. & C. RR. Co. in 1872 conducted comparative trials to determine the ammonia locomotive's economies over animal propulsion. It was found that to operate the ammonia locomotive cost $6.775 per day as compared to $9.910 per car per day for animal traction. Expenses of animal upkeep and feed, also labor and track work (plank walkway), were cut out by Lamm's invention. May 27, 1872 saw the charter filed for The Ammonia & Thermo-Specific Propelling Co. of America. New Orleans' "social register" staffed the Board of Directors. Dr. Emile Lamm, Mr. Leon Godchaux, Mr. P. J. McMahon, Mr. W. C. Wilson, Mr. Jules Brudy, Gen. Beauregard, Mr. G. L. Laughland (elected President of the company), and Mr. H. C. Millaudon put their signatures to the company's charter.

Mention of the ammonia engine showed in the "Daily "Picayune", February 21, 1871. The engine, tendered by Dr. Lamm, made several trips from the Clay Statue, out Canal Street to Halfway House and back. The engine was referred to as a "motor". Its workings were simple and very similar to a steam engine. Aqua-ammonia (1/5th part of Ammonia to 4/5ths part of water) was heated in tubes (flues) surrounded by water. The water was heated by a small coal flame (one barrel of coal required for three trips). The Ammonia effervesced rapidly, provided motivating power in cylinders. Ammonia was not allowed to escape, was retained to be mixed with water anew. However, the Thermo-Specific engine was more practical. Loss of energy in the transformation of the fuel into energy doomed the Ammonia engine. The Thermo-Specific engine used superheated water in 18" diameter tanks located on the roof of the "motor" (it was not clear in newspaper accounts if a "dummy" or a standard mule car was employed). Steam from the superheated water propelled the engine. However, having to constantly replenish the tanks rendered the experiment unwieldy for tight street railway operation. Dr. Lamm did not discontinue experimentation. August 24, 1872, The Combination Propelling Co. of New Orleans, Louisiana was chartered to build and sell the "motor" patented by Sylvester L. Langdon. Lamm joined forces with Langdon, and on December 10, 1874, the company was reorganized as The Lamm Fireless Engine Company. The product was similar to the earlier Lamm experiments. Several were bought by the Crescent City RR. Co. and the New Orleans & Carrollton RR. Co. All were converted to standard steam locomotive type propulsion. The engines were 0-4-0s and 2-2-0s with exposed boilers, both horizontal and vertical types. Incidentally, some of Lamm's Thermo-Specific engines saw street railway service in Paris, France beginning 1878.

Other companies in New Orleans testing locomotive propulsion were: Ammonia Motor & Railway Co., chartered September 2, 1890 to build and sell motor cars, organized by Atwood Violett, Thomas Woodward, and J. L. Byrne. Company dissolved 1891 and sold

15

to Standard Fireless Engine Co. of Chicago. Ill. In 1886, earlier tests were carried out with Ammonia cars on the New Orleans & Carrollton RR. Co. under the name, "Standard Fireless Engine Co.", but research failed to tie in this company with the later Chicago outfit. A little known company was the United States & European Propelling Car Co. Chartered March 22, 1872, its aim was to purchase from Henry Clay Bull and Benjamin Bloomfield certain patents for propelling street cars. These obscure organizations are mentioned and recorded in hopes someone can come forward with more information regarding their patents and products. Authors' research was fruitless.

This sidetrack into the world of the unreal—the intriguing attempts to replace the mule before electricity became predominant—should be closed in mentioning the most bizarre, fantastic, and "way-out" propulsion idea ever invented, barring VERY FEW. We won't say it was the "most"—surely man in his almost infinite imagination has ascribed to wilder schemes. This was none other than General Beauregard's overhead cable experiment, handled by his own company, The New Orleans Car-Traction Company (chartered March 29, 1870). A cable was supported over railway tracks by means of bracket poles. Two retired steam locomotives (stationary) were re-modeled to pull the cable. Cable was in constant motion. The "grip" extended from the car's roof, could be released when a stop was necessary, or closed about the cable to start the car. Experiments were conducted June-November,

1870. Yes, it was unsuccessful—but actually not to be criticized. It preceded the Halliedie and Casebolt cable street railway experiments in Oakland and San Francisco.

General Labuzan could watch and study his street railway from his North Claiborne Avenue home. His Canal & Claiborne Streets RR. Co. was constantly improving its operation. On May 8, 1869, the C. & C. Sts. RR. Co.'s "Grand Trunk Route" was opened, the outside tracks from North Basin to the foot of Canal Street, allowing the company's Canal and Claiborne Line to operate to the river. Labuzan's company was the only one seen by the authors to carry paid ads in the "Daily Picayune" promoting pleasure and Sunday riders.

Around-the-clock street railway service had not yet come to New Orleans, although late at night schedules were tried on at least one line. The New Orleans & Carrollton operated 12:30 A.M. and 1:00 A.M. cars on the Carrollton Line, on a trial basis, from November 14, 1869 to May 7, 1870.

Safety devices were tried by the New Orleans City RR. Co. in 1869. A rubber tube fender, the invention of Mr. Felix M. Dannoy, was fixed under a number of "City Railroad" cars.

November 6, 1870 was the starting date for the Orleans RR. Co.'s French Market Line. The year 1870 also saw a new street railway start construction. It was an ambitious plan—a second route between New Orleans and Carrollton, from Carondelet and 8th, up

Louis C. Hennick Collection

Lamm engines on New Orleans & Carrollton RR. Co., about 1875.

Carondelet and other streets to the upper limits of Carrollton. Service to downtown New Orleans via trackage rights over St. Charles St. RR. Co. Formed in 1870 as Carondelet Street & Carrollton City RR. Co., the new line built one mile of double track on Carondelet between 8th and Upperline Streets only to find the St. Charles St. RR. Co. would not permit trackage rights. Mr. Edmund Burke and Mr. N. Commandeur, principal backers of the project, considered building trackage into downtown New Orleans, but capital was not to be had. The project was closed down in August of 1872 and dismantled two years later. Newspapers commented upon the line's completion, but reference to actual service never could be found.

January 8, 1870, the city awarded a contract to John Roy & Co. to build the Protection Levee, the present boundry between Orleans and Jefferson Parishes. Consolidation of Algiers and Jefferson City with New Orleans was approved March 18, 1870. Population of New Orleans in 1870 was 191,418—a 13.5% increase over the previous census (1860).

Freight service (on a local, light basis) was provided by the New Orleans & Carrollton RR. Co. between New Orleans and Carrollton for many years until its discontinuance February 1, 1871. A solitary boxcar pulled by mule constituted the N.O. & C. RR. freight services. A new car line opened in 1871, Canal & Claiborne Sts. RR. Co.'s Canal and Common Line.

Ill tidings for the Pontchartrain RR. was the opening of the New Orleans Mobile & Texas RR. between New Orleans and Mobile, late in 1870. By 1871, Pontchartrain RR.'s business had dropped considerably— the freight that used to be unloaded from ships at Milneburg was coming into New Orleans over the N.O.M. & T. RR. The Pontchartrain was located strategically in downtown New Orleans, with its tracks extending along the waterfront between Girod and Elysian Fields. The directors of the Pontchartrain decided to hand over control of their property to the New Orleans Mobile & Texas RR. This was done December 12, 1871, although the Pontchartrain retained its corporate identity. March 12, 1872, some of the tracks between Girod and Elysian Fields were sold to the Morgan's Louisiana & Texas RR. & Steamship Co. "Pontch" passenger service returned to the pre-1868 operation, Milneburg to Elysian Fields and Decatur.

The New Orleans City RR. Co. opened the Barracks and Slaughter House Line on June 1, 1872. This year began a "doldrum" period for the company that lasted into 1874. In December of 1872 an epidemic of the "epizooty" struck beasts of burden in the New Orleans area—so many of the company's mules were ill that street railway service was practically non-existant for over a week. The 1873 annual report of the New Orleans City RR. Co. bemoaned "the deplorable financial condition of the whole community". The N.O. C. RR. Co. handled 1,128,135 LESS passengers in 1873 than in 1872. During 1873, the company complained

of receiving $2,500.00 in counterfeit nickels. This latter problem no doubt arose when the wheel of the first streetcar turned.

The year 1874 marked the twelfth year of carpetbag rule for New Orleans. On September 14, 1874, thousands of white New Orleans citizens took arms and rebelled. The infamous Metropolitan Police, upholders of the shameful carpetbag regime, were put to rout after a few moments of battle. Fighting lasted sporadically for fifteen or more hours. Some mule cars were used to buttress barracades for the white citizens' army. These cars were returned to their respective companies when fighting ceased. Several days were required for the city to return to normal, during which time no street railway service was run. A full and glorious account of 14 September, 1874 can be read in Mr. Stewart Omer Landry's "The Battle of Liberty Place".

There was some street railway construction in New Orleans in 1874. The Orleans RR. Co. opened its Canal, Dumaine and Fair Grounds Line (later Broad Line) and the St. Charles Street RR. Co. opened its Clio Line extension down Bourbon and up Royal (see: Routes). The New Orleans City RR. Co. opened a new line in 1874, the Levee and Esplanade (later French Market).

Jewell's "Crescent City, Illustrated" compiled accurate data of the various street railway lines in New Orleans for 1874. There were six street railway companies serving New Orleans at that time. The largest company was the 5' 2½" gauge *New Orleans City Railroad Co.* The company employed 400 men and carried about twelve million riders annually. Revenue averaged $625,432 annually (average determined by the company over the period 1871-74). Two and a half minute headways were maintained during rush hours. Frequency for rest of daytime service was five minutes. Dark to 10:00 P.M., ten minutes headways, cut to 15 minutes from 10:00 P.M. to last car at midnight. New Orleans City RR. Co. at this time repaired and BUILT cars at Canal Station. From 1872 to 1874, eleven open "excursion" cars were built for mule car service on Canal Street. The Canal Station also mixed feed for mules, performing that task for all the other N. O. C. RR. stations.

List of routes and car assignments, as follows:

| ROUTES | CARS ASSIGNED | | EXTRA CARS | |
|---|---|---|---|---|
| | 1873 | 1874 | 1873 | 1874 |
| Magazine | 28 | 24 | 2 | 8 |
| Prytania | 17 | 16 | 3 | 2 |
| Canal | 10 | 10 | 6 | 3 |
| Esplanade | 18 | 10 | 2 | 1 |
| Levee and Esplanade | | 10 | | 2 |
| Dauphine | 20 | 18 | 4 | 5 |
| Levee and Barracks | 19 | 16 | 2 | 5 |
| Barracks and Slaughter House | 6 | 6 | 0 | 0 |
| Bayou Bridge and City Park | 2 | 2 | 0 | 0 |
| TOTALS | 120 | 112 | 19 | 26 |

Re-capitulations of equipment, as follows:

| | 1873 | 1874 |
|---|---|---|
| Cars running (on the timecard) | 120 | 112 |
| Cars — extra | 19 | 26 |
| Open "excursion" cars | 2 | 3 |
| TOTAL CARS | 141 | 141 |

Animal-power (mules) stationed, as follows:

| | NUMBER OF MULES | |
|---|---|---|
| STATIONS (BARNS) | 1873 | 1874 |
| Camp | 87 | 89 |
| Canal | 73 | 69 |
| Esplanade ("Bayou Road") | 98 | 132 |
| Magazine | 152 | 147 |
| Poland | 248 | 234 |
| TOTAL MULES | 658 | 671 |

The second company in size was the *New Orleans & Carrollton Railroad Co.* with four lines, all 4' 8½" gauge (Carrollton, Jackson, Louisiana, and Napoleon). Two barns (one at St. Charles and Felicity, the other at St. Charles and Napoleon) handled the company's 59 cars and 249 horses and mules. Ten of Lamm's engines were providing motive power on the Carrollton Line in connection with mule cars. Steam trains made the run from Carrollton to Napoleon Avenue while mule cars operated from Napoleon Avenue down to Baronne and Canal. This steam operation was the last used by the New Orleans & Carrollton. The Carrollton to Napoleon service lasted from 1874 to 1889. Other phases of the railroad's steam train service were: 1835 to late 1830s, Canal and Baronne to Carrollton; late 1830s to mid 1840s, Poydras and Baronne to Carrollton; mid 1840s to 1862, Perdido and Baronne to Carrollton. From 1862 to 1867 trains terminated at Tivoli Circle station. Between 1867 and 1874 the N. O. & C. RR. did not use steam locomotives. Before steam trains were discontinued in 1867, mule cars and trains were used together on the Carrollton Line. Mule cars operated as local service from Canal Street to Jackson Avenue, while the steam trains were operated as express runs.

In 1874 the New Orleans & Carrollton RR. Co. was employing 140 men. Patronage averaged 4,863,354 riders annually during the period 1871-74. General Beauregard's constant improvements and increased efficiency were reflected in the company's stock value. In 1865, each share sold for $7.50. The value had increased to $110.00 by the early 1870's.

Third in size (but second in patronage) was the *Canal & Claiborne Streets RR. Co.* The company operated three 5' 2½" gauge lines (Girod and Poydras, Canal and Claiborne, and Canal and Common), employed 100 men to operate 12 miles, 40 cars, and 218 mules. A two year (1873-74) average of 6,000,000 riders supported the $59,000 annual payroll. C. & C.

Sts. RR. Co. had two barns (Rocheblave and Claiborne —see chapter on BARNS). Service was held to following headways: Daytime — Claiborne, three minutes; Common (Tulane), seven minutes; and Girod and Poydras, eight minutes. After dark and until midnight —fifteen minutes.

*St. Charles Street RR. Co.* operated three lines, all 5' 2½" gauge (Clio, Dryades, Carondelet), served by two barns, one at Clio and Magnolia and another at 8th and Carondelet. Although a driver may have worked on a car for sixteen hours, the mules were rotated so as to work only four or five hours at a time. St. Charles St. RR. Co. allotted four mules to each car on Clio and Carondelet Lines, but five per car on the Dryades Lines (because of curves and the rough condition of streets).

*Orleans RR. Co.* was operating three lines in 1874 —Bayou St. John, Broad, and French Market. Barns of this 5' 2½" gauge system were at Gentilly Boulevard, North Dupre and Laharpe Streets.

*Crescent City RR. Co.* maintained two lines (Annunciation, Tchoupitoulas) with 35 cars. Gauge was 5' 2½".

*Magazine St. RR.* had ten cars and two miles of track. Gauge was 5' 2½".

There was but one suburban steam operation (besides the N. O. & C. RR., mentioned earlier)—the *Pontchartrain RR. Co.* Local passenger traffic on the line was still impressive (half hour frequency during 1873 Fourth of July National Holiday) but freight service had dropped considerably. Lost forever were the through-travellers disembarking at Milneburg.

Pleasure-seekers increased with the growth in population. Most popular with these holiday travelers in the early 1870's was Milneburg. The pavilion of Denechaud & Jartoux, famous Taisconi's Restaurant, other night spots, shaded walks, and a beach, attracted those with leisure time. In fact, there was no other spot within such easy reach. Establishment of additional recreation and pleasure grounds on Lake Pontchartrain's shores had been actively discussed since the War Between the States, and since the 1864 abandonment of the railway to Bucktown (the Jefferson & Lake Pontchartrain Ry.).

On May 19, 1873, the Canal Street City Park & Lake RR. Co. was chartered. The route began at Basin and Customhouse (now Iberville), extended down Basin, out Bienville, Bernadotte, crossing and thereupon following the Orleans Ave. Drainage Canal to Lake Pontchartrain, then turning right and running to Spanish Fort, an amusement ground and boat landing built upon the site of an old Spanish fortress dating back to 1770. The new railway was steam powered and started service in 1875 (its timetable was printed for

*From New Orleans Times*
This railway later became the New Orleans Spanish Fort
& Lake RR. — schedule late 1875.

the first time in the New Orleans "Times" on October 3, 1875). Financial difficulty jolted the company through three presidents in as many years—1874, 1875, and 1876 respectively witnessed Mr. Joseph Sands, Col. Thomas H. Handy, and Mr. Joseph L. Smith.

The Canal Street City Park & Lake RR. did perform a small freight service. One of several lake steamers touching at Mandeville and other small lakeshore communities was the "Marie". Freight was unloaded from the steamers and taken to downtown by the railway. Competition from the Pontchartrain RR. was keen, as Lake Pontchartrain traffic was not immense by any stretch of the imagination, and the P. RR. had better transfer facilities at Milneburg.

More successful than the C. S. C. P. & L. RR. was the 5' 2½" gauge steam railway opened to West End in 1876. West End is that part of New Orleans at and below the Protection Levee, along the shore of Lake Pontchartrain for a quarter of a mile. The building of a railroad to this location from New Orleans was promoted by the New Orleans Metairie & Lake RR. Co., chartered April 29, 1869. Lack of capital prevented any construction. The New Orleans City RR. Co. decided to revive the N. O. M. & L. RR. Co. project and acquired that corporation's franchise rights through stock exchange, consummated December 21, 1875. During February and March of 1876, the N. O. C. RR. Co. built the new line, laying track from Half Way House out City Park Avenue to New Basin Canal, and alongside New Basin Canal to West End. On April 15, 1876, the first of the order for Porter "dummy" locomotives arrived in New Orleans for service on the West End Line. Service commenced April 20th, from Half Way House to West End. After citizen protests against anticipated smoke nuisance subsided, service was operated in Canal Street to Carondelet Street, beginning June 18, 1876. New cars for the dummies were built at Canal Station. These were single truck models, double end, seating 28 on reversible seats, with blinds to ward off the terrible heat and bright sunlight. Each car cost all of $700.

After the N. O. C. RR. Co. opened the West End Line (also called the "Canal Street Steam Railway" by the locals), Milneburg was referred to as "Old Lake End" and West End as "New Lake End". Fare to "New Lake End" was 25 cents at first, lowered to 10 cents July 5, 1878 (15 cents round trip, but 5 cents Carondelet Street to Half Way House, and five cents Half Way House to Lake).

Street railway improvements of 1876 were highlighted by the Crescent City RR.'s extension of the Tchoupitoulas Line to Upper City Park (now Audubon Park). The Crescent City RR. built a large dancing pavilion in the park. Lamm motors were being used on the Tchoupitoulas Line at this time, incidentally. These efforts to attract riders were accomplished by the Crescent City RR.'s President, Mr. Hugh Kennedy.

Pressure of the New Orleans City RR. Co. and Canal Street City Park & Lake RR. competition for pleasure-seekers forced the Pontchartrain RR. to lower the fare

*From Daily Picayune July 6, 1876*

to Milneburg. After April 1, 1876, fare was 20 cents one way, 10 cents for children under 12. This same month, the road went under. Mr. Daniel B. Robinson was appointed receiver (Robinson was also Superintendent of the New Orleans Mobile & Texas RR. Co.).

In 1877, the Chicago St. Louis & New Orleans RR. Co. (later Illinois Central RR.) planned a belt line for freight service, beginning at foot of Louisiana Avenue, extending out Louisiana Avenue, then down Claiborne Avenue to Calliope, connecting with the C. St. L. & N. O. RR. Co. To achieve this plan, the Commercial Transit Company was chartered July 20, 1877 (name changed to New Orleans Belt RR. Co.—not to be confused with later New Orleans Public Belt RR.—August 30, 1877). Construction started in July of 1877. There was one obstruction—the Louisiana Line of the New Orleans & Carrollton RR. Co. This line was very lightly patronized, and although the N. O. & C. RR. publicly fought to preserve it, nonetheless all trackage on Louisiana Avenue was sold to the N. O. B. RR. Co. in 1877 for only $7,500. The New Orleans Belt RR. Co. chartered an inspection trip over its completed line May 25, 1878, and the year 1878 can be regarded as the last for the New Orleans & Carrollton's Louisiana Line.

New Years Day, 1878, must have been too much for a Lamm motor operator on the Crescent City RR.'s Tchoupitoulas Line. That day involved a head on collision between two trains, each pulled by one of the Lamm steam engines. The operator of one leapt from the machine, leaving the throttle wide open. No casualties, save two ruined motors. New Orleans city ordinance A.S. 3243 (September 1875) extended to October 1, 1877, the time the C. C. RR. was permitted to operate the motors on Tchoupitoulas Street. Yet, the year 1878 saw an end to steam engines on the Crescent City RR. Co.

Street railways commonly charter their operations for a period of 99 years. There was a good reason, and the plight of the New Orleans City RR. Co. in 1879 illustrates it. During that year, the city noted that the original lines' franchises were "running out" of time. Cities are deadly in observing means to raise additional revenues. The city of New Orleans threatened to sell the original N. O. C. RR. franchises at public auction unless the railroad would renew them through purchase. In October 1879, President Wintz of the N. O. C. RR. borrowed the necessary $630,000 from an old friend and then New York banker, Mr. Samuel Smith. Mr. Smith, incidentally, was an ex-New Orleanian. Famous New Orleans city ordinance A.S. 6148 of October 2, 1879, re-sold the franchises to the "City Railroad".

The first eight years of the Canal Street City Park & Lake RR.'s life were financially spectacular in a manner quite opposite the dreams of the railroad's founders. The line went bankrupt in 1876 and was seized by the Sheriff on July 28th of that year. Mr. James A. Shakespeare (later Mayor of New Orleans) was appointed Receiver by the District Court in New Orleans. Shakespeare could do nothing with the property, turning it over to Mr. Thomas H. Handy on

July 14, 1877. Handy sold the line to M. Schwartz & Bro. in 1879 for $90,848.49. The Schwartz brothers effected a corporate reorganization—they chartered the New Orleans Spanish Fort & Lake RR. Co. with Mr. Moses Schwartz as President on March 31, 1879 and conveyed the Canal Street City Park & Lake RR. Co. to the new corporation the 9th of April. Still, some creditors and investors were not satisfied. A session in the New Orleans courts followed with the Schwartz brothers successfully contending innocence and avoiding judgment. This was not the end of financial turbulence, apparently. The Spanish Fort "Daily Herald" of August 5, 1883, reports the New Orleans Spanish Fort & Lake RR. had been upgraded, steel rails replacing old iron rails. The seven and a half mile railroad was praised by the paper for having convenient service and clean trains. The road's new General Manager and Lessee, Mr. W. S. Saiter, was commended for his efficient management — trains were able to run eight minutes apart, made the trip from New Orleans to Spanish Fort in twenty minutes, still charged only 15 cents for a round trip. A new locomotive was put in service, named the "W. S. Saiter" (no other data available).

The shops of the N. O. S. F. & L. RR. Co. remained in the same location after all those reorganizations, behind the Beauregard School, in the block bounded by Patrick, Olympia, Bienville, and Customhouse Streets. Office was at No. 26 St. Charles Street and depot at No. 9 Basin Street.

According to the U. S. Census Report of 1880, New Orleans had a population of 216,090, a 12.1% increase over 1870. Street railway service was provided by 21 car lines, 313 cars, 1,641 horses and mules, and 671 employees. Over twenty three million people were carried in mule cars in 1880 for the nickel fare. On August 24, 1881, the Southwestern Brush Electric Light & Power Co. was granted permission to build a steam generating plant on Dryades opposite the end of Union St. (where present N. O. P. S. I. office building now stands). This was the beginning of electric street lighting in New Orleans.

The 1880's did not have the exciting street railway news of the 1860's and 1870's for New Orleans. No new companies came into existence and only one new line began service. The Canal and Coliseum and Upper Magazine Line of the Crescent City RR. Co. started service in 1881. There were two corporate re-organizations during the 1880's—New Orleans City RR. Co. became New Orleans City & Lake RR. Co. in 1883 and Canal & Claiborne Streets RR. Co. changed to Canal & Claiborne RR. Co. in 1888. The first known strike in New Orleans of operating street railway employees took place in 1885. Hours and wages were the issues.

The predecessors of our giant World Fairs of today were the "Expositions" of grand yesteryear. One of

St. Charles Ave., looking up from Lee Circle. Car on left C.C.RR. Coliseum Line. Photo circa 1890. Note walkway for mules in St. Charles Ave. neutral ground. Walkway extended up to Carrollton Ave.

these expositions was the New Orleans Cotton Centennial Exposition, opened December 16, 1884 and lasting until May 31, 1885. Besides the towering and flowery exhibition pavilions of many nations at the exposition grounds (encompassing ALL of present day Audubon Park—then, Upper City Park), there were two displays that caught the eye and caused passing, tittering comment among the spectators. These were two ELECTRIC railways, full size, carrying visitors who desired (or who were brave enough) to ride.

One system was operated by the Daft Electric Light Company. Their dynamo operated lights and a small one-fifth of mile long electric railway connecting the Main Building and the U. S. Government Building. The system employed the patented invention of Mr. Leo Daft, an Englishman. The motor unit, the "Volta", operated with a third rail, laid in the center of the track. The motor used small phosphor-bronze contact wheels.

The other system utilized the overhead trolley method of gathering power. This was Mr. Charles J. Van Depoele's one mile long railway. This Belgian's operation was spectacular with its motor car and two large open cars. The motor car actually had an overhead trolley with wheel pressing against and contacting underside of wire. Montgomery, Alabama adopted this system for revenue service in 1886, but New Orleans waited seven years to do the same.

Before the overhead trolley system of electric railway operation was adopted to public service in New Orleans, the electric battery car principle was tested—without success.

June 15, 1889, The Electric Traction & Manufacturing Co. was chartered under the auspices of the Crescent City RR. Co. and the New Orleans City RR. Co. Officers signing the charter included: Mr. J. A. Walker (President, New Orleans City RR. Co.), Gen. W. J. Behan (President, Crescent City RR. Co.), Mr. A. N. Meyer, and Mr. Philip Thompson. Purpose of the corporation was to purchase franchises, privileges, patents, and to manufacture, sell and lease cars—even operate lines, if the need ever arose (which it didn't). This was the very first attempt to electrify street railway operations in New Orleans. It failed. Honest attempts were made. Early in 1889, the Crescent City RR. Co., then under the Presidency of Gen. W. J. Behan, bought one Gibson Electric Co. car with Daft motor and Gibson cells. The car arrived April 6th for tests on the Coliseum Line. Twelve hp was the capacity of the Daft motors, yet the little car could attain speeds up to 25 mph. Unlike the "bobtail" mule cars, the Gibson storage battery car had platforms at each end. Although this type of car was successfully used on Fourth Avenue in New York City, it was not adopted in New Orleans. Later, in the early 1890's, cars of the Julien system of battery operation were tested. April 30, 1890, the Crescent City RR. Co. signed a contract with E. T. & M. Co. to equip 40 cars, five at a time, with battery power. One of these cars, No. 3, was tested August 8, 1890 on the Coliseum Line. The car weighed 4,500 lbs., seated 13 people to each side, was 16' long, could run 15 mph and had an endurance of 96 miles between battery charges. Inside, the car was illuminated with two 16 candle power lights, and on the outside boasted a bright electric headlight. However, in 1891, the battery cars were discarded. The Crescent City contract was annulled in 1892.

The year 1890 saw the establishment (April 26) of the last mule car line in New Orleans—the South Peters Line. New Orleans boasted a population of 242,039. Yet, the city would not consider allowing the overhead trolley system of electric railways to be employed. Mule cars, with their average speed of something like five to eight mph, seemed quite satisfactory. The New Orleans City RR. Co., answering a query put to it by the *Street Railway Journal,* said in part: "We use on an average five animals to a car; mileage per car ranges from 90 to 102 miles per day. The average per animal per day appears severe, but to meet this we have a very clean and level track and special attention is given the journal boxes of the cars. We use only the 'Sugar Mule', an especially bred animal of better than ordinary strength. Instead of bell straps we use electric bell push buttons in staunchion posts. For ventilation, an air siphon (Ed. note—an air ventilation system at that early date on MULE CARS may be a record!). Patents for both the bell system and the air siphon ventilation system have been granted us. We hope to go to electric cars in the near future". Incidentally, what is probably as early a one-man, pay-as-you-enter operation as one could hope to find was in use in New Orleans, and had been since immediately before the Civil War. The "Bobtail" cars (beginning 1861) with rear entrance required passengers to drop fare in box at front of car. Motorman (DRIVER) could see through glass front of fare-box. If change was necessary, he would make it, then drop it into a gravity slot for passenger to get. This system prevailed on the mule cars as long as they were operated in New Orleans. The fareboxes were designed by Mr. J. B. Slawson in the 1850's, used on omnibuses in St. Louis as well as in New Orleans, adopted by mule cars in New Orleans in 1861.

*Louis C. Hennick Collection*

Looking up St. Charles from Canal, circa 1890. Old St. Charles Hotel visible next block. St. Charles Street RR. white car in foreground. This was starting point for that company's Carondelet and Dryades Lines.

## "AND AFTER US, THE DELUGE"
# THE GOLDEN ERA OF ELECTRIC TRACTION
### 1893-1926

Superintendent C. V. Haile of the New Orleans & Carrollton RR. Co. visited Richmond, Va. in late 1888. Haile noted the progress there with electric traction and the overhead trolley system for street railways. During 1889, the N. O. & C. studied Haile's report and in 1890 the road's President, Mr. J. Hernandez, decided to petition the New Orleans city council for permission to electrify, using the overhead trolley system. The city fathers showed no great devotion to the idea until 1891. Ordinance CS 5847 of December 15, 1891 gave the go-ahead signal for New Orleans & Carrollton RR. Co. electrification.

For some time the N. O. & C. had realized that a new form of car propulsion was necessary for rapid street railway service. Steam engines were permanently withdrawn from service May 1, 1889. The very last order for mule cars arrived in January of 1890—three Stephenson models. It is possible these three cars inaugurated "smoking car service" on the Carrollton Line, starting March 24, 1890, from Canal Street to Napoleon Avenue. Service ran from 7:00 A.M. to 10:00 A.M. and from 4:00 P.M. to 7:00 P.M. With this elegant flourish, who could believe mule cars were preparing to vanish from the New Orleans street railway scene?

Work was launched on the New Orleans & Carrollton electrification by a silver spike ceremony held at Lee Circle on July 13, 1890. The respected New Orleans business leader (no connection with the N. O. & C.), Mr. A. L. Abbott, was honored to drive the spike. It was hoped to have service operating by October of 1892, but the usual delays attendant with ordering varied equipment and work dependent upon weather conditions stalled the opening day until February of the following year. Experimental runs were made beginning January 25, 1893 to test the St. Louis Car Co. single truck closed cars and the new overhead system put in by J. G. White & Co. of New York City.

The first line to switch to electric cars and the overhead trolley system was the Carrollton Line (re-named "St. Charles" Line on day of electrification). A procession of seven cars, led by No. 21, commenced service on the St. Charles Line, February 1, 1893. By February 10th, the N. O. & C. RR. Co.'s other two lines, Jackson and Napoleon, were running electric cars. Thomson-Houston motors and controls were employed on all N. O. & C. cars at this beginning.

The "Picayune" of February 2, 1893, commented thusly: "Electric cars are started on St. Charles Avenue. They create as much excitement as a Rex parade. Yesterday, for the first time, New Orleans rode by wire.

The experience proved delightful, safe and successful . . . and now that the system is perfected, New Orleans will desire to speedily forget the fact that all over the North and West, even in the smallest towns, the electric cars have for a long time been in popular use. Those persons who persistently fought against the introduction of this means of rapid transit will now have to take a back seat.

"Promptly at 10, the gay, spic and span green cars were drawn up on Carrollton Avenue for the trip to Baronne and Canal, the present terminus of the road. The camera fiend took a shot, Mr. Haile gave the signal to start, and as gently as a leaf drifting on a summer river, the cars rolled along Carrollton Avenue into St. Charles and as pompously as any Carnival king, the procession made its triumphant way to Canal Street".

Preparing for electrification, the N. O. & C. RR. Co. extended the Carrollton Line out Carrollton Avenue from St. Charles to Jeanette, and built new shops and barns on the corner of Jeanette and Dublin, one block up from Carrollton. After the electric cars started, daytime headways were 1½ minutes with all night service offered—on 30 minute headways from midnight to daybreak. For a few weeks, N. O. & C. conductors used fare boxes. These were cumbersome contrivances, each conductor having one strapped to himself. These fare boxes no doubt were dispensed with when the N. O. & C. adopted the straight 5 cents fare system, effective March 1, 1893.

Electrification of the Crescent City RR. Co. and the New Orleans City & Lake RR. Co. was of a somewhat more elaborate undertaking. New York capital was interested. On November 29, 1892, the New Orleans Traction Company Limited was chartered to buy control of both properties, plus the Electric Traction & Manufacturing Co. New Orleans Traction Co. was a holding company from its start. Officers of the new holding company were Mr. E. E. Denniston, President, and Mr. Henry Seligman, Treasurer and Secretary. Ten million dollars were raised through the J. & W. Seligman & Company to get the New Orleans Traction Co. started.

Thus, the second company to order electric cars was New Orleans Traction Co. This name appeared on only a few cars, and then only in small letters at the end of the lower curved side panel (see photo of car No. 50 on page 112). Two separate orders of cars were necessary for electrification of the 86 miles of track comprising the C. C. RR. Co. and the N. O. C. & L. RR. Co. Fifty open cars, single truckers, were ordered from an unknown source in 1892 and arrived

Canal St., looking from Royal St. "out". Snow storm of 1895 stopped electric cars, calling forth the mulecars. Lack of equipment to remove ice from trolley wires kept electrics in the barns.

in 1893. These cars sat idle until the first few lines were finally electrified in 1894. The second order of cars was more impressive. TWO HUNDRED AND TWENTY-SIX closed cars with Brill 22-E "Eureka" maximum traction trucks were ordered from Brill of Philadelphia in 1893 and 1894. The first line to be electrified was the Canal Line. On July 28, 1894, wire was tightened and current activated for the first time. On July 30th, a test run was made with a car. Regular service commenced August 1st.

In quick succession, other lines of the Crescent City and New Orleans City & Lake systems, controlled by New Orleans Traction Co. Ltd., were electrified. Peters Avenue Line, a new line, was tested with open cars on August 10th and officially opened August 18th. Brill closed cars bumped the opens the following day. Four lines followed apace: Prytania on September 15th, Esplanade on November 12th, Dauphine on November 22nd, and Barracks and Slaughter House on December 22nd. Barracks and Slaughter House was consolidated with Dauphine on the 22nd of December. In all, six N. O. T. Co. lines were electrified in 1894.

Electric power for New Orleans Traction Co.'s streetcars was being purchased from the Louisiana Electric Lt. Co. (formerly Louisiana Electric Lt. & Pwr. Co.) during 1894, 1895, and 1896. In 1897, N. O. T. Co. began upgrading its newly purchased power facility on Market Street, near the River (for more data, see chapter titled "Powerhouses and Substations"). While N. O.

T. Co. at first purchased power, other New Orleans' street railway systems began electric operations with their own power stations.

Eight New Orleans Traction Co. lines were electrified in 1895—Coliseum on February 22, Magazine on March 15, Annunciation on April 2, Tchoupitoulas on April 20, South Peters on May 8, French Market (not to be confused with Orleans RR. Co. Line of same name, still a mule car line) on May 21, Henry Clay (a new line, electric when opened) on June 13, and Villere (also a new line) on October 15, 1895.

New Orleans Traction Co. electrification was a determined project. On January 14, 1896, Levee-Barracks Line got electric cars. West End was electrified July 16, 1898, and the last mule car hold out in New Orleans, the Bayou Bridge and City Park Line, retained mule cars until late 1899 or early 1900 (exact date unobtainable).

The West End operation (steam) was electrified with large double-truck cars built by Barney & Smith Car Co. (see Chapter 4, Equipment). On July 17, 1898 the New Orleans "Times-Democrat" commented on the first run of the double-truck cars to West End under the heading "Lightning to the Lake". The first run was a commemorative affair held on the afternoon of July 16, 1898—regular service commenced July 18.

West End was in its prime in 1898. Between 1890 and 1911, West End was a unique and likeable place for relaxation and pleasure with its many entertain-

Circa 1900 shot of an 1894 Brill on modified St. Louis type 8 truck. 1894 Brills for New Orleans varied between 7 and 8 side windows, and arched or notched side windows.

ment devices and restaurants. "Tranchina's", an imposing white building (all West End buildings were white with canary yellow trim) with a broad gallery roof extending the length of the structure afforded an unsurpassed spot at which to dine. The galley and great inside dining room offered the finest New Orleans style cuisine bedecked with snow white napery and superbly served.

There were many other restaurants, all forms of popular rides, the usual concessions offering games, stands selling peanuts, pop corn, and crackerjack, drinks, ice cream, and sodas—in fact, everything that went to make a first class amusement park. West End, sometimes called a "park", was mostly a vast expanse of timber platform extending almost a thousand feet out over the waters of Lake Pontchartrain.

There was a long jetty, or mole, extending further out, leading to the exclusive Southern Yacht Club. The mole was open to the public and was quite popular, featuring a long walk out its full length with an unobstructed view of the lake, sailboat regattas, sunsets —and an opportunity for courtship of the walking and discourse degree (only). The Yacht Club was off to

the side of the jetty and was a classical white structure built on piling over the water. The Club house had broad verandas running around three sides.

The usual train after electrification consisted of one motor car hauling up to three double truck trailers. Service commenced from Canal and Baronne instead of from Canal and Carondelet, as in the steam operation days. During the summer season, headways were roughly, as follows: from 5:30 A.M. to noon, half hourly; from noon to early evening, twenty minutes; during the evening, ten or fifteen minutes until 10:30 P.M. when crowds had returned home. Service diminished until midnight, then hourly service prevailed until 5:30 A.M. During the balance of the year, hourly service was provided through the night with a single car, and half hourly service operated during daytime. Summertime Sunday service during pleasant weather was the heaviest—five minute headways. Sunday service throughout the year also required more frequent schedules.

Weather affected the service since West End was really an open air playground and amusement center. When a squall rushed forth during an evening performance it was quite a feat to reach shelter before clothes were absolutely soaked.

The "Vitascope" (moving pictures) was an interesting device. A unit in itself, it was moved on wheels to a certain point to project pictures on an immense screen (about 20' by 40'—covering the bandstand at West End). After the "moving pictures", the unit was rolled back, screen removed, benches placed into the space occupied by the "Vitascope" track, and the regular stage show presented.

Fare to West End was 15 cents per round trip, and this permitted one to occupy a bench for the band concert, "Vitascope", and Orpheum Vaudeville. A reserved section "down front" called for twenty-five cent tickets, obtainable in town at the Starter's House (then located on the neutral ground of Canal at Bourbon Street).

There were some private residences at both West End and Bucktown, with the two areas connected by an embankment. The lake was on one side, the yacht basin on the other. Trees, shrubs, and grassy expanses graced this part of West End, and the stroll up to Bucktown was a pleasant affair.

Lake Pontchartrain is forty miles long and 24 miles wide at its extreme dimensions—with an average depth of only 18 feet. When a storm comes, the effect is more like blowing across a saucer of water.

Three more companies electrified street railway operations in New Orleans during 1895 and 1896. The Orleans RR. Co. contracted the firm of engineers from New York City, Ford & Bacon (later Ford, Bacon & Davis), to supervise and plan electrification. C. E. Ross & Co. were subcontracted to erect wiring, and Brill to provide cars. On Nov. 16th a test run was successful on the O. RR.'s Bayou St. John Line, and service commenced the next day, November 17, 1895. The company's two other lines, Broad and French Market, started electric service a few days later (see: ROUTES). June 22, 1897, the O. RR. Co. barns at Gentilly Boulevard, North Dupre and Laharpe Streets burned. The building was replaced before the end of the year. Twelve FB&D cars for O. RR. arrived in November of 1897. Early in 1898, the Orleans RR. started the City Park Line.

The next system to start electric service was the St. Charles Street RR. Co. In 1895, 300 workers of the Messrs. Loss & Co. of Chicago got to work rebuilding the St. C. St. RR. Co. roadbed—forty single truck Pullman cars were ordered for the twelve mile street railway. The Clio and Carondelet Lines started electric service on January 2, 1896, followed by the Dryades Line on January 14th: All night service was offered. Even during last years of St. C. St. RR. Co. mule car operation, a half hourly owl service was provided, midnight to daybreak.

Only thirty cars were necessary to electrify two lines of the last company on the "city" side of the river to start electric service. President Joseph H. De Grange of the Canal & Claiborne Railroad Co. contracted the

New York firm, Ford, Bacon & Davis, to design thirty cars and other physical improvements. Thus, the famous "FB&D" car was originated which later became the standard single truck car in New Orleans, besides being later ordered by other city railways (Shreveport, Pine Bluff, Birmingham to name three). Both the Claiborne and Tulane Lines were electrified on October 10, 1896. The Girod and Poydras Line was never electrified, remained a mule car operation until its abandonment in late 1899. As of January 1, 1897, the Canal & Claiborne RR. Co. reported to Poors: Sixteen miles of electric railway—4' 8½" gauge; Four miles of horse (sic—actually mule) railway—5' 2" (sic—actually 5' 2½") gauge; 30 electric cars, ten mule cars. It is interesting to note the change of gauge—C. & C. RR. Co. then joined the New Orleans & Carrollton RR. Co. in operating standard gauge electric street railway lines. In fact, the two systems also co-operated with one another in this respect. On January 30, 1896, the N. O. & C. RR. Co. commenced using Canal Street from Baronne to the foot of Canal, all three lines running to the River. The outside tracks on Canal which belonged to the Canal & Claiborne RR. Co. were the first tracks of that company converted to standard gauge. Obviously, wide gauge C. & C. RR. Co. mule cars turned back at Canal and Baronne while the N. O. C. RR. Co. standard gauge electric cars entered Canal at Baronne and proceeded to the river, for operating mule and electric cars on the same trackage is awkward (but not impossible. A third rail would have enabled a dual gauge operation, but speed and acceleration differences between electric and animal powered cars would have been aggravating). After electrification, dual gauge was installed on Canal Street's outer tracks from Claiborne to the River.

New Orleans gained a new railroad in 1896. The New Orleans & Western RR., chartered January 17, 1895 and opened January 11, 1896, operated a fourteen mile steam railroad extending from Chalmette to Shrewsbury, through New Orleans but by-passing the downtown section. Chalmette is below New Orleans, on the river, and is separated from the city by the small industrial community of Arabi. Shrewsbury is across the Orleans-Jefferson Parish Line, above New Orleans, about a mile and a half above the line. The N. O. & W. crossed the New Orleans, Spanish Fort & Lake RR. Co. in the vicinity of the present intersection of Orleans and Florida Avenues. From there to Chalmette, frequent steam passenger train service was provided. The principal source of revenue for the New Orleans & Western was transfer freight, as the line connected with every railroad entering New Orleans on the "city" side. Industrial tracts were developed in Chalmette. On July 1, 1897, the New Orleans & Western RR. purchased control of the New Orleans, Spanish Fort & Lake RR. Co., the latter company retaining its corporate identity. "Official Guides" indicate that N. O. & W. trains then began running to

North Basin and Iberville over the N. O., S. F. & L. RR. Co. The New Orleans & Western RR. was a locally owned operation in 1896, with Mr. Charles E. Levy, President and Mr. J. G. Preston, Superintendent. Defaulting on bonds in 1897 threw the road and its subsidiary into receivership with New York capital taking over the management.

The New Orleans & Carrollton RR. Co. was the first street railway in the United States to issue for its patrons weekly or semi-weekly news pamphlets placed in holders secured to its cars' window stanchions. This practice started in 1897, according to Mr. George H. Davis of Ford, Bacon & Davis in a letter to the *Electric Railway Journal,* published by that magazine in its March 18, 1916 issue.

Early in 1899, the New Orleans & Carrollton RR. Co. absorbed the Canal & Claiborne RR. Co. New officers were: J. K. Newman, President; Joseph H. De-Grange, Vice President; Walter J. Crouch, Superintendent; and George H. Davis, General Manager. The expanded operation gave the New Orleans & Carrollton RR. Co. forty miles of standard gauge electric railway operation and 120 electric cars, four miles of 5' 2½" gauge mule car trackage with ten mule cars, five electric car lines (St. Charles, Jackson, Napoleon, Claiborne, and Tulane) and the solitary mule car operation, the Girod and Poydras Line. The mule car line was operating at infrequent and long intervals—patronage had been falling (so much that the Canal & Claiborne RR. Co. had no intention of electrifying it in 1896). New Orleans city ordinance C.S. 15489 of July 26, 1899 relieved the New Orleans & Carrollton RR. Co. of the burden of operating the line. Ordinance C.S. 15823 (December 27, 1899) permitted removal of most Girod and Poydras Line trackage.

After the merger, the New Orleans & Carrollton RR. Co. painted its cars the olive green and cream livery of the former Canal & Claiborne system. This color scheme later became official for all street cars in New Orleans and is still used at the present time (with much reduction in cream trim, however).

A more grandiose re-organization of street railway interests in 1899 applied to the New Orleans Traction Co. Ltd. A new corporation bearing the name "New Orleans City Railroad Company" (the second to have this name) was formed and chartered in 1899. Local interests financed the reorganization which absorbed all properties, franchises, and rights of the New Orleans Traction Co. Ltd., New Orleans, City & Lake RR. Co., and Crescent City Railroad Co. The newly organized system comprised 114.85 miles of 5' 2½" gauge street railway, almost totally electrified. The last mule car operation, the Bayou Bridge and City Park Line, succumbed to electric cars late in 1899 or early 1900 (exact date unobtainable). Offices of the New Orleans City RR. Co. were in New Orleans with Mr. R. M. Walmsley, President; Mr. Albert Baldwin, Vice-President, Mr.

A. H. Ford, Secretary and Treasurer; and Mr. C. D. Wyman, General Manager.

The turn of the century was colorful in all our large cities, but New Orleans with its two distinctive sections and (at that time) two languages was indeed in a

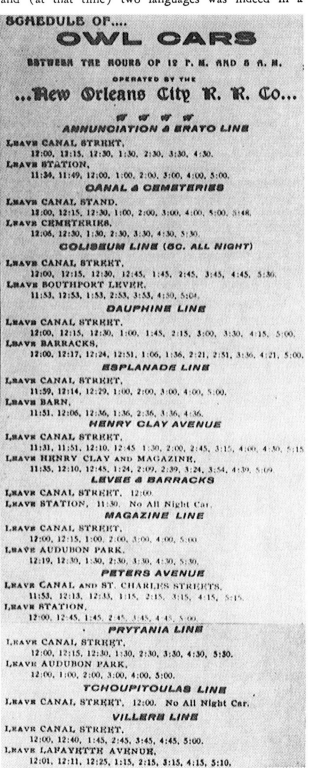

Owl schedule effective Jan. 1901.   *Louis C. Hennick Collection*

period with a flavor once tasted, never forgotten. The superb restaurants, the racing, the Carnival, the opera, the mixture of new blood striving to create a new, advanced city above Canal Street together with the French Quarter's atmosphere of Sans Souci was captivating, to say the least. Much additional color was contributed by the multi-hued street cars. White car bodies designated St. Charles St. RR. rolling stock, red was the Orleans RR. Co's color, the New Orleans City RR. Co. combined orange and yellow, while the old pioneer New Orleans & Carrollton RR. Co. chose the well known olive green and cream. With these various basic colors and their different trim, plus gold or silver striping and lettering, the cars by day presented an attractive picture. By night, a gay and kaleidoscopic effect was created by the cars' many-colored route signs in the front glass of the clerestory deck. This sight intrigued the stranger and fascinated even those used to the sight. These destination signs were of almost every color combination one could imagine, and are described in the chapter on "Routes". Car body liveries at the turn of the century consisted of several coats of paint, then several applications of varnish rubbed by hand. When completed, the car sides reflected images almost with the faithfulness of a mirror.

There were, then, only four street railway systems operating in New Orleans in 1900, on the "city" side, with the trend to group all systems into one corporation well on the way:

1. New Orleans & Carrollton RR. Co. 4' 8½" gauge, 40 miles, 120 cars, five lines.
2. New Orleans City RR. Co. 5' 2½" gauge, 115 miles, 300 motor cars, 39 trailers, sixteen lines.
3. Orleans RR. Co. 5' 2½" gauge, 11 miles, 31 cars, four lines.
4. St. Charles St. RR. Co. 5' 2½" gauge, 12 miles, 40 cars, three lines.

Two improvements highlighted 1900: the start of the New Orleans & Carrollton RR. Co's. St. Charles and Tulane Belts, and a revision of Canal Street trackage. Ford, Bacon & Davis completed the track work which encompassed a nine-track terminus at the foot of Canal Street. This track improvement and later track laying programs are described in detail in chapter 5, "Track, Paving and Overhead".

In 1901, the New Orleans & Carrollton RR. Co. was reorganized as the New Orleans & Carrollton RR. Light & Power Co., with plans to purchase Edison Electric Co. and Merchants Electric Co. The idea was to provide electric power as well as street railway service. The company's Carrollton Barn, built in 1892, was expanded with new equipment for servicing and rebuilding rolling stock. New cars from St. Louis and American Car Co's. were added. The New Orleans City RR. Co. started the Canal and Esplanade Belts on June 1, 1901.

The New Orleans & Western RR. and its subsidiary, the New Orleans, Spanish Fort & Lake RR. Co. were reorganized in 1901. The N. O. & W. became the New Orleans Belt & Terminal Co. while the subsidiary property, the N. O. S. F. & L., retained its identity while being controlled by the new company.

City wide consolidation of street railway companies in New Orleans took place in 1902. This was merely a consolidation, *not* a true merger. The four street railway systems did not lose their corporate identity — on paper. Cars were repainted and lettered "New Or-

*Courtesy Rita Ann Collins*

During 1902 strike of carmen—not a streetcar in sight on Canal Street.

leans Railways Company", the new corporation incorporated in New Jersey to lease the street railway lines on the "city" side of New Orleans. E. C. Jones & Co. of New York City provided capital for the venture, headed by Mr. H. H. Pearson, Jr. N. O. Rys. Co. stock was exchanged for that of the New Orleans & Carrollton RR. Lt. & Pwr. Co., New Orleans City RR. Co., Orleans RR. Co., and St. Charles St. RR. Co. The change in ownership was quickly felt. All cars were painted orange and yellow, except the Carrollton Division Lines (St. Charles, Tulane, Jackson, Claiborne, and Napoleon) which retained the olive green and cream.

The year 1902 included great expansion and city wide improvement, as sewerage, drainage, and extensive street paving work was in progress. Plans for a water purification plant were on the board. The old practice of obtaining drinking water from cisterns was on the way out. It was a year of great change — the city was on its way to modernization.

On June 5, 1902, the first of the luxurious "Palace" cars were received from the St. Louis Car Co. The first ten of these large double truck cars did not have air brakes. It was soon learned that motormen could not handle these giants with the old hand brake — even on New Orleans' grade-less streets. Air brakes were thereupon installed on the "Palace" cars (also on the West End cars) and subsequent orders of the "Palace" type arrived with air brake equipment installed. The posh "Palace" cars bumped smaller 1900 maximum traction truck Americans from the Canal and Esplanade Belts.

In 1902 work was begun on the first motor cars built in New Orleans. Canal shops turned out twelve large wooden electric cars named "Morris" cars, after Mr. E. J. Morris, the N. O. Rys. Master Mechanic. Canal had built double truckers previously (since 1891), but all were trailers.

When N. O. Rys. Co. consolidated all street railway operations under one management in 1902-03, unanimity was achieved in all areas except one. Before the consolidation, each company had a separate agreement with its operating personnel. These agreements varied as to pay scale and hours. The carmen wanted a single and new agreement, an increase in pay, and recognition of their union (Amalgamated Association of Street and Electric Railway Employees of America). New Orleans Rys. Co. would agree to nothing — a threatened strike earlier in the year did not come to pass, but on September 27, 1902, operating personnel did not return to work. The strike lasted for fifteen days. There was violence, some rioting, dynamiting, and a few fatalities. The strike was settled by a 2¢ per hour raise, partial recognition of the union, and a promise to prepare a new agreement. In 1903, N. O. Rys. Co. fully recognized the union and drew up an acceptable agreement.

In late 1902, Mr. H. H. Pearson, Jr. resigned as N.O. Rys. Co. president. Vice-president Miller took over the position temporarily until Mr. E. C. Foster was elected president.

All in all, the street railways in New Orleans were embarked upon full-scale modernization by 1902, a year that can be called the "middle age" of street railway history in New Orleans. With all deference to 1893, from here to 1926 was a true "hey-day" of the trolley.

In 1902 New Orleans' streetcars were even carrying mail! There were no R. P. O. cars in New Orleans at any time on the street railways, but mail in the form of closed pouch service was carried for many years, from about 1900 to 1924. The cars carried bags from the main post office to the various postal branches, and vice versa. When carrying mail, cars carried a dash sign reading "U. S. Mail" in red and white. When bags were unloaded, the sign was removed (the bags were always handled by post office employees). Exact dates of this service are probably unobtainable, but Assistant Postmaster Frank J. Graff has verified the above in substance.

Mail was also carried on West End trains and on the Orleans-Kenner Traction Company (see Vol. I).

Nuns, letter carriers with pouch, policemen, and firemen in uniform were (and still are) carried free. Detectives rode free by displaying a badge, although dressed in "civvies".

One of the foremost achievements of the New Orleans Rys. Co. was the "Royal Blue Line", opened to service January 1, 1903. The new line commenced at St. Charles and Napoleon, and ran out Napoleon, South Broad, Washington, South Carrollton, and New Basin Shell Road (later Pontchartrain Boulevard) to Metairie Road (soon built up Metairie Road to Orleans—Jefferson Parish Line at 17th Street Canal). Plans to build such a line were formed in 1897, under the projected The Orleans & Jefferson Ry. Co., Ltd., chartered June 1, 1897. Company officers were: Mr. William R. Hall, President; Mr. Robert R. Zell, Vice-President and Engineer; and Mr. Cyrus B. Buchanan, Secretary-Treasurer. First attempts to start construction were unsuccessful. The company's new President, Mr. Thomas W. Castleman, Esq., was likewise unable to get things moving. The heavily indebted line, with little construction and no operating service to show, was reorganized in 1901 as the New Orleans & Pontchartrain Railway Co., with Mr. Adolphe H. Prentzel as President and Mr. George S. Kansler as Vice-President. New Orleans Rys. poured capital into the N.O. & P. in 1902 and service finally commenced in 1903. Old 1894 Brills were used at first on the 5' 2½" gauge line. To avoid confusion with the 4' 8½" gauge ex-New Orleans & Carrollton Napoleon Line, operating in Napoleon from St. Charles to Tchoupitoulas, the N. O. & P. Ry. was referred to simply as the "N.O.& P. Line". Sometime in 1906 (exact date not found by research), the Napoleon Line from St. Charles to Tchoupitoulas was widened to 5' 2½" gauge and through service then operated from

Metairie Road and 17th Street Canal to Tchoupitoulas. The line was officially designated "Napoleon" Line but locally called the "Royal Blue Line". Soon Jackson & Sharp cars replaced the 1894 Brills, and the J&S cars were later replaced by "Palace" cars.

On July 12, 1903, the New Orleans Spanish Fort & Lake RR. Co. was closed. Dismantling followed almost immediately, and the Louisiana Railroad Commission officially recorded the abandonment in 1904. Spanish Fort did not have the attraction of West End, and passengers preferred either the electric service to West End or even "Smoky Mary" to Milneburg. The New Orleans Belt & Terminal Co. passenger operation to Chalmette continued. The N.O.B. & T Co. was consolidated with the New Orleans Terminal Co. in September of 1903. The N.O.T. Co. was owned by the Queen & Crescent Route and the St. Louis & San Francisco RR. Co. New Orleans Terminal Co. built a large railway station at North Basin and Canal Streets, opening it in 1908. Railroads using it were: Frisco Lines, Queen & Crescent Route, New Orleans Great Northern RR., Louisiana Railway & Navigation Co., and N.O.T.Co's. own trains to Chalmette.

Vestibules were required by an act of the Louisiana Legislature in 1904. N. O. Rys. complied with this law in the spring of the year. Both Magazine and Carrollton Shops were busy for some time fabricating and installing vestibules.

In 1905, New Orleans Rys. Co. went into receivership and was reorganized as New Orleans Ry. & Light Co. From this point until 1922, N. O. Ry & L. Co. was the big name in street railway and power services on New Orleans' city side. It seems strange that receivership and reorganization should have transpired in 1905. There were SIXTY FOUR MILLION riders handled by N.O.Rys. Co. — N. O. Ry. & L. Co. that year over the 191 mile rail system.

A new line was opened in 1905, a double track extension beside Orleans Avenue Drainage Canal from City Park Ave. to the City Park Race Track. Called the City Park Race Track Extension, it soon gained the shorter nickname, "Orleans Avenue Line". The Line sported the very first 600 volt catenary for city service cars in the United States, plus a six track stub terminus within a loop to store extra cars during the races. The race track and grandstand were opened to the public in March of 1905. Until the City Park Race Track Extension was opened on November 30, 1905, passengers going to the races rode Canal Belt cars to City Park Avenue and St. Louis Street where a transfer was made to special free race track trains operated by the New Orleans Terminal Co. Trains were operated on a five minute headway during the races. After N.O. Ry. & L. Co. opened the extension, a threefold service was provided. During the races, West End type trailer trains operated to the grandstand from Baronne and Canal Streets, stopping only at Claiborne, Galvez, and Broad.

Service commenced at 11:00 AM, with trains following at 11:30 AM, 11:45, 12:00 Noon, 12:15 PM, 12:30, 12:40, 12:50, and 1:00 PM, and thereafter on a seven minute headway throughout the afternoon. In addition to this high-capacity service, Canal Belt cars ran out to the grandstand during races. There also was tripper service from City Park Avenue to the grandstand. When there were no races, only the tripper operated to accommodate track personnel.

Incidentally, at one time New Orleans had no less than three race tracks. The City Park Race Track, mentioned above, was located in what is now City Park but which during the life of the track (1905-1908) did not extend that far out. The race track was a short distance from the New Orleans Terminal Co's. railroad as one goes out Orleans Avenue to the lake. The life of this track was short, a scant three years, because of the passing of a Louisiana State law abolishing racing. The law was passed in 1908, and passing with it was the City Park Race Track Extension car line. The law was later rescinded, but the number of race tracks was restricted to certain limits as regards population and area.

*Louis C. Hennick Collection*
Original of this timetable is four times this size, was posted in waiting sheds and stations. West End lost popularity after 1911, when Spanish Fort amusement grounds were opened by N. O. Ry. & L. Co.

The Fair Grounds Race Track is the oldest of the three, and still is used. It is located on the Fair Grounds, a few blocks down from Grand Route St. John. Before 1908, the track was used every year with about 120 days of winter season racing. Cars of the Esplanade, and Canal Belts, Broad, and Bayou St. John Lines served the track during racing days only. Service was provided by diversionary access routes visible on the large track map in this volume.

Jefferson Park race track was in Jefferson Parish and when first built was served by Illinois Central (Yazoo & Mississippi Valley RR.) New Orleans Div. gas-motor cars. Later, electric railway service was provided by the Orleans-Kenner Electric Ry. (see Vol. I). Located near Shrewsbury, this track had its financial ups and downs, was finally closed. Today, a residential area covers the race track site.

Semi-convertible cars made their appearance in New Orleans in 1906 — 25 double truck cars of that type went into service on the Coliseum Line. The Coliseum Line was operating to Southport (Jefferson Parish Line) then, carrying thousands of people to the gambling spots just across the line (the cars are gone today, but not the gambling).

Mr. E. C. Foster, formerly N.O.Rys. Co. President, held the same office with New Orleans Ry. & Lt. Co. in 1906. The company was operating with a $26,000,-000 bonded indebtedness while combined street railway and electric power operations grossed over five million dollars. Preferred stock dividends in 1906 were five dollars per share. Earned surplus amounted to $298,274.

The last order placed in New Orleans for FB&D cars was in 1908 (35 cars, from McGuire-Cummings, Nos. 325-360).

Street railway mileage in New Orleans increased in 1909 with the opening of the St. Bernard Shuttle. The next year saw the last order for single truck cars by N.O.Ry. & Lt. Co. — fifty from St. Louis Car Co. for the Prytania Line. The cars were locally called "Prytania" cars. N.O.Ry. & Lt. Co. Master Mechanic William Dickinson designed a new type fender, dubbed "Herr Fender" in honor of his father-in-law. This fender became standard in New Orleans until 1922 when life guards were adopted. The "Herr Fender" was used in other Louisiana cities, and in other places (see Vol. 1—Shreveport). With 201.27 miles of track in 1910, the company had 557 motor passenger cars, 36 passenger trailers, 48 service cars, three freight cars and one baggage car (as of December 31).

Also in 1910, the Villere Line made permanent its "St. James" extension. In 1909, the Villere Line was extended out Almonaster and Franklin Avenues to St. James Avenue (now Dreux). A grade crossing was necessary for the car line to cross the New Orleans Terminal Co. yard tracks at Florida Walk. The N.O. T. Co. promptly initiated litigation to prevent such a crossing. While the hassle was raging, the Villere's

E. Harper Charlton Collection
St. Charles St., looking toward Canal, about 1910 shows semi-convertibles as delivered.

divorced segment operated with a shuttle car, and the Gentilly Land Development & Realty Corp. (developing homes at the end of Villere Line) and the Gentilly Automobile Co. ran a bus line from downtown to the vicinity of Franklin and St. James Avenues (see: ROUTES, Villere Line). The N.O.Ry. & L. Co. agreed to build a substantial trestle, the N.O.T.Co. accepted specifications, and through Villere service commenced May 15, 1910. The only casualty was the bus line.

The double track extension from the West End Line, along Adams Avenue (now Gen. Robert E. Lee Boulevard to Spanish Fort was opened in 1911. As a recrea-

31

Building Spanish Fort pier, 1916.                                            *Courtesy N.O.P.S.I.*

tion and gathering area, Spanish Fort has had an interesting career. As far back as 1825, boats landed there from Lake points. Milneburg was not New Orleans' only lakeside spot to have this distinction. Railway service opened to Spanish Fort in 1875 enhanced its importance, but development of West End and the popularity of both West End and Milneburg overshadowed Spanish Fort. Steam rail service ended to Spanish Fort in 1903. The only factor reviving the place was the failure of the city and N.O. Ry. & Lt. Co. to agree upon plans to improve West End, and means to share the expense. So, New Orleans Ry. & Lt. Co. in 1910 began developing Spanish Fort into a rubber stamp sort of amusement park. The car line was opened March 26, 1911. Electric trains, motor unit plus three trailers (West End equipment), began running to Spanish Fort probably soon after the resort was formally opened to the public May 28, 1911. The newly created park was not as unique or spacious as West End, or as popular. The company tried several times to improve the place (perhaps there should have been no quibbling over improving West End). During the late Teens, a pier was built out over the Lake, extending nearly a mile, to bath houses and fishing piers. A single track electric line was built out this pier with a shuttle car providing service (5¢ fare) from pier's end to Spanish Fort loop. Spanish Fort's popularity declined through the years. The last service to the spot operated in 1932. Experimental car 288 was running as a shuttle car from West End Junction to Spanish Fort when the service ceased.

Other improvements instituted in 1911: Beginning June 10, 1911, an "independent" daily freight service was operated from Canal at North Liberty to Spanish Fort and West End. Four trips were run daily, handled by regular trains carrying the baggage car. Also, the long Tchoupitoulas Line was joined with the French Market Line. One could ride without transfer from

Villere and Esplanade, in Esplanade, then through the French Quarter, downtown, the waterfront, all the way to Audubon Park.

In 1912, the Paris Avenue Shuttle commenced service and two-unit operation with FB&D cars was inaugurated on the St. Charles-Tulane belts. A giant re-routing scheme was accomplished the following year that saw two new lines created, one abolished and two-re-routed. The Henry Clay Line was discontinued. A new line, Louisiana, was created, assuming a portion of the old Henry Clay. The Coliseum Line gave up its upper portion to the Magazine Line. The Coliseum took over part of the Henry Clay, while the Magazine Line began running to Southport. The Magazine Line gave up its old running on Laurel and Chestnut Streets. A new line, Laurel, was started to serve this part of the old Magazine Line. For clarification in detail, see chapter "ROUTES" for lines affected.

New track construction was impressive in 1915. The South Claiborne Line and "Shrewsbury Extension" of the Napoleon Line were opened. New Orleans' first steel, arch roof cars, the 400s, were placed in service. Built by Southern Car Co. of High Point, N. C., these cars were indeed a "new look" for the city. New Orleans finally got an interurban line in 1915 — the Orleans Kenner Electric Railway Co. Service commenced in February. A complete history of this operation appears in Vol. I.

The jitney bus threat to organized and regulated operation of public transit came to New Orleans in 1914. It was finally curbed and almost stopped by the passage of the so-called "jitney" ordinance on April 27, 1915. The ordinance set forth strict conditions for the operation of jitneys with the result that most transit services of that nature had "evaporated" from New Orleans before the close of 1915. This piracy was reflected in the revenue and passengers carried

# New Orleans Railway & Light Co.

## OWL CAR SCHEDULE.

**Leaving or crossing Canal Street going up town (South.)**

HENRY CLAY—
1:00 a. m.; 1:30 a. m.; 2:00 a. m.; 2:30 a. m.; and every half hour thereafter.

PETERS AVENUE—
1:00 a. m.; 1:30 a. m.; 2:00 a. m.; 2:30 a. m.; and every half hour thereafter.

MAGAZINE—
1:10 a. m.; 2:10 a. m.; and every hour thereafter.

CLIO (Uptown)—12:45 a. m.; 1:57 a. m.; 2:57 a. m.; 3:57 a. m.

ST. CHARLES AVE.—
1:20 a. m.; 1:50 a. m.; 2:20 a. m.; 2:50 a. m.; and every half hour thereafter.

PRYTANIA—1:00 a. m.; 1:30 a. m.; 2:30 a. m.; and every hour thereafter.

TCHOUPITOULAS—
1:30 a. m.; 2:30 a. m.; and every hour thereafter.

JACKSON AVENUE—
12:50 a. m.; 1:35 a. m.; 2:30 a. m., last car.

CARONDELET—
1:10 a. m.; 1:40 a. m.; and every half hour thereafter.

COLISEUM—
12:45 a. m.; 1:30 a. m.; 2:15 a. m.; every 45 minutes thereafter.

**Going down town (North.)**

CLIO (down town)—
1:37 a. m.; 2:42 a. m.; 3:42 a. m.; 4:47 a. m.

VILLERE—
12:40 a. m.; 1:45 a. m.; 2:45 a. m.; 3:45 a. m.; 4:45 a. m.

DAUPHINE—
12:45 a. m.; 1:45 a. m.; 2:45 a. m.; 3:45 a. m.; 4:45 a. m.

CLAIBORNE—
1:00 a. m.; 2:00 a. m.; 3:00 a. m.; 4:00 a. m.; 5:00 a. m.

CARONDELET—
1:10 a. m.; 1:40 a. m.; 2:10 a. m.; 2:40 a. m.; 3:10 a. m.; 3:40 a. m.; 4:10 a. m.; 4:40 a. m.; 5:10 a. m. Downn.

LEVEE AND BARRACKS—
1:00 a. m.; 2:00 a. m.; 3:00 a. m.; 4:00 a. m.

**Going back of town (West.)**

CANAL—
1:00 a. m.; 2:00 a. m.; 3:00 a. m.; 4:00 a. m.; 5:00 a. m.

TULANE—
1:00 a. m.; 2:00 a. m.; 3:00 a. m.; 4:00 a. m.; 5:00 a. m.

ESPLANADE—
1:00 a. m.; 2:00 a. m.; 3:00 a. m.; 4:00 a. m.; 5:00 a. m.

BAYOU ST. JOHN—
12:45 a. m.; 1:45 a. m.; 2:45 a. m.; 3:45 a. m.; 4:45 a. m.

WASHINGTON AND NAPOLEON AVE. LINE—
Leaves Napoleon Avenue and Tchoupitoulas, 12:40 a. m.; 1:00 a. m.; 2:00 a. m.; 3:00 a. m.; 4:00 a. m. Leaves Tulane Street Canal, 1:30 a. m.; 2:30 a. m.; 3:30 a. m.; 4:30 a. m.

*Louis C. Hennick Collection*

Owl schedule effective about 1911 shows citywide and consolidated transit system.

statistics of the street railway company for the three following years:

| Year | Passengers Carried | Gross Revenue |
|------|-------------------|---------------|
| 1914 | 87,239,968 | $4,398,507 |
| 1915 | 83,184,938 | 4,198,235 |
| 1916 | 87,680,288 | 4,422,777 |

It has been shown heretofore that the New Orleans Ry. & Lt. Co. was somewhat austere, and that fact is evident when one considers that the company made all its own brass and bronze castings. A foundry was operated at Magazine Shops that turned out trolley wheels, bearings, hardware, and other car fittings. All nickel plating was done at Magazine Shops, also.

A trend to two car trains for the rush hour on Canal Street started during 1916-17. Six of the Morris cars were converted to trailers, and many of the trailers built for West End service were revamped and modernized. Some route changes were made in 1916. The South Peters Line was abandoned, the South Peters and South Claiborne Shuttles started service. The Prytania and Villere Lines were united, and the South Claiborne Line was extended.

During 1917, a comprehensive survey of the New Orleans street railways was finished by the St. Louis firm, James E. Allison & Co., transit engineers. The survey, dated July 16, 1917, embraced every angle of street railway service, recommending elimination, consolidation, and re-routing of many lines. Also suggested was elimination of some "owl" service, disposal of all single-truck cars, and re-arrangement of routes using Canal Street so that some would run from one to three blocks on Canal instead of all the way to the loop. Re-routings occurring as a consequence of the Allison Report can be seen in chapter 3, Routes. Mr. D. D. Curran, President of N.O. Ry. & L. Co. was quick to act. Two lines were discontinued — Annunciation and Levee-Barracks. Jackson-Claiborne and Tchoupitoulas-City Park consolidations were put into effect shortly after the report was accepted. Prytania "owl" service was eliminated (St. Charles "owl" service remained, parallelling Prytania one block away for three miles).

The "fish bellies" made their appearance in 1918. The idea of rebuilding car sides was sound from an engineering standpoint (reduced number of parts needed to assemble side sections), but as for looks — very ugly in the authors' opinions.

New Orleans Ry. & Lt. Co. was operating 555 motor cars over a system of 219 miles of track in 1918, with 42 passenger trailers, one baggage trailer, and 68 work and service cars.

Taxes in 1918 charged against revenue had increased to $349,000 — operating expenses touched $600,000 for the railway department, while the company grossed only $850,000 more than in 1917. Judge Foster of the U.S. District Court at New Orleans appointed Mr. J. D. O'Keefe receiver for N.O. Ry. & Lt. Co. on January 9, 1919. An application by the American Cities Co. (for several years past, this power trust had controlled the New Orleans company), holder of defaulted notes, brought about receivership proceedings. Fares went to 6¢ in 1918.

Despite receivership, numerous improvements were instituted in 1919. The Tchoupitoulas-French Market union was severed. The Tchoupitoulas Line was then joined with the French Market-City Park Line, forming an even longer and more interesting "thru-town" line. The French Market Line, down North Peters, out

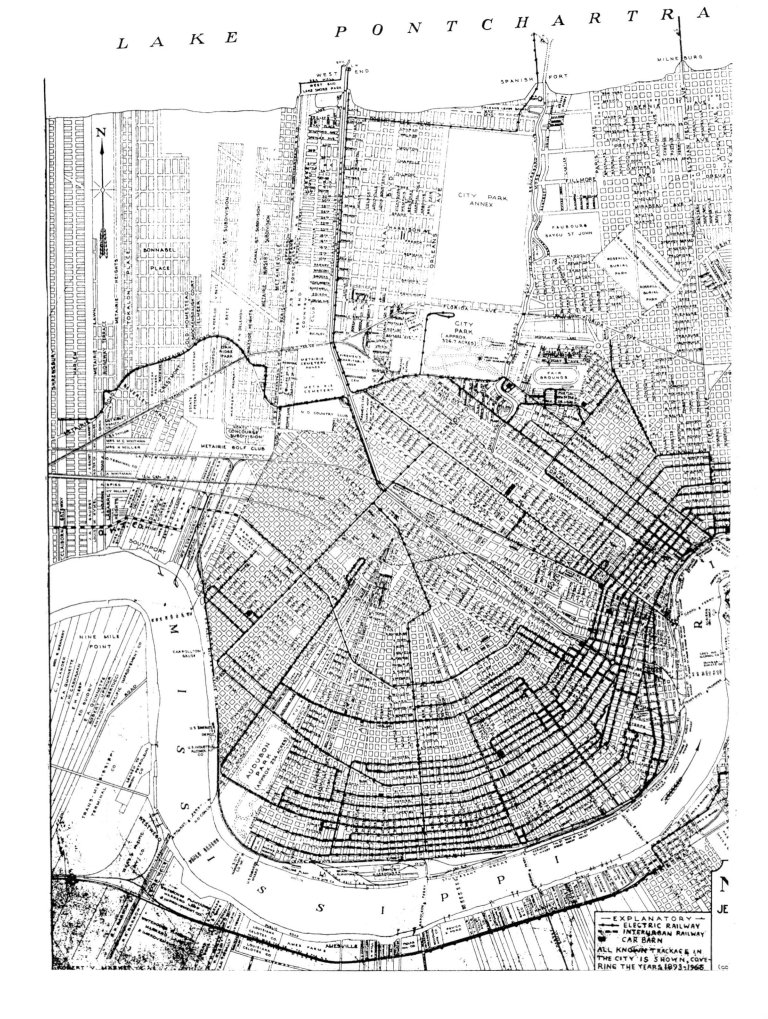

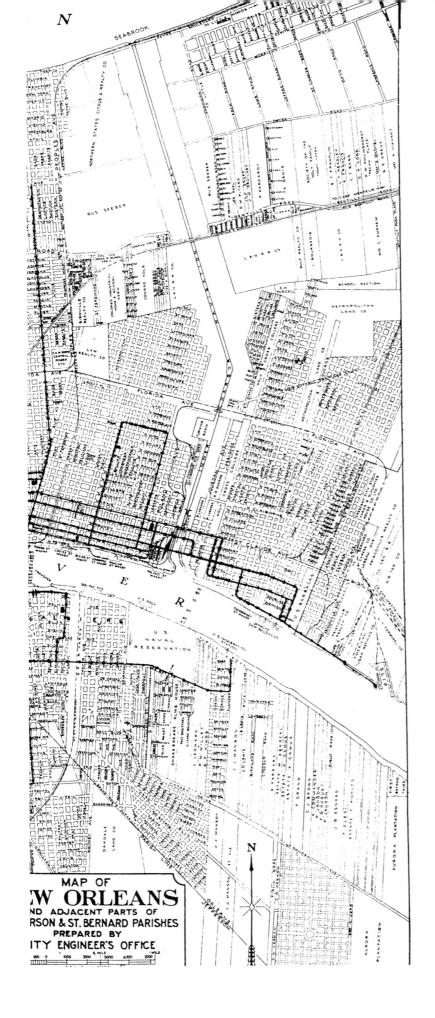

MAP OF
W ORLEANS
ND ADJACENT PARTS OF
RSON & ST. BERNARD PARISHES
PREPARED BY
ITY ENGINEER'S OFFICE

Esplanade to Villere, was renamed "North Peters" Line. Of more interest was the extension of the Carondelet Line to the industrial area about the Industrial Canal (the Canal was still under construction at the time, was not completed until 1922). The Carondelet Line Extension was opened December 20, 1919 (SEE: Routes, Carondelet Line). Another new item for New Orleans transitwise in 1919 was the use of cash fare tokens which began that year.

Street railway service in New Orleans suffered through a troublesome strike in July of 1920. Over a wage dispute, operating personnel walked off their jobs beginning July 1. With the help of Federal Marshalls, the New Orleans Police, and the sanction of the Governor, New Orleans Ry. & Lt. Co. tried to break the strike by restoring the car lines to operation. Although all but one line was "in operation" by July 9, service was unsatisfactory. Not enough strikebreakers were to be had — headways were infrequent and the threat of violence kept people from the car stops. Although jitneys were outlawed in New Orleans, there was much "jitneying" during the strike. The strike ended July 25th with full restoration of car service, and a satisfactory wage settlement. After the strike, there were some car service changes and improvements.

The lower end of the Carondelet Line was severed at Canal Street and made into two distinct routes, Desire and Louisa. Carondelet's upper end continued as usual (See: Routes, Chapter 4, for lines affected). Steam passenger train service of the New Orleans Terminal Co. to Chalmette was discontinued. On October 22, 1920, street railway cash fares were increased to 8¢ — increased operating costs and wages being the cause.

Service changes continued in 1921, but without decrease in rail mileage. The French Market-City Park Line was divorced from the Tchoupitoulas Line and renamed "City Park" Line. Two operations were discontinued. The Cemeteries Franchise Car and the South Peters Shuttle, both short working operations, ended service. The Magazine Line was cut back and the Oak Street Shuttle began service over former Magazine Line trackage. The use of train, or run, numbers began in 1921. These numbers are still displayed by N.O.P.S.I. streetcars, trackless trolleys, and buses.

In February of 1922, the upper floors of the New Orleans Ry. & Lt. Co. office building at Baronne and Common Streets were gutted by fire. This catastrophe destroyed invaluable records — photographs, car plans, drawings of plants and structures, maps, and some dates of car service changes. The loss is sorely felt by the

Spanish Fort pier, 1923. Track extended to the end of the pier.                    *Courtesy N.O.P.S.I.*

36

Canal and University Place, 1924.                                          *Chas. L. Franck Photo*

authors. After the fire, the company moved to temporary offices at 421 Baronne Street.

A complete reorganization of New Orleans' street railway, power, and light companies was begun in 1922. August 18, 1922, New Orleans Public Service Inc. was chartered under Louisiana Law with domicile at New Orleans. The new corporation was empowered through its charter to buy various street railway, electric, and gas lines — also to build railway and BUS lines. For the first month of its existence, the company did not have a President, rather was managed by a Board of Directors. On September 27 ,1922, the company was reorganized, retaining the same name, but with a chief executive. New officers took charge of the affairs of the newly created organization, New Orleans Public Service Incorporated. Mrs. R. S. Hecht was elected President on September 27.

Since September 27, 1922, there has been only one corporation, *N.O.P.S.I.,* controlling and/or owning all street railway, power, and natural gas services in New Orleans. From August 18, 1922 to January 1, 1926 can be regarded as the formative years of the great corporation. During this time, the following companies were absorbed into "Public Service" (exact dates for street railway companies given at end of this chapter in section titled "Succession of Companies"): New Orleans & Carrollton RR. Lt. & Pwr. Co., Orleans RR. Co., New Orleans & Pontchartrain Ry. Co., St. Charles St. RR. Co., New Orleans City RR. Co., New Orleans Gas Light Co., Consumers Electric Lt. & Pwr. Co., and Citizens Electric Co. Actually, as far as the casual observer was concerned, all street railway companies in the Crescent City appeared unified as early as 1903. The corporate changes of 1922-26 were "paper" transactions — the "form" having been fashioned nearly twenty years earlier. After January 1, 1926 (a final consolidation in a legal sense of N.O.P.S.I. properties), no further reorganizations or changes in corporate structure have taken place.

37

One of N.O.P.S.I.'s first improvements was reducing cash fares from 8¢ to 7¢. Owl cars began charging a 7¢ fare October 21, 1922 (owl fare had been a dime). The company was operating 225.364 miles of street railway (single track equivalent) at the close of 1922. As far as can be officially determined, this was the peak of street railway mileage for New Orleans.

Another extensive transit report was presented in 1923 to solve New Orleans' public transit problems. The J. A. Beeler Co. of New York submitted findings similar to those of the former Allison survey. However, some "owl" service that had been eliminated was restored and the "nightowls" of "The City That Care Forgot" were able to get about with all the abandon that the natives were used to. Again, a short walk at normally (in OTHER cities) odd hours, would bring a rider to a street car stop that had service.

Some changes suggested by the report were implemented immediately. In 1923, the North Peters (old N. O. C. RR. French Market Line) was discontinued, the Louisiana Line stopped terminating at the Ferry Building and a new line was created to provide that service (the Ferry Line).

Seeming oddities of New Orleans streetcar travel intrigued the authors of the Beeler Report. These quotes bear testimony:

"Mr. A. Morris Buck, New York representative of J. A. Beeler, has made an unexpected discovery: If the capacity loads carried by the cars of the N. O. Ry. & L. Co. after 9:00 P.M. and through midnight and thereafter are criterions by which the experts are to be guided, the people of New Orleans are *human bats*, as the street traffic there is different in this respect from any other city in the U. S. which Mr. Buck has studied.

"Another peculiarity of streetcar travel in New Orleans is that of Mondays. There appears no difference in volume between Saturdays and Mondays—one is as heavy as the other. This is due largely to the fact that all the big Canal Street department stores have their bargain day on Monday."

Owl service was frequent—20 minutes was the headway on the Canal, Esplanade, St. Charles, and Tulane Belts; 30 minutes on the Magazine, Coliseum, Carondelet, Clio, Broad, Peters Avenue, Dauphine, Annunciation and Villere Lines. The remainder of the lines had headways of from 45 minutes to one hour all night long. Even West End had cars hourly from midnight to 5:00 A.M. Some of the lines that normally operated double truck cars used single truckers for the "owl" service.

New Orleans is also known as "The City That Never Sleeps". Poetic license is not abused too greatly by this title, if the reader considers the aforementioned testimony.

Much rebuilding of equipment took place in 1923 and 1924. N.O.P.S.I. replaced "curative" maintenance with "preventive" maintenance. The new 800's were rolling and the 900's were on the way. A considerable number of "Palace" cars were rebuilt, getting new trucks, four motors, Tomlinson couplers (to haul trailers), and enclosed platforms. Experimental single truck car 288 was built at Carrollton Shops. The new car could be operated as a one or two man car—perfect for light lines (one man crew) for rush hour traffic (two man crew). However, New Orleans City Council would not change city ordinances which required two man crews on all streetcars. This failure to allow the one man streetcar operation accelerated the motor bus conversion program that was soon in coming. In 1924, N.O.P.S.I. started its first motor bus line. White built buses were installed on the new North Carrollton Line from Tulane to the main entrance to City Park, through a section of the city that never had regular street railway service (there had been a single track special service car line on Carrollton between Tulane and Canal for baseball crowds and non-revenue car movements, lasting several years and discontinued about 1924).

In 1924, the Freret Line was established and the Carondelet Line discontinued. The Carondelet duplicated other car lines, thus there was no bus service substituted. Track mileage was 221 with 367 double truck passenger motor cars, 42 double truck passenger trailers, 241 single truck passenger cars, 1 baggage trailer, and 74 work cars.

Three lines were abandoned in 1925 (without bus substitution): Ferry, Bayou St. John, and Peters Avenue. There were five motor bus lines in operation by August of 1925 (North Carrollton, Frenchman, St. Claude—a shuttle connecting with the Dauphine car line, Gentilly Road, Canal Boulevard). The Jackson-Claiborne united line was severed when the Jackson Line was widened to 5' 2½" gauge, October 28, 1925.

Two new car lines were established in 1926. The Dauphine was renamed "St. Claude" and rerouted, the Villere was renamed "Gentilly" and also rerouted. The Claiborne car line's gauge was widened to 5' 2½".

Street railway patronage in New Orleans reached an all-time peak in 1926. One hundred and forty-eight MILLION passengers rode over N.O.P.S.I.'s twenty-six street railway lines and five motor bus lines during this year. Although there had been years showing more revenue for N.O.P.S.I., 1926 was the GREAT year of transit patronage in New Orleans—in the era of the street railway. Abandonments up to this time constituted elimination of duplicating street railway service. After 1926, new bus lines meant a decrease in trolley service. Automobile registration figures began reflecting a shift in the public's attitude and frame of reference in regards to mass transportation. Individualized private transit began its erosion of public transportation at an accelerating pace. The "Golden Era" of the trolley had drawn to a close.

# THE DECLINE OF THE STREET RAILWAY
## IN
## NEW ORLEANS
### 1927 - 1964

Track mileage had decreased to 191.5 by the end of 1927. This year saw over two million fewer passengers on the streetcars and buses in New Orleans over the previous year. N.O.P.S.I. purchased the 1000 class of streetcars in 1928 from Perley A. Thomas and St. Louis Car Companies—these were the LAST streetcars purchased for use in New Orleans.

A disastrous year for public transportation in New Orleans was 1929. On July 1 at 10:00 P.M. began one of the lengthiest and most violent street railway strikes the nation has ever witnessed. The operating personnel struck over the company's unwillingness to accept a closed shop provision plus stronger curbs on the company's power to discharge men. Wages and hours did not enter the picture. Attempts to restore car service on July 5th were met with unbelievably intense violence. Streetcars were mobbed by crowds of strikers, sympathizers, out-of-town "professional" troublemakers—some cars were overturned. Mounted police and Federal Marshalls were unable to protect the street railway service—attempts to break the strike ceased. N.O.P.S.I.'s Vice-President A. B. Paterson began arbitration with President Green of the A.F. of L. and President Mahon of the union of street railway operating personnel. Although the men agreed to go back to work in August, and beginning August 15th gradual restoration of car service commenced, the strike was not settled until the strikers voted on October 10th to accept the Paterson-Green Agreement. The strike hit the company severely—1929 revenue was nearly two million dollars less than in 1928. FORTY MILLION fewer people rode cars and buses in New Orleans in 1929 as compared to 1928. Five street railway lines were abolished. Coliseum, Dryades, Oak Street Shuttle (replaced by New Orleans' first trackless trolley), St. Bernard (buses substituted), and Tchoupitoulas Lines ceased running.

Gauge of the St. Charles and Tulane Belts was converted to 5' 2½" in 1929, and the Orleans-Kenner Traction Co. discontinued running its interurban cars to downtown New Orleans (see Vol. I, page 117 and Errata and Addenda to Vol. I in this volume).

Despite the trials and set-backs in 1929, the year 1930 witnessed one of the largest outlays, visually and financially, that N.O.P.S.I. had ever undertaken at one time. This was the beautification of Canal Street. Nearly two miles of the street, beginning at the loop and extending out to North Claiborne Avenue, were bedecked in dazzling mosaics and ornate lighting standards. This three and a half million dollars project put Canal Street in the front rank as the most brilliantly lighted street in America. New Orleans Public Service Inc. paid for almost half the cost of this improvement, since the neutral ground and lighting standards were under its operation and maintenance.

Two streetcar lines faded out in 1931—France and South Claiborne Shuttle. Mileage had shrunk to 168.09, while rail equipment had fallen to 389 double truck passenger cars, 24 single truck passenger cars, 36 double truck passenger trailers, and 48 work cars.

There is nothing that can be recorded concerning rail operation from this point forward except cold, matter of fact figures, each year diminishing in total. Five rail lines were retired in 1932: Broad, Clio, Paris Avenue, Prytania, and Spanish Fort. Rail mileage had eroded to 143.85. The old Pontchartrain Railroad discontinued passenger service this year, after one hundred and one years of service—under the original corporate name (a record in this sense). N.O.P.S.I. began operating the Milneburg motor bus line, serving the area once, and for so long, covered by the Pontchartrain RR. The Louisville & Nashville RR. operated freight service on the "Pontch" for a few years, but by 1935 the Pontchartrain was dismantled—"Smoky Mary" was gone.

The Universal Transfer System made its appearance in New Orleans in the depths of the depression, on July 1, 1933. Rail abandonments again highlighted the New Orleans transit scene. Claiborne (North), Louisiana, Canal and Esplanade Belts, and the Shrewsbury Extension of the Napoleon Line were discontinued in 1934. During the depression, some barns were closed, including Carrollton (reopened 1943 to facilitate repairs and storage during WW II transit boom)—see chapter 7, "Barns", for greater detail.

Two more rail abandonments took place before World War II. Laurel Line closed down in 1939, followed by City Park Line in 1941. N.O.P.S.I. entered the transit boom of WW II with 109 miles of street railway trackage, 116.9 miles of motor bus and trackless trolley lines, 243 motor passenger cars (all double truck), 7 passenger trailers (out of service), 17 work cars, and 168 motor bus and trackless trolley units. In 1940, streetcars turned in 73.7% of the company's gross revenue from transit operations while logging 58.3% of vehicle miles. Trackless trolley provided only 1.4% of gross revenue and 2.2% of vehicle miles. Motor buses made up the 24.9% remaining of gross revenue and the 39.5% of vehicle miles. Employees in N.O.P.S.I.'s Railway Department comprised 1,327 people in 1941, including 59 in the Roadway Division, 172 in the Equipment Division, 1,084 in Transportation Division, and 12 in the Schedule Division. The Railway Department handled all modes of city transit,

Only FB&D type car in existence (1964)—first "fan" trip conducted in New Orleans, 1962.        *Courtesy Otto A. Goessl*

bus, trackless trolley, and streetcar. Patronage for 1940 constituted 124 million riders. The increase compared to the lean 1930's was due mainly to the expanded city area served by transit vehicles, made possible by the motor bus. Also, by 1940 New Orleans' population had burgeoned to 490,000.

Ownership of transit operations in New Orleans had wavered through the years between local and outside groups. When World War II began, the outside group stage was in force. N.O.P.S.I. was then controlled by Electric Light & Power Corp. of New York City, in turn controlled by Electric Bond & Share Co.

Without adding new equipment during the war, N.O.P.S.I. handled a tremendous increase in transit riding. The peak was reached in 1945 when 246,000,000 people used streetcars, motor buses, and trackless trolleys in New Orleans. The manpower shortage dictated the employment of women as "conductorettes' on streetcars from 1943 to 1946.

When WW II ended in 1945, there was a fanatic return to the private auto, at great expense to the taxpayer who had to pour millions of dollars into elevated expressways. All this sacrifice to avoid a few minutes of waiting—while the car and bus fare in New Orleans remained a whopping seven cents! Further conversions of rail lines to rubber tired transit continued. In 1946, the Freret Line was replaced, followed by Jackson in 1947. Three heavy lines capitulated in 1948—Magazine, Gentilly, and the immortalized Desire Line.

Trackless trolleys replaced streetcars on the St. Claude Line in 1949. West End Line was motorized in 1950. In 1951, the St. Charles and Tulane Belts operation was discontinued. Trackless trolleys replaced streetcars on Tulane Avenue while streetcars remained on St. Charles Avenue and South Carrollton Avenue (from St. Charles to Dixon only) carrying the route name "St. Charles". In August of 1952, the St. Charles Line was cut back to South Carrollton and South Claiborne (where—in what place or city—can one find two streets prefixed by "SOUTH" that INTERSECT? Disbelievers please refer to a New Orleans map).

Through a quarter of a century, the most hectic and turbulent years, of city transit operation in New Orleans, one man held the President's chair of New Orleans Public Service Inc. This was Mr. A. B. Paterson. The enthusiast of electric traction may be disappointed with the record, the rapid erosion of rail mileage and the upshooting growth of the less captivating rubber tired transit vehicle. However, were the trying times of the late 1920's, the awful 1930's, and the not much better 1940's put into the hands of the Beauregards, the Labuzans, the McCoards, and the Nicolsons—the results would have been no doubt similar, except that streetcars MAY have disappeared from New Orleans earlier. Where else in this nation has city transportation functioned so well during the transit decline, and with a static fare? Where else can one ride a city bus for a dime?

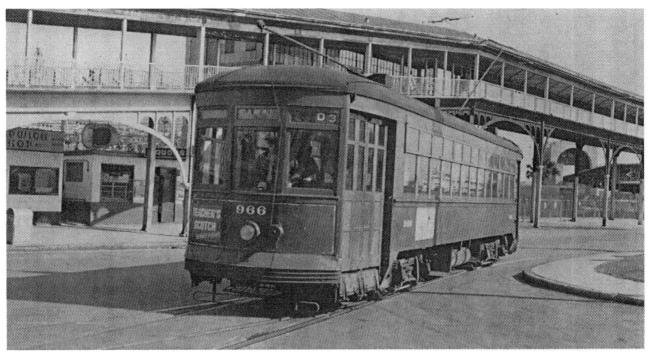

Foot of Canal, about 1960. Walkway to Ferry Building shown in background.          *Courtesy Otto A. Goessl*

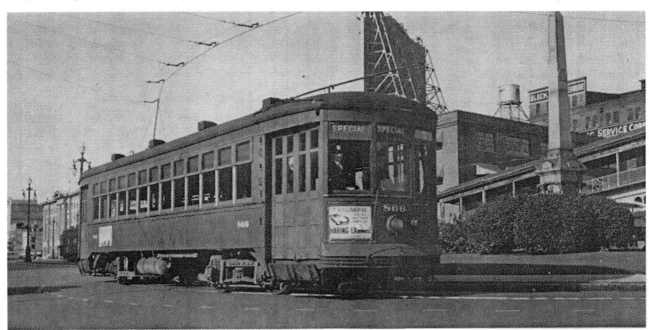

*Courtesy Otto A. Goessl*
December 1963 Texas ERA chartered tour, turning at Liberty Monument, Foot of Canal Street. The 866 is one of the Brill built 800s.

Presidents of N.O.P.S.I. and Their Tenures of Office

R. S. Hecht ........................from September 27, 1922
to April 15, 1923
Herbert B. Flowers ..................from April 15, 1923
to July 11, 1930
A. B. Paterson ......................from July 11, 1930
to May 16, 1951
George S. Dinwiddie ..............from May 16, 1951
to May 20, 1959

Gerald L. Andrus ....................from May 20, 1959
to August 27, 1962
Clayton L. Nairne ..................from August 27, 1962

New Orleans Public Service Inc. began 1953 with 277.748 miles of transit route mileage, divided as follows: Motor bus—193.131; Trackless trolley—48.391; Street railway—36.226. Revenue equipment consisted of 702 units (349 motor buses, 212 trackless trolleys, and only 141 streetcars). At this time as is true today,

South Claiborne at Nashville—September 4, 1951.

N.O.P.S.I. was controlled by Middle South Utilities, Inc. of New York.

Two lines were motorized in 1953, South Claiborne and the popular "Royal Blue Line", Napoleon. Only two car lines remained—Canal and St. Charles. Ten years passed that demonstrated an almost infinite capacity for endurance these lines seemed to enjoy. It is a mystery to many observers how the two lines with their circa-thirty year old streetcars survived in New Orleans while elsewhere in the United States such streetcar lines were being refitted with modern equipment or were being motorized. However, a peculiar situation does exist in New Orleans. First, rather than buying new streetcars, N.O.P.S.I. is demonstrating that the old, conventional type of streetcar is timeless. The company has just completed refurbishing thirty five of the Perley Thomas cars in the 900 series. These cars are in better condition now than when they were delivered in 1924. Secondly, most of the St. Charles Line's route is in the lovely neutral ground of St. Charles Avenue (see: Routes, Chapter 3 for a description of this line). Many residents along St. Charles Avenue do not want to see the street railway removed for fear this would give the city "carte blanche" to widen the Avenue at the expense of the neutral ground. Fortunately, threats to the life of the 129 year old rail line (the oldest street railway line in the world still in operation) have been few and, until now, harmless.

Alas, not so fortunate was the Canal Line. Early in the morning of May 31, 1964, the last regularly scheduled Canal Line car, No. 958 (run No. 14), pulled up to the Canal Station (Barn), transferred its passengers to car No. 972, and then "put in" for the last time. Car 972, a "Special" run and the last streetcar to run

on the Canal Line, carried a banner reading, "See Me On St. Charles" out to the Cemeteries then back to St. Charles Street where a "last car and first bus" ceremony of short duration was held. The 972 then sped out to the Carrollton Station. Buses took over the Canal Line at 5:00 A.M. on May 31st.

The change in Canal Street is evident. From North Claiborne out to City Park Avenue, Canal Street has a narrower neutral ground minus trees. The neutral ground from North Claiborne in to Front Street, and the Liberty Monument, has had rails removed and has been paved for motor bus use (except for the ONE block between Carondelet and St. Charles, where the St. Charles Line turns to begin outbound trips—this track is on the "up" side of the Canal Street neutral ground and does not interfere with the two paved bus lanes). The transit improvement is there to be seen. Three bus lines that used to end at City Park Avenue and Canal Street, transferring passengers to the Canal Line cars, now run all the way in to the Liberty Monument at the foot of Canal Street.

What has been the real cost of this transit improvement? The *world-wide* image of Canal Street has been severely altered. Immutability is necessary for the preservation of historic charm and character—and the disappearance of the streetcars has torn the heart out of Canal Street's image. Could something have been done to retain streetcars on Canal Street?

It takes no great explaining to show that saving the Canal Line was not the responsibility of N.O.P.S.I. The company is not an historical foundation. Rather, it is a private enterprise in business for one and only one purpose—to make a fair return on operations that satisfies owners and investors after all expenses, payrolls,

Last of the Canal Line, St. Charles and Canal Streets. May 31, 1964, about 5:00 A.M.
*Courtesy Otto A. Goessl*

and taxes have been paid. N.O.P.S.I. can alter or upgrade its services for economy, or other, purposes so long as the public is not harmed.

The task—if not DUTY—of saving the streetcars on Canal Street rested upon other shoulders.

The New Orleans city government, embodied in its City Council, almost to the man blindly followed N.O.P.S.I.'s plan to substitute buses for streetcars on the Canal Line. The city government offered or suggested no plan whereby the car line could have been saved, and encouraged no one else to do so. From the City government, no official concern was expressed for the state and/or preservation of New Orleans' worldwide image—only the usual unctuous platitudes on "progress".

The city's syndicated press system of two papers, the "Times-Picayune" and the "States-Item", both violently opposed retaining streetcars on Canal Street.

Few if any of the many historical and preservation societies of New Orleans concerned themselves with the loss of the Canal cars. They were quiet with their ideas as to what removal of the cars would do to Canal Street.

A small group of citizens, organized under the name "Streetcars Desired, Inc.", tried earnestly to save the Canal Line. The organization was sincere and devoid of ulterior motives or petty affectations—as were most of its members. The majority of its members were not fanatics merely infatuated with streetcars, but were New Orleanians concerned over what the loss of streetcars on Canal Street would do to the city's charm and well-known character. However, "Streetcars Desired" suffered from several drawbacks. The organization did not have the funds or the necessary number of constituents to wage a long, drawn-out and well advised battle through the public communications media, the papers,

television, and radio. The group did not devise or publicize any plan outlining how the Canal Line could be saved. Refusal of the city government to allow the streetcar issue to be settled by referendum was unfortunate, although the New Orleans City Charter did not have a provision for referendum at the time.

What plan or plans should have been proposed and actively publicized by "Streetcars Desired" and at least "considered" by New Orleans city government? The most feasible plan for saving the Canal Line probably would have entailed a partial subsidy to N.O.P.S.I. to cover any losses incurred in the operation of streetcars over the line. A public well alerted to the value of streetcars to Canal Street's and the city's image possibly would have endorsed such a plan, and certainly would NOT have censored anyone else supporting the plan.

What of the North Claiborne to the River neutral ground operation of buses, so important to those citizens weary of transferring at City Park Avenue and Canal Street? Buses could be run non-stop via the expressway from City Park Avenue to North Claiborne, thence over North Claiborne to Canal (a specially arranged system of traffic lights, police direction, and the prohibition of trucks from North Claiborne between Canal Street and the overpass from 8:00 A.M. to 9:30 A.M. and from 4:00 P.M. to 6:00 P.M. would facilitate the movement of traffic and buses during the rush hours). Buses could operate with streetcars on the paved neutral ground of Canal Street between North Claiborne and the River. They have done it in the past on city streets. Since most West End, Lakeview, and Lake Vista bus riders are destined for downtown, the problem of transferring would not be so annoying.

There was a rather slim chance that the public would

43

Howard Ave. at Baronne, about 1960. Lee Monument in background. *Courtesy Otto A. Goessl*

ask that streetcars be restored to Canal Street. "Streetcars Desired" circulated a petition in 1963-64 asking for referendum, asking that the matter of retaining the cars be put in the public's hands at the voting booths. Over 11,000 signatures were collected (New Orleans has a voting registration of nearly 200,000. The city government scoffed at the petition as they could well afford to, knowing that the majority of the people are indifferent). The issue of saving the streetcars was never voted upon, but the matter of having in the City Charter an amendment allowing referendum was voted upon in the General Election of November 3, 1964. The amendment was not approved by the electorate. Fully 162,479 New Orleanians cast votes for one or the other Presidential candidate, but only 48,606 bothered to vote for or against the referendum amendment. Had referendum been voted in, "Streetcars Desired" would have circulated a petition for an election to restore streetcars to Canal Street.

With but one rail line left in New Orleans, some remarks outlining the disappearance of the streetcar should be made.

Clearly, the change in the American mind that calls for individual and private transportation as opposed to public transit is the chief factor determining conversion from rail to rubber tired transportation. The loss of patronage suffered by public transit calls for a minimum of operating costs—and buses are much cheaper than streetcars to operate. Maximum flexibility is likewise a necessity with present day city transit. New city residential areas have a lower density of population than do the older sections nearer the business district. The older sections are losing their populations quickly to the apartment projects and suburbs. The motor bus is the least expensive vehicle that can attain maximum flexibility. Establishment of giant shopping centers has altered the flow of traffic in American cities. Less people shop downtown now, and most shopping is done in the shopping center. Cities have been cut into self-sufficient cells wherein the private auto is almost the exclusive transit vehicle.

In some very large cities, commuting and travel to the central business district is being handled—at great expense—by rapid transit. Electric railways traveling on private rights of way, with station stops and large auto parking areas, handle enormous numbers of people that would otherwise be forced to ride buses or drive in autos. In cities, such as Toronto, Ontario, New York City, N. Y., Boston, Mass., San Francisco, Cal., and Cleveland, Ohio, the saturation point has been reached with road transportation (auto and bus)—the downtown areas simply cannot handle any more autos. In such cases, rapid transit is being instituted. The *street* railway, however, has actually passed out of the American city transit spectrum.

In New Orleans, the above conditions apply, and are magnified by the following factors:

1. Circuitous and duplicating rail lines requiring straightening and simplifying.
2. Major expenditures arising when cars and trackage needed replacements—a new street railway or merely a fleet of buses?

44

3. Increasing operating costs and the almost prohibitive task of finding streetcar parts as time passes.
4. The impact of the 1929-1934 depression upon business and city travel.
5. Major expenditures often resulting from civic improvements, especially street paving and re-alignment projects.
6. Seeing heavy car lines going bus in this country, while in Europe, even small cities are retaining streetcars and upgrading the service to semi-rapid transit in many instances (even with auto registration rising), makes the authors wonder whether some of the bus conversions here are more fad than finance.

The last named factor was often an immediate cause of an abandonment, although the abandonment would occur sooner or later anyway. Many streets in New Orleans were unpaved up to very recent years. As late as World War II, many minor streets were dirt, gravel, or crushed oyster shells. When the city began to pave streets, to construct new streets and/or otherwise re-align them, it was advantageous to discontinue the car line affected at the same time.

By a glance at the track map or the all-time electric railway map in this volume, the reader can readily see that N.O.P.S.I.'s inherited rail system was a tangle. Some parts of town were over-served while new sections had no service. There was little opportunity for crosstown travel. By 1943, the system had evolved into a functional network that carried riders in any direction they may have desired. Lines were spaced at a reasonable distance from one another, yet no one had to walk any great distance to a bus or car stop. Due to this spacing, service could be frequent, even on the crosstown bus lines.

One matter pertinent to the straightening of lines was the question of each line's primary function. Was it a radial, crosstown, or feeder type of service? A study of the old route layouts reveals that some lines tried to combine some or all of these functions. The service requirements are not the same for the three types of lines, thus a bi or tri-purpose line was wasting car mileage. Furthermore, such lines are not convenient for most passengers—a Louisiana Line patron going downtown would not wish to ride all the way out to La Salle Street before finally reaching University Place and Canal. Much unnecessary transferring was mandatory—and riders do not like to transfer. Thus, in some cases the crosstown portion of a line was supplanted by buses or trackless trolleys while the radial portion continued in operation, as a car line.

World War II brought the Office of Defense Transportation into being. The ODT at once ordered all street railway lines then in service to be continued for the duration and for trackless trolley and bus lines to be re-routed wherever practicable to act as feeders for the rail lines. This held up abandonment programs in U. S. cities, New Orleans included, for three years. The ODT "freeze" was lifted in 1945.

As lines were trimmed, equipment became surplus and was at first sold for use as dwellings, businesses, or other. In no time the countryside near New Orleans became cluttered with old transit vehicles which shortly became eyesores. After the war, N.O.P.S.I. was ordered to sell cars only for scrap within a hundred mile radius of the city. In only a few instances were New Orleans streetcars sold to another company for continued use on rails (see page 111).

And now the time has come for the story to be recorded memories—now closes an era that arose with staggering force and that contributed mightily to the development of cities, towns and country, yet started to die within a brief span of years seemingly much too short for the enormous investment involved. Electric traction appeared to be the perfect answer to mass transit, and for a half century successfully met all demands upon it. Changing times have made new demands and presented new and more complex problems. Today we are searching for the answer to mass transportation's challenge and problems with no clear solution yet at hand.

## SUCCESSION OF COMPANIES
(Companies that constructed trackage and performed no service are not listed)

1. Pontchartrain Railroad Company (see Note A)
   Chartered:    January 20, 1830
   Abandoned:    1935
2. New Orleans & Carrollton Railroad Company
   Chartered:    February 9, 1833
   Reorganized (by sale):
      To 22, September 26, 1901
3. Jefferson & Lake Pontchartrain Railway Company (see NOTE B)
   Chartered:    March 25, 1840
   Abandoned: November 23, 1864 (last train)
4. New Orleans City Railroad Company
   Chartered:    June 15, 1860
   Reorganized (by sale): To 16, June 11, 1883

5. Jefferson City Railroad Company
   Chartered:    February 18, 1863
   Reorganized (by sale):
      To 6, August 29, 1865
6. Magazine Street Railroad Company
   Chartered:    May 30, 1866 (organized 1865)
   Reorganized (by sale): To 7, May 20, 1873
7. Sixth District & Carrollton Railroad Company
   Chartered:    May 6, 1873
   Merged: To 8, October 7, 1880
8. Crescent City Railroad Company (see NOTE C)
   Chartered:    August 30, 1866
   Merged: To 20, June 1, 1899

9. St. Charles Street Railroad Company
   (see NOTE D)
   Chartered: September 27, 1866
   Consolidated: To 25, December 14, 1923

10. Canal & Claiborne Streets Railroad Company
    Chartered: September 2, 1867
    Reorganized (by sale): To 17, July 3, 1888

11. Orleans Railroad Company (see NOTE E)
    Chartered: July 31, 1868
    Consolidated: To 25, September 27, 1922

12. New Orleans Metairie & Lake Railroad Company
    (see NOTE F)
    Chartered: April 29, 1869
    Purchased: By 4, December 21, 1875

13. Carondelet Street & Carrollton City Railroad
    Company
    Chartered: July 18, 1870
    Construction suspended: July, 1872
    Dismantled: Late 1876

14. Canal Street, City Park & Lake Railroad Company
    Chartered: May 19, 1873
    Reorganized (by sale): To 15, April 9, 1879

15. New Orleans, Spanish Fort & Lake Railroad
    Company (see NOTE G)
    Chartered: March 31, 1879
    Abandoned: July 12, 1903 (last train)

16. New Orleans City & Lake Railroad Company
    (see NOTE H)
    Chartered: May 17, 1883
    Reorganized (by sale): To 20, May 8, 1899

17. Canal & Claiborne Railroad Company
    Chartered: June 26, 1888
    Merged: To 2, April 3, 1899

18. New Orleans Traction Company Limited
    Chartered: November 29, 1892
    Franchises and Rights sold: To 20, 1899

19. Orleans & Jefferson Railway Company, Limited
    (The)
    Chartered: June 1, 1897
    Reorganized (by sale):
    To 21, September 25, 1901

20. New Orleans City Railroad Company
    (see NOTE I)
    Chartered: February 28, 1899
    Consolidated: To 25, May 27, 1925

21. New Orleans & Pontchartrain Railway Company
    (see NOTE J)
    Chartered: July 8, 1901
    Consolidated: To 25, September 27, 1922

22. New Orleans & Carrollton Railroad,
    Light & Power Company (see NOTE K)
    Chartered: August 28, 1901
    Consolidated: To 25, September 27, 1922

23. New Orleans Railways Company
    Incorporated IN NEW JERSEY:
    January 28, 1902
    Reorganized (by sale): To 24, July 16, 1905

24. New Orleans Railway & Light Company
    Chartered: June 12, 1905
    Reorganized (by sale):
    To 25, September 27, 1922

25. New Orleans Public Service Incorporated
    (see NOTE L)
    Chartered: August 18, 1922

---

NOTES:

A) Retained its identity throughout its history, although controlled by New Orleans, Mobile & Texas R.R. Co. from December 12, 1871 to October 4, 1881 and by Louisville & Nashville R.R. Co. from October 5, 1881 to abandonment date.

B) J. & L. P. Ry. Co. both built and owned by New Orleans & Carrollton R.R. Co. Although abandoned in 1864, its stock with ownership of land titles remained in hands of N. O. & C. RR. Co. and followed all corporate changes of same. As late as 1932, J. & L. P. Ry. Co. existed on paper as a corporation controlled by N.O.P.S.I.

C) Leased by New Orleans Traction Co. Ltd. 1892 to 1899.

D) Leased by New Orleans Rys. Co. 1902 to 1905 and by New Orleans Ry. & Lt. Co. 1905 to 1922.

E) Same as NOTE D.

F) Purchased by New Orleans City R.R. Co. (No. 4) before construction commenced.

G) Acquired by East Louisiana R.R. November 15, 1895, sold to New Orleans & Western R.R. July 1, 1897, and in turn sold to New Orleans Belt & Terminal Co. April 9, 1901. N. O. B. & T. Co. sold all property EXCEPT N. O. S. F. & L. RR. Co. to New Orleans Terminal Co. December 26, 1903. Retaining its identity through these corporate changes, the N. O. S. F. & L. RR. Co. was abandoned 1904 and lasted twenty-one years "on paper". Receiver J. F. Fitzwilson sold the "paper corporation" to the New Orleans Terminal Co. June 24, 1935.

H) Same as NOTE C.

I) Same as NOTE D.

J) Same as NOTE D.

K) Same as NOTE D.

L) For several years, N.O.P.S.I. did have a comma in its corporate name, thusly: N.O.P.S,I. However, research could not confirm that the comma was legally part of the name.

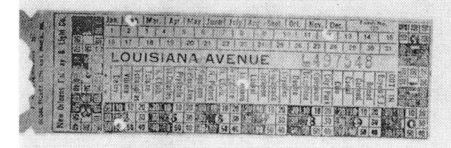

**TAKE ONE.**

# The New Orleans and Carrollton R. R. Weekly.

Vol. II.    New Orleans, Feb. 7, 1901.    No. 2.

Passengers are requested not to present large bills in payment of fare, as it is often impossible for conductors to make the change. The Company requires conductors to have with them at all times change to the amount of two dollars, this being the largest amount which it is practicable for them to carry around with them to accommodate any one passenger.

It is well known that for years it has been an almost universal practice in street railway operation for conductors to be required to furnish change to the amount of $2.00 only, therefore passengers should not be disappointed at not getting change on the car.

If there is any reasonable way of furnishing change, conductors will gladly do so to accommodate patrons.

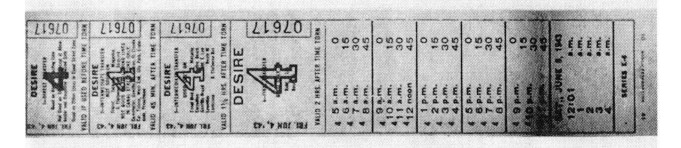

*Louis C. Hennick Collection*

Tickets, left to right: circa 1866, circa 1870, 1899. Transfers, top to bottom: 1920, circa 1925, circa 1933, 1943, and 1951.

An unknown artist captured Canal St. in the late 1840s or early 1850s. Note omnibuses.

Chas. L. Franck Photo

48

# CANAL STREET DOWN THE YEARS

## CHAPTER 2

When New Orleans was mapped in 1719, the upper limits of the city extended along what is now Canal Street, from the River to North Rampart Street. City limits, in terms of today's streets, were: Canal Street, North Rampart Street and Esplanade. The city faced the River. During the 18th century, New Orleans was a walled city. The limits set by Bienville were made into earthen and stone ramparts, with the ground in front cleared to deny cover to any potential enemy. Drainage ditches parallelled the walls outside the city. The cleared area along the upper wall, down what today is Canal Street, was called "Terre Commune"—public ground, or "common". After the Louisiana Purchase of 1803, the Americans removed the ramparts in 1804. The walls were leveled and the old limits became thoroughfares. Shortly after 1804, the upper limit thoroughfare was named "Canal", influenced by the large drainage ditch in its center. After the War of 1812, Canal Street became important as new business and residential construction proceeded up the River from the older part of town. By 1825, the street had become an avenue of commerce. For some time during the middle of the 19th century, there was talk of building a navigation canal down Canal Street, bringing the coastwise and lake vessels right to the center of town. This was the dream of Mr. Judah P. Touro, wealthy and prominent New Orleans citizen. Canal Street was renamed "Touro Avenue" in the 1850's. Citizens persisted in using the name "Canal". In a short while the street officially regained its traditional name.

New Orleans prided itself in its "Grand Boulevard", which was Chartres Street until 1866. Canal Street officially captured this distinction that year, so claim several local papers of the time.

The "canal" in Canal Street, the drainage ditch from North Claiborne to the River, had been filled long before 1866. By that time, the 170' 6" wide street sported a neutral ground well lined with street railway tracks over the filled in "canal" portion. However, the section of Canal Street from North Claiborne out to City Park Avenue (then Metairie Road) still had a large open drainage ditch. Tracks of the New Orleans City RR. Co.'s Canal Line were suspended OVER the ditch. In 1872, a contracting firm chartered under the unusual name "Louisiana Portable Railway Company" filled in the ditch from North Claiborne to Metairie Road, with N. O. C. RR. Co.'s tracks removed and placed beside the road in the neutral ground. Trees were planted over this section in the neutral ground. As each year passed, the street became increasingly pleasing to see.

Canal Street is THE main and central artery of traffic in New Orleans, the traditional line of demarcation between the French and American sections of the city. The division goes further to separate two distinct eras of history and three basic forms of architecture. French and Spanish architecture dominate the French section ("Vieux Carre") and hark back to pre-1825 times when that section or quarter was the principal economic force of the city. The American section with its more modern buildings denotes later periods in the city's growth and development.

New Orleans' fine retail establishments for years have lined Canal Street between Camp and North Rampart. The street is also a grand promenade. With thousands of tourists, New Orleans' own cosmopolitan population, and hundreds of ships monthly putting in, bearing many flags, a short walk on Canal Street will reveal many nationalities and different faces. Canal Street is a focal point of the fantastic Carnival Season, "Mardi Gras".

The term "Mardi Gras" so frequently applied to the Carnival festivities is loosely used, but has become almost the accepted reference. Literally, "Mardi Gras" is a French expression designating "Shrove Tuesday", the LAST day of the Carnival season. Festivities end at the midnight before Lenten season begins.

The first of the Carnival Balls is that of the exclusive Twelfth Night Organization in January—without parade.

Many groups do hold balls and present magnificent parades as well. The oldest and best known are: Krewes of Momus, Proteus, Comus, and the Parade and Ball of Rex, himself—Rex, of course, is king.

The first "Mardi Gras" celebration was a spontaneous affair held about 1830. The practice of general masking by participants came into being some five years later. The Carnival became a yearly throw from that point to the present day, seeming to increase in vitality through the years as various organizations were formed to participate. The annual institution feature of the festival has been compromised only a few times —during war years.

"Mardi Gras" is a riot of color with joy reigning supreme. In spite of the enormous crowds and seemingly unrestrained masses, there is surprisingly little disorder or crime. Floats built by the various groups join annually in the parades day and night. The night parades are the most brilliant with their flaming torches and myriad of colored lights decorating buildings and strung along streets. The monumental day parade carries Rex through the central section of the city and the "royalty" is toasted at the various clubs, such as the Boston, Pickwick, and others. This parade passes old City Hall where Rex is given the key to the city. Rex rules throughout Mardi Gras Day (Tuesday), until midnight, the end of Mardi Gras.

Canal St. in late 1870s with usual saturation of transit vehicles.

The official "Mardi Gras" anthem in use since the 1870's is played by all bands participating in the festivities. The lyrics are short, paying homage to Rex, as follows:

"If I ever cease to love,
If I ever cease to love—
May the cows lay eggs
and the fish have legs,
If I ever cease to love."

During the heyday of the trolley, much rerouting and severing of lines entering and crossing Canal Street took place during the parades. The following is typical for the period of 1910-15:

The lines from uptown were turned back at Canal Street. The same practice applied to lines from down-town. Lines coming in on Canal Street were turned back at Liberty Street. On side streets with double tracks, cars swung trolleys, crossed over, and proceeded back on their routes. The few streets with single track (such as Royal, Bourbon, etc.) alternated cars, seeing two-way operation by groups of four or five cars, running in this manner from Canal to Dumaine. Up to about 1898, cars were run on Canal Street during parade time and were frozen there.

Only during the year 1899 did a carnival parade in New Orleans have electrically lighted floats on streetcar trucks, believed to be the first time this was done anywhere. The route of the parade thus became restricted, and the rigidity of the rails did not permit the floats to be drawn up alongside the various club

Carnival Scene, about 1896. Streetcars are 1894 Brills with 22-E trucks.　　　　*Louis C. Hennick Collection*

Mardi Gras, 1926.　　　　*Courtesy N.O.P.S.I.*

Late 1890s Rex Parade.

*Louis C. Hennick Collection*

Mardi Gras of 1951 — cars lined up due to Rex parade.

*Courtesy Otto A. Goessl*

*Courtesy N.O.P.S.I.*

Early 1895 Canal Street scene, looking "out" toward Lake from Camp Street. In foreground, terminus for New Orleans City & Lake RR Co's. Magazine and Prytania Lines (Magazine Line still mulecar). Orleans RR. Co. mulecar seen looping around Henry Clay Statue (O.RR. lines were not electrified until November of 1895). Canal, Dauphine, and Esplanade Lines' (NOC&LRRCo.) electric cars—1894 Brills—seen grouped at their terminus on Lake side of Clay Statue. West End Line steam dummy visible in next block.

53

balconies where toasts were given to the rulers of the Mystic Krewes. Although elaborate in presentation and decoration, there was not the fantastic aura lent by the flaming multi colored torches. Hence, electricity was used but once.

In the old days, and until recently, teams of horses or mules pulled the floats. Lately, truck chassis have been used. However, the bright flambeaux and flares carried by the hooded, marching figures surrounding the floats remain the most colorful way of illuminating the night parades.

In these pages, we offer a kaleidoscopic assortment of Canal Street and "Mardi Gras" festival views spanning more than a century. All but one view have one thing in common: Public transit vehicles, be they omnibuses, mule cars, electric cars, or motor buses. That one photo has been included for its (up till now) uniqueness—not one single trolley car to be seen, as there was a transit strike in progress at the time. The strike photo is on page 28 .

The photo of Canal at Camp on page 57 taken in March of 1902 is not a traffic "block", but rather is the normal movement of cars at nine o'clock in the morning. Depicted here is the transit scene immediately prior to New Orleans Railways' consolidation of street railway properties in New Orleans. The *Street Railway Journal* used this photo in an article presenting and attempting to solve the problems created by the growing number of streetcars on Canal Street.

Even before 1902 there were five tracks on Canal Street between North Claiborne and the loop at Liberty Place (Delta Street). Four tracks were through and the fifth (middle) track was used for a stub end terminal by several lines that did not go all the way in to the loop. For instance, in 1902, cars of the Orleans RR. Co.'s Bayou St. John, Broad, and City Park lines used the middle track for their terminus between St. Charles and Camp. Inbound, cars of these three lines swung from the outside river-bound track into the middle track and swung trolleys. Outbound, these cars proceeded over to the outside lower side track and turned into Dauphine (later into Burgundy) to thread their way through the old French Section by various ways out "back o' town" to their respective destinations. Other lines using the middle track for stub end terminus were: South Peters, Tchoupitoulas, Levee-Barracks, West End, French Market (N. O. C. & L. RR., later combined with Tchoupitoulas for a line CROSSING Canal, and renamed North Peters after the union was severed), and, for a while, Annunciation.

The two outside tracks were dual-gauge (4' 8½" and 5' 2½") while the two second tracks and the middle track were 5' 2½" gauge.

Cars using the outside track loaded and unloaded from the usual "on" side, while cars using the second tracks had passengers boarding and alighting from the "off" or left side. Passengers using cars that terminated on the middle (fifth) track were literally "in the

*Street Railway Journal*
Rex Parade and Mardi Gras crowds, 1897.

middle" if they tried to board cars while on the "stand".

This situation existed until about 1920 on the block mentioned (Canal, from St. Charles to Camp). After this year, the old Orleans RR. lines came up Dauphine Street and, swinging onto the outside lower side track, proceeded one block on Canal, turned into Burgundy, and resumed their outbound journeys.

In 1905, a double track was built from the loop at the foot of Canal (Liberty Place—Delta Street) out to the Ferry House, about fifty feet from the waters edge at the docks. The first line to use this extension was the Dryades Line. In 1917, the Louisiana Line assumed this task. The primary purpose of the extension was to handle the Algiers ferry (Fifth District) customers.

*Photo (right) courtesy Rita Ann Collins*
Looking out Canal toward Lake, about 1890. Light tower at Canal and Carondelet, terminus for West End steam trains. Henry Clay Statue visible in foreground at Canal and St. Charles (to the left) and Royal (to the right). Turntable in foreground for New Orleans City & Lake RR. Magazine and Prytania Lines. On the "Lake" side of the statue, on Canal Street, is the terminus for the N.O.C.&L.RR. Canal, Dauphine, and Esplanade Lines. Orleans RR. lines came in on Canal from Burgundy and looped around Clay Statue. Canal & Claiborne Sts. RR. Co. terminus at foot of Canal, using outside tracks on Canal Street. St. Charles St. RR. Co. terminus on Canal between Camp and Magazine. Note starters' houses and open-top feed and supply car on siding. This photo well illustrates the track complex at Clay Statue, the ballast block paving on Canal, the covered walks, the street cars—all the vanished charms that once graced Canal Street with a world wide image.

54

Canal St., looking toward Lake from N. Peters, about 1897. FB&D type car in left foreground, followed by a St. Charles Street RR. Co: Pullman. Right is an 1894 Brill. Large building in right foreground is U.S. Custom House.

The last line to use the multi-track layover and terminus at the foot of Canal Street was the old "Cemeteries", or Canal Line. Where there were as many as nine tracks at the layover, there were only four when the Canal Line was motorized on May 31, 1964.

During the rush hour, three tracks were used for loading. It was a novel arrangement, and operated as follows: Outside track cars proceeded almost to North Peters to load; second track cars loaded in the block above North Peters; cars using the third track loaded in the first block (with the loop as the base). The only other car line still in operation today, the St. Charles Line, uses Canal Street only between Carondelet and St. Charles—one block.

The once proud street railway operation in New Orleans eclipsed other large cities in some respects. The terminus at Liberty Place, the loop at the foot of Canal Street, saw in 1902 more lines terminating and grouping there than did the famous streetcar terminus at the Ferry Building in San Francisco. Very few cities had long stretches of five-track operation and the multi-track terminus at Liberty Place was quite uncommon.

March 1902, taken five minutes after famous photo in Charlton's 1955 "Street Railways of New Orleans", page 20.

E. Harper Charlton Collection

Canal St. in early 1920s,                                    *Chas. L. Franck Photo*

*Courtesy Otto A. Goessl*

Streetcars looped at the foot of Canal Street during the period 1869-1964.  This photo taken about 1960.

Canal and Carondelet Sts., 1948.

*Courtesy N.O.P.S.I.*

Canal St., 1958. Beautification of 1957 just completed.

*E. Harper Charlton Collection*

Canal at St. Charles, looking toward Lake. Fall of 1961. *Courtesy A. E. Brown*

Canal Street today. Modern GM and Flxible buses shown. *Louis C. Hennick Collection*

*Chas. L. Franck Photo*

Carondelet and Common, circa 1939, in center of New Orleans' financial district. Building at right foreground is old Hennen Building, New Orleans' first "Skyscraper" (now the Maritime Building)

# ROUTES

In this chapter, the various street railway and steam suburban railroad routes are individually covered. Instead of sentencing the reader to labor through listings for selected years, each route's history is given under one heading. The routes are listed by official designation, by the route sign nomenclature as displayed by each route's cars.

During the animal traction era, streetcars were gaily painted with nearly all streets served by a particular route inscribed across cars' sides, letterboard, and dash. Older illustrations in this book reveal this empirically. When electric cars entered the scene, the gilt-edge quaintness of route designation took a more simple form. Route signs began appearing in streetcars' clerestory front light, dash and/or upper sash of vestibule windows.

Route designations as used in the Compendium of Routes were more or less uniform after electrification, with only minor variations—the addition of "Ave." here or the dropping of "St." there.

An historical summary enables readers to find cru-

cial dates without a tiring search. Lists of abandonment dates, etc. will be helpful, also.

Note that some routes are not given dates for electrification, merely a dotted line. This indicates a line was opened with electric cars. In instances certain animal powered lines were abandoned, the word "NEVER" implies the line was never electrified. The profusion of street names in this chapter requires the use of many abbreviations.

Below capsule list of street railway mileage for New Orleans outlines eras of expansion and demise of rail service, beginning from 1905 only:

| | | | |
|---|---|---|---|
| 1905: | 191 | 1931: | 168 |
| 1910: | 201 | 1932: | 144 |
| 1915: | 217 | 1940: | 109 |
| 1920: | 222 | 1945: | 108 |
| 1922: | 225 | 1950: | 48 |
| 1925: | 219 | 1955: | 25 |
| 1927: | 191 | 1960: | 25 |
| 1929: | 174 | 1964: | 15 |

France at N. Galvez, April 29, 1948—Desire Line had one month left.                    *Courtesy Otto A. Goessl*

# CHRONOLOGICAL LIST
of
## ABANDONMENT DATES

### Street Railway Lines

| Line | Date |
|---|---|
| Poydras-Magazine | March-April, 1836 |
| La Course Street | 1840's |
| Louisiana Avenue (N.O.&.C.RR.Co.) | 1878 |
| City Park Race Track | July, 1908 |
| Henry Clay | August, 1913 |
| South Peters | Late 1916 |
| Levee-Barracks | Late 1918 |
| South Peters Shuttle | April 18, 1921 |
| Cemeteries Franchise Car | October 10, 1921 |
| French Market (North Peters) | March 27, 1925 |
| Ferry | August 22, 1925 |
| Bayou St. John | September 23, 1925 |
| Peters Avenue | September 23, 1925 |
| Coliseum | May 11, 1929 |
| Dryades | July 2, 1929 |
| Oak Street Shuttle | July 2, 1929 |
| St. Bernard | July 2, 1929 |
| Tchoupitoulas | July 2, 1929 |
| South Claiborne Shuttle | January 1, 1931 |
| France | July 26, 1931 |
| Paris Avenue | January 31, 1932 |
| Broad | July 16, 1932 |
| Clio | September 1, 1932 |
| Prytania | October 1, 1932 |
| Spanish Fort | October 16, 1932 |
| Canal Belt | December 27, 1934 |
| Claiborne (North) | December 27, 1934 |
| Esplanade Belt | December 27, 1934 |
| Louisiana | December 27, 1934 |

| Lines | Date |
|---|---|
| Shrewsbury Extension of Napoleon | December 27, 1934 |
| Laurel | July 5, 1939 |
| City Park | January 1, 1941 |
| Freret | December 1, 1946 |
| Jackson | May 19, 1947 |
| Magazine | February 11, 1948 |
| Desire | May 29, 1948 |
| Gentilly | July 17, 1948 |
| St. Claude | January 1, 1949 |
| West End (Cemeteries-West End) | January 15, 1950 |
| St. Charles Belt | January 8, 1951 |
| Tulane Belt | January 8, 1951 |
| South Claiborne | January 5, 1953 |
| Napoleon | February 18, 1953 |
| Canal | May 30, 1964 |

### Steam Railroads

| | Date |
|---|---|
| Jefferson & Lake Pontchartrain Ry. Co. (all services) | November 23, 1864 |
| New Orleans, Spanish Fort & Lake RR. Co.* | 1904 |
| New Orleans Terminal Co. (passenger only) | December 26, 1920 |
| Pontchartrain RR. Co. (passenger only) | March 15, 1932 |
| Pontchartrain RR. Co. (freight service) | 1935 |

NOTE—*Passenger service suspended July 12, 1903. Rails removed 1904.

# CHRONOLOGICAL LIST
of
## LINE CONSOLIDATION AND NAME CHANGES

| | Date |
|---|---|
| Magazine (6th District) consolidated with Coliseum* | September 1, 1881 |
| Barracks and Slaughter House consolidated with Dauphine | December 22, 1894 |
| Bayou Bridge and City Park consolidated with Esplanade | 1899-1900 |
| Tulane became Tulane Belt | February 19, 1900 |
| St. Charles became St. Charles Belt | February 19, 1900 |
| Canal became Canal Belt | June 1, 1901 |
| Esplanade became Esplanade Belt | June 1, 1901 |
| Oak Street (Southport) Shuttle consolidated with Coliseum | 1903 |
| French Market (Orleans RR. Co.) renamed French Market-City Park | 1905 |

| | Date |
|---|---|
| Napoleon (N. O. & C. RR. Co.) consolidated with Napoleon (N. O. & P. Ry. Co.) | 1906 |
| French Market (New Orleans City RR. Co.) renamed North Peters | 1919 |
| Annunciation consolidated with Laurel | December 23, 1917 |
| French Market-City Park renamed City Park | 1921 |
| Louisa renamed France | July 7, 1923 |
| Dauphine renamed St. Claude | February 21, 1926 |
| Villere renamed Gentilly | February 21, 1926 |

NOTE—*This date consolidated service started—legal conveyance date 6th Dist. & Carrollton RR. Co. — Crescent City RR. Co. was Oct. 7, 1880.

St. Charles St. about 1920, looking from Lee Circle toward Canal St. Prytania car on right, FB&D on left.

Chas. L. Franck Photo

65

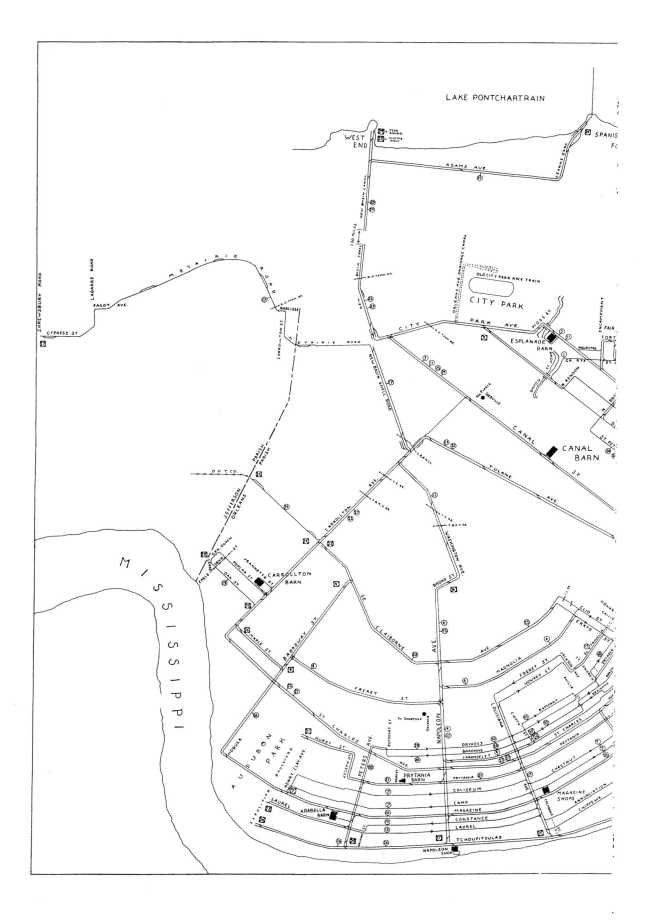

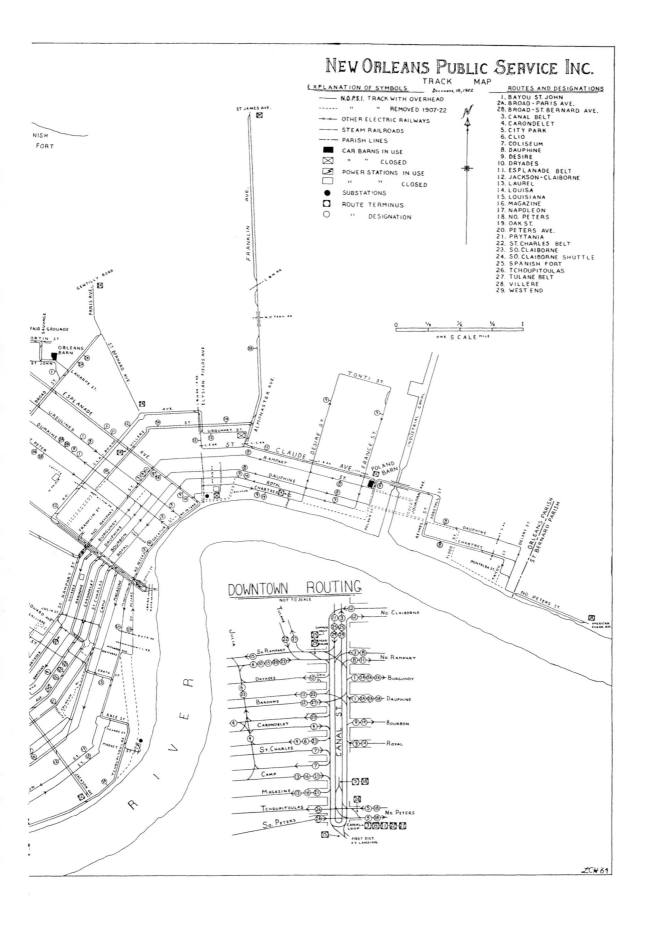

# HISTORICAL SUMMARY
## Street Railway Lines

| Route Designation | Opened | Electrified | Disappeared |
|---|---|---|---|
| ANNUNCIATION | February 27, 1867 | April 2, 1895 | December 23, 1917 |
| BARRACKS AND SLAUGHTER HOUSE | June 1, 1872 | December 22, 1894 | December 22, 1894 |
| BAYOU BRIDGE AND CITY PARK | Mid 1861 | April-May 1899 | same date |
| BAYOU ST. JOHN | July 4, 1868 | November 17, 1895 | September 23, 1925 |
| BROAD | 1874 | November 23, 1895 | July 16, 1932 |
| CANAL | June 15, 1861 | August 1, 1894 | May 30, 1964 |
| CANAL BELT | June 1, 1901 | | December 27, 1934 |
| CARONDELET | July 29, 1866 | January 2, 1896 | September 7, 1924 |
| CEMETERIES FRANCHISE CAR | June 1, 1901 | | October 10, 1921 |
| CITY PARK (first phase) | July 1, 1898 | | 1905 |
| CITY PARK (second phase) | December 24, 1910 | | January 1, 1941 |
| CITY PARK RACE TRACK | November 30, 1905 | | July 1908 |
| CLAIBORNE (NORTH) | May 13, 1868 | October 10, 1896 | December 27, 1934 |
| CLIO | January 23, 1867 | January 2, 1896 | September 1, 1932 |
| COLISEUM | September 1, 1881 | February 22, 1895 | May 11, 1929 |
| DAUPHINE | July 1, 1861 | November 22, 1894 | February 21, 1926 |
| DESIRE | October 17, 1920 | | May 29, 1948 |
| DRYADES | November , 1866 | January 14, 1896 | July 2, 1929 |
| ESPLANADE | June 1, 1861 | November 12, 1894 | May 31, 1901 |
| ESPLANADE BELT | June 1, 1901 | | December 27, 1934 |
| FERRY | August 14, 1923 | | August 22, 1925 |
| FRANCE | July 7, 1923 | | July 26, 1931 |
| FRERET | September 7, 1924 | | December 1, 1946 |
| FRENCH MARKET (N. O. C. RR. Co.) | 1874 | May 21, 1895 | March 27, 1925 |
| FRENCH MARKET (O. RR. Co.) (later FRENCH MARKET-CITY PARK) | November 6, 1870 | November 25, 1895 | December 24, 1910 |
| GENTILLY | February 21, 1926 | | July 17, 1948 |
| GIROD AND POYDRAS | April 14, 1868 | (never) | July 1899 |
| HENRY CLAY | June 13, 1895 | | August 27, 1913 |
| JACKSON | January 13, 1835 | February 10, 1893 | May 19, 1947 |
| LA COURSE STREET | March-April, 1836 | (never) | Circa 1840 |
| LAUREL | August 12, 1913 | | July 5, 1939 |
| LEVEE-BARRACKS | May 14, 1866 | January 14, 1896 | Late 1918 |
| LOUISA | October 17, 1920 | | July 7, 1923 |
| LOUISIANA (N. O. & C. RR. Co.) | February 4, 1850 | (never) | 1878 |
| LOUISIANA (N. O. Ry. & L. Co.) | August 27, 1913 | | December 27, 1934 |
| MAGAZINE (N. O. C. RR. Co.) | June 8, 1861 | March 15, 1895 | February 11, 1948 |
| MAGAZINE (J. C. RR. Co.) | 1864 | (never) | August 31, 1881 |
| NAPOLEON (N. O. & C. RR. Co.) | February 4, 1850 | February 10, 1893 | 1906 |
| NAPOLEON (N. O. & P. Ry. Co.) | January 1, 1903 | | February 18, 1953 |
| OAK STREET (first phase) | February 19, 1900 | | 1903 |
| OAK STREET (second phase) | April 25, 1921 | | July 2, 1929 |
| PARIS AVENUE | March 6, 1912 | | January 31, 1932 |
| PETERS AVENUE | August 18, 1894 | | September 23, 1925 |
| POYDRAS-MAGAZINE | January 1835 | (never) | March-April, 1836 |
| PRYTANIA | June 8, 1861 | September 15, 1894 | October 1, 1932 |

| | | | |
|---|---|---|---|
| ST. BERNARD | July 13, 1909 | ............................. | July 2, 1929 |
| ST. CHARLES | September 26, 1835 | February 1, 1893 | STILL OPERATING |
| ST. CHARLES BELT | February 19, 1900 | ............................. | January 8, 1951 |
| ST. CLAUDE | February 21, 1926 | ............................. | January 1, 1949 |
| SOUTH CLAIBORNE | February 22, 1915 | ............................. | January 5, 1953 |
| SOUTH CLAIBORNE SHUTTLE | May 8, 1916 | ............................. | January 1, 1931 |
| SOUTH PETERS | April 26, 1890 | May 8, 1895 | 1916 |
| SOUTH PETERS SHUTTLE | 1916 | ............................. | April 18, 1921 |
| SPANISH FORT | March 26, 1911 | ............................. | October 16, 1932 |
| TCHOUPITOULAS | August 10, 1866 | April 20, 1895 | July 2, 1929 |
| TULANE | January 15, 1871 | October 10, 1896 | February 18, 1900 |
| TULANE BELT | February 19, 1900 | ............................. | January 8, 1951 |
| VILLERE | October 15, 1895 | | February 21, 1926 |
| WEST END | April 20, 1876 | July 17, 1898 | January 15, 1950 |

## MARRIED LINES

| Designation | Joined | Separated |
|---|---|---|
| JACKSON-CLAIBORNE | December 23, 1917 | October 29, 1925 |
| MAGAZINE-DAUPHINE | October 13, 1902 | December 29, 1902 |
| PRYTANIA-VILLERE | November 1916 | December 23, 1917 |
| PRYTANIA-ESPLANADE BELT | August 28, 1902 | December 20, 1902 |
| TCHOUPITOULAS-CITY PARK | December 23, 1917 | February 14, 1921 |
| TCHOUPITOULAS-FRENCH MARKET (N. O. C. RR. Co. ) | 1911 | 1917 |
| TCHOUPITOULAS-NORTH PETERS | July 24, 1923 | March 27, 1925 |

## STEAM RAILROADS

| Company | Passenger Service Opened | Passenger Service Closed |
|---|---|---|
| Jefferson & Lake Pontchartrain Ry. Co. | April 14, 1853 | November 23, 1864 |
| New Orleans, Spanish Fort & Lake RR. Co.* | October 3, 1875 | July 12, 1903 |
| New Orleans Terminal Co.* | January 11, 1896 | December 26, 1920 |
| Pontchartrain RR. Co. | April 23, 1831 | March 15, 1932 |

NOTE—* Not original corporate name.

**Carrollton and Julia, October 3, 1949—865 and 808 wait for a KCS passenger train.**          *Courtesy Otto A. Goessl*

# SELECTED ROUTE MILEAGES

| Routes | In-bound | Out-bound | Round Trip | Date (as of) |
|---|---|---|---|---|
| Annunciation | 4.500 | 4.650 | 9.150 | 1916 |
| Bayou St. John | 3.198 | 2.383 | 5.581 | 6/ 8/25 |
| Broad (to Broad and St. Bernard) | 2.788 | 2.726 | 5.514 | 10/25/27 |
| Canal (Cemeteries) | 3.684 | 3.822 | 7.506 | 5/ 1/30 |
| Canal | 3.496 | 3.614 | 7.110 | 1964 |
| Canal Belt | | | 8.434 | 10/25/27 |
| Canal Belt | | | 7.136 | 5/ 1/30 |
| Carondelet (to Maple and Broadway) | 7.040 | 6.970 | 14.010 | 1921 |
| Carondelet (to South Claiborne and Broadway) | 7.780 | 7.710 | 15.490 | 1921 |
| City Park | 3.539 | 3.848 | 7.387 | 6/ 8/25 |
| City Park | 3.444 | 3.369 | 7.123 | 1/21/30 |
| Claiborne (NORTH) | 3.207 | 3.350 | 6.557 | 5/ 1/30 |
| Clio | 3.819 | 3.700 | 7.519 | 5/ 1/30 |
| Coliseum | 4.835 | 4.733 | 9.568 | 10/31/27 |
| Dauphine | 6.349 | 6.351 | 12.700 | 6/ 8/25 |
| Desire | 3.879 | 3.479 | 7.358 | 5/ 1/30 |
| Dryades (during operation to Ferry) | 2.790 | 2.918 | 5.748 | |
| Dryades | 4.753 | 4.413 | 9.166 | 11/ 3/27 |
| Esplanade Belt | | | 8.437 | 5/ 1/30 |
| Ferry | .872 | .872 | 1.744 | 6/ 8/25 |
| France | 2.632 | 2.520 | 5.152 | 5/ 1/30 |
| Freret | 5.953 | 5.839 | 11.792 | 10/28/27 |
| Gentilly | 4.822 | 4.700 | 9.522 | 5/ 1/30 |
| Jackson | 2.679 | 2.649 | 5.328 | 10/28/27 |
| Jackson-Claiborne | 6.662 | 6.652 | 13.314 | 11/23/24 |
| Laurel | 5.335 | 5.724 | 11.059 | 5/ 1/30 |
| Laurel | 3.432 | 2.995 | 6.427 | 11/28/32 |
| Levee-Barracks | 5.240 | 5.008 | 10.248 | 1915 |
| Louisiana | 3.714 | 3.488 | 7.202 | 10/29/27 |
| Louisiana (during operation to Ferry) | 4.384 | 4.270 | 8.654 | |
| Magazine | 6.500 | 6.381 | 12.881 | 10/31/27 |
| Magazine | 5.300 | 5.218 | 10.518 | 11/28/32 |
| Napoleon (to Shrewsbury) | 8.421 | 8.427 | 16.848 | 5/ 1/30 |
| Napoleon | 3.580 | 3.577 | 7.157 | 11/22/34 |
| Napoleon | 2.409 | 2.410 | 4.819 | 11/14/40 |
| Oak Street Shuttle | .575 | .749 | 1.324 | 1929 |
| Paris Avenue | .438 | .438 | .976 | 10/25/27 |
| Peters Avenue | 4.840 | 4.940 | 9.780 | 1921 |
| Prytania | 4.702 | 4.536 | 9.238 | 10/29/27 |
| Prytania | 4.676 | 4.526 | 9.202 | 5/12/29 |
| St. Bernard | .790 | .790 | 1.580 | 10/25/27 |
| St. Charles | 6.508 | 6.625 | 13.128 | 1964 |
| St. Charles | 7.526 | 7.639 | 15.165 | 12/15/50 |
| St. Charles Belt | | | 10.316 | 1/ 8/48 |
| St. Claude | 5.585 | 5.614 | 11.199 | 11/22/34 |
| South Claiborne | 4.628 | 4.497 | 9.125 | 5/ 1/30 |
| South Claiborne Shuttle | .805 | .805 | 1.610 | 10/29/27 |
| Spanish Fort (to South Rampart and Canal) | 7.913 | 7.868 | 15.781 | 5/ 1/30 |
| Spanish Fort (to Adams Avenue and West End Blvd) | 2.184 | 2.184 | 4.368 | 5/ 1/30 |
| Tchoupitoulas | 5.928 | 5.796 | 11.724 | 6/ 8/25 |
| Tchoupitoulas | 1.567 | 1.430 | 2.997 | 12/17/27 |
| Tulane Belt | | | 11.229 | 5/ 1/30 |
| Villere | 5.339 | 5.318 | 10.657 | 7/ 1/21 |
| West End (to Canal Loop) | 6.444 | 6.538 | 12.982 | 5/ 1/30 |
| West End (to City Park Ave.) | 2.954 | 2.935 | 5.889 | 5/ 1/30 |

South Claiborne at Second St., November 1, 1951.

*Courtesy Otto A. Goessl*

St. Charles St. at Poydras, looking toward Canal. Early 1920s.

Chas. L. Franck Photo

71

# CHART SHOWING COLORS USED TO ASSIST PERSONS
## IN DISTINGUISHING CAR ROUTES

| COMPANIES | Mule Car Body and Night Light Colors | | Electric Car Destination Sign Colors | |
|---|---|---|---|---|
| Routes Listed Beneath | Cars | Light | Glass | Letters |
| **Canal & Claiborne Railroad Co.** | | | | |
| CLAIBORNE | yellow | red | white | green |
| GIROD AND POYDRAS' | yellow | green | --------- | --------- |
| TULANE AVE. | yellow | white | purple | white |
| **Crescent City Railroad Co.** | | | | |
| ANNUNCIATION | red | white | purple | red |
| COLISEUM | green | green | green | white |
| SOUTH PETERS | red | red | red | white |
| TCHOUPITOULAS | green | green | dark green | white |
| **New Orleans City & Lake Railroad Co.** | | | | |
| BAYOU BRIDGE AND CITY PARK | --------- | --------- | --------- | --------- |
| CANAL | green | white | green | white |
| BARRACKS AND SLAUGHTER HOUSE | red | white | --------- | --------- |
| DAUPHINE | red | white | red | white |
| ESPLANADE | yellow | red | yellow | brown |
| FRENCH MARKET | yellow | red | purple | red |
| LEVEE-BARRACKS | green | red | green | white |
| MAGAZINE | green | white | green | white |
| PRYTANIA | yellow | red | yellow | tan |
| WEST END | --------- | --------- | white | purple |
| **New Orleans & Carrollton Railroad Co.** | | | | |
| JACKSON | red | red | red | white |
| NAPOLEON AVE. | yellow | yellow | yellow | red |
| ST. CHARLES | green | green | green | white |
| **New Orleans & Pontchartrain Ry. Co.** | | | | |
| NAPOLEON AVE. | --------- | --------- | royal blue | white |
| **Orleans Railroad Co.** | | | | |
| BAYOU ST. JOHN | blue | blue | red | white |
| BROAD | green | green | blue | white |
| CITY PARK | --------- | --------- | green | white |
| FRENCH MARKET | red | red | --------- | --------- |
| **St. Charles Street Railroad Co.** | | | | |
| CARONDELET | white | white | blue | white |
| CLIO | red | red | red | white |
| DRYADES | green | green | green | white |

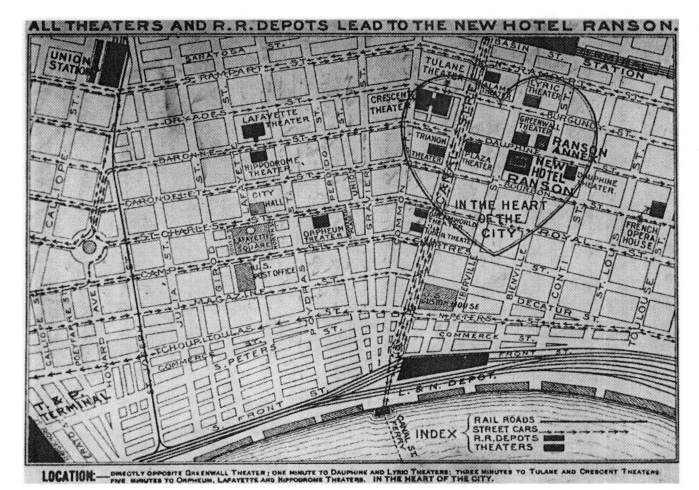

LOCATION— DIRECTLY OPPOSITE GREENWALL THEATER; ONE MINUTE TO DAUPHINE AND LYRIC THEATERS; THREE MINUTES TO TULANE AND CRESCENT THEATERS; FIVE MINUTES TO ORPHEUM, LAFAYETTE AND HIPPODROME THEATERS. IN THE HEART OF THE CITY.

Hotel stationery had this circa 1910 downtown map.                    *Courtesy Jack Stewart*

# COMPENDIUM OF ROUTES

1. ANNUNCIATION.
   Original Company: Crescent City RR. Co.
   Opened: Feb. 27, 1867.
   Electrified: April 2, 1895.
   Consolidated with Laurel: December 23, 1917.

Original route: from Canal and Camp, in Canal, up Tchoupitoulas, Annunciation, in Louisiana to Tchoupitoulas. RETURN: Louisiana, Chippewa, Race, Annunciation, Delord (now Howard Ave.), South Peters. After *1877*: upper terminus changed, as follows: up Annunciation, in Toledano to Tchoupitoulas. RETURN: out Toledano, down Chippewa. Beginning *April 26, 1890*, route was as follows: from Canal and Camp, out Canal, up Carondelet, Clio, Camp, Erato, Annunciation, Toledano to Tchoupitoulas. RETURN: Toledano, Chippewa, Race, Annunciation, Erato, Camp, Calliope, St. Charles, Canal. From about *1910 to 1916*, Annunciation operated in a one-direction circuit, thusly: from Canal and South Peters to Toledano and Tchoupitoulas terminus as formerly, but returning via Toledano, Chippewa, Race, Annunciation, Howard Ave. and South Peters. Final routing, after *1916:* From Canal and

Camp, up Camp, Erato, Annunciation, Louisiana to Howard St. (La Salle St. now). RETURN: Louisiana, Chippewa, Race, Annunciation, Erato, Camp, Clio, Carondelet, Canal.

The Annunciation was an Uptown-near-riverfront line, all street running, through the factory, warehouse and poorer sections, as well as the old, famous "Irish Channel" district. Streets traversed were narrow and poorly paved—track was awful (see photo, page 193). Original electric cars on the line were single truck six-window models in banana yellow livery with light brown trim. Later cars were the FB&D's and finally, the Palace cars. Route sign was purple with red letters in front light of clerestory.

2. BARRACKS AND SLAUGHTER HOUSE.
   Original company: New Orleans City RR. Co.
   Opened: June 1, 1872.
   Consolidated with Dauphine on day of electrification, Dec. 22, 1894.

Original Route (unchanged): from Poland and N. Rampart, in Poland, down Dauphine, Delery, N. Peters to Slaughter House. RETURN: N. Peters, Flood, Dau-

73

Canal and City Park Ave., May 1951.

*Courtesy Otto A. Goessl*

phine, Poland. This was a "shuttle" operation serving the Jackson Army Barracks and large plant of the Crescent City Live Stock Landing & Slaughter House Co. at N. Peters and Esteban Streets. Most of the route was through dirt or shell paved streets.

3. BAYOU BRIDGE AND CITY PARK (also known as CANAL AND BAYOU ST. JOHN).
   Original company: New Orleans City RR. Co.
   Opened: Fall of 1861.
   Electrified: April-May 1899.
   Absorbed by Esplanade: Same time.

Original route: from Half Way House at New Basin Canal, down Metairie Road (now City Park Ave.) to bridge across Bayou St. John at Sportsman Park. RETURN: same route. Line was nicknamed "The Ridge Line" because Metairie Road runs along a "ridge", long known as "Metairie Ridge". In its early days the line was lightly travelled, served by only two mule cars. At various times there were threats to close the line and its trackage was usually in terrible shape. On *May 1, 1897*, line was reduced to running on City Park Ave. from Canal St. to Alexander St. entrance to City Park, due to Esplanade Line extension. In this form the line lasted until electrified and absorbed by Esplanade Line.

4. BAYOU ST. JOHN. (originally CANAL, DU-MAINE AND BAYOU ST. JOHN).
   Original company: Orleans RR. Co.
   Opened: July 4, 1868.
   Electrified: Nov. 17, 1895.
   Discontinued: Sept. 23, 1925.

Original route: from stand on Canal at Exchange Place (before electric cars, from Canal and St. Charles only), between St. Charles and Camp, on middle track, out

Canal on the outside track, down Dauphine, out Dumaine, Moss, Grand Route St. John, Bayou Road, N. Broad, Ursulines (every fifteen minutes via St. Peter), Burgundy, and in Canal on outside track to Exchange Place. Route remained unchanged until about *1920*, when inbound cars came UP Dauphine to Canal, out Canal's outside track to Burgundy, and DOWN Burgundy.

The Bayou St. John Line was a downtown back o' town line. It's passage through the old dairying district around Bayou St. John inspired the nickname "The Cream Cheese Line". The line featured some neutral ground running. Inbound on Ursulines it ran down neutral strip from N. Broad to N. Claiborne where the street narrows from there to the River. It served residential areas and passed through the French Quarter for the greater part of its route. Track was poor to fair, save the well kept portion on Ursulines' neutral ground. Bayou St. John Line had single truck cars for its entire life. First electrics were Brill single truck open platform cars painted dark red with cream trim. Later, FB&D cars were assigned. Clerestory route signs were red with white frosted letters.

5. BROAD (originally CANAL, DUMAINE AND FAIR GROUNDS).
   Original company: Orleans RR. Co.
   Opened: 1874.
   Electrified: Nov. 23, 1895.
   Buses substituted: July 16, 1932.

Original route: same as Bayou St. John Line to Dumaine, out Dumaine, N. Broad, Laharpe, Grand Route St. John, Sauvage, ending at Fair Grounds. RETURN: Sauvage, Grand Route St. John, Bayou Road, N. Broad,

Canal Line loop at Liberty Place, 1960.

Ursulines (every fifteen minutes via St. Peter—Ursulines alternate cut out about *1895*), Burgundy and returning same route as Bayou St. John Line. Ordinance CCS 2108 dated *Jan. 26, 1915* permitted Broad Line to absorb both St. Bernard and Paris Ave. shuttles, and operate with alternate cars turning from N. Broad, right into St. Bernard and left into St. Bernard to reach Paris Ave. About *1920*, Broad began same revised routing as Bayou St. John—UP Dauphine and DOWN Burgundy. Final routing *1929*, after St. Bernard leg replaced by buses: from Burgundy and Canal, Canal, N. Rampart, Dumaine, N. Broad, St. Bernard, Paris Ave. to Gentilly Road. RETURN: Paris Ave., St. Bernard, N. Broad, St. Peter, Burgundy to Canal.

Broad was another downtown, back o' town line, also with some neutral ground running. Type of area served was mainly French Quarter and old residential. First electric cars were same type as mentioned for Bayou St. John Line, except Broad's clerestory route sign was blue with white frosted letters. At the end, the line was using the 1910 Prytania cars.

6. CANAL—(at different times, known as CANAL-CEMETERIES and CEMETERIES).
   Original company: New Orleans City RR. Co.
   Opened: June 15, 1861.
   Electrified: Aug. 1, 1894.
   Last day of service: May 30, 1964.
   Last cars (No. 958, Run 14 and No. 972 Special Run): May 31, 1964.
   Buses substituted.
Original route: from St. Charles and Canal, out Canal

to White St. Extended *August 24, 1861* out Canal to Cemeteries, terminating at the Half Way House. This phase of operation ceased *May 31, 1901* as the Canal and Esplanade Belts began service June 1, 1901. In *1925*, under the name Canal-Cemeteries Line, the Canal Line operation resumed the pre-1901 service. Route name changed to "Canal" on December 27, 1934. The Half Way House has been gone for years, and since *August 20, 1951*, the Canal Line had been terminating at Canal and City Park Ave.

First electrics were Brill seven-window, maximum traction trucks (Brill 22-E "Eureka"), open platforms, longitudinal seats. Cars boasted orange-yellow livery with cream trim and clerestory route signs were green with white frosted letters. Later cars were the 1899 Americans, Palace Cars, and lastly, on December 27, 1934, the 800-900's.

The Canal Line has operated entirely on neutral ground, 1861 to 1964.

7. CANAL BELT.
   Original company: New Orleans City RR. Co. (second corporation).
   Opened: June 1, 1901.
   Always electric.
   Discontinued: Dec. 27, 1934.
Original Route: from loop at foot of Canal, out Canal, City Park Ave., Moss St., Esplanade Ave., N. Rampart, and in Canal to the loop. Effective *November 29, 1929*, operation to the Canal loop discontinued with cars turning at N. Rampart and Canal. The route was all neutral ground operation. Opened with American Car

Heavy snow of December 31, 1963—Canal Line did not stop rolling. Photo at Canal Station. *Courtesy Otto A. Goessl*

Co. eight-window cars (1899 order), 22-E maximum traction trucks. Beginning in June, 1902, and up to 1934, the famous St. Louis "Palace" cars serviced this route. The entire nine and one half mile circuit over the original Canal Belt Line afforded lovely views of City Park, Bayou St. John, residential areas, the business district, and the Cemeteries. Track was smooth and well maintained. Also see: route No. 19, ESPLANADE BELT.

8. CARONDELET.
   Original company: St. Charles St. RR. Co.
   Opened: July 29, 1866.
   Electrified: Jan. 2, 1896.
   Discontinued: Sept. 7, 1924.
Original route: from St. Charles and Canal, up St. Charles, Delord (now Howard Ave.), Baronne, Philip, Baronne (note off-set intersection) to 8th St. RETURN: 8th St., Carondelet, Canal. On *February 5, 1902,* line was extended up Carondelet from 8th St. to Napoleon. At the same time, the line began crossing Canal, operating uptown-downtown. New operation saw cars coming down Carondelet, crossing Canal, continuing down Bourbon, Esplanade, Decatur, Elysian Fields, Chartres, Louisa to Royal. RETURN: up Royal, crossing Canal, up St. Charles and as originally to 8th and Carondelet, and on up Carondelet to Napoleon. By *1910,* Carondelet Line had been extended from Carondelet and Napoleon, out Napoleon, Freret, Broadway, to Maple. On

*March 1, 1916,* Carondelet absorbed a portion of South Claiborne given up when South Claiborne began running all the way up S. Claiborne to Carrollton. This trackage was in Broadway from Freret St. to S. Claiborne. Carondelet Line then had two "legs" at its upper end, splitting at Broadway and Freret and running out Broadway to S. Claiborne and in Broadway to Maple, respectively.

This rambling line sprouted an extension effective *December 20, 1919,* this time on its below Canal St. section. Cars carrying the "Carondelet" route sign and a new destination sign, "Desire", proceeded down Chartres past Louisa to Desire St., out Desire to Tonti, down Tonti to France, in France to Royal, and back up Royal to join Carondelet tracks at Royal and Louisa. Carondelet cars still carried the "Louisa" destination sign, these cars turning at Chartres and Louisa for return trips. Thus, the world famous Desire Line had its beginning (see: route No. 16, DESIRE). Barely a year later, the Carondelet Line began suffering re-routing and shortening changes. On *October 17, 1920,* Carondelet cars discontinued crossing Canal St. The upper portion of the line operated as formerly, but turning off Carondelet, going in Canal one block, and resuming outbound trips at Canal and St. Charles. Lower portion continued as Desire and a short working, Louisa (both distinct routes). In *1924,* the Freret Line was created, assuming portions of the Carondelet Line—the Carondelet

76

Even as late as 1962, one could usually see plenty of streetcars on Canal Street. *Courtesy Otto A. Goessl*

was abolished the day Freret started service (see: route No. 22, FRERET).

At its peak, Carondelet Line offered a long and interesting journey, from the Industrial Canal area, through the French Quarter, across Canal, passing Loyola and Tulane Universities, almost to the city's upper limits. All trackage except short stretches in Louisiana and Napoleon were street running. First electric cars were Pullman models, followed by American FB&D seven-window cars, painted white with gold trim. Route sign was blue with white frosted letters. Although for a brief time New Orleans "Times-Democrat" announced notices that double truck cars provided extra service during rush hours (1911), regular service was always single truck equipment.

9. CEMETERIES FRANCHISE CAR.
   Original company: New Orleans City RR. Co. (second corporation).
   Opened: June 1, 1901.
   Always electric.
   Discontinued: Oct. 10, 1921.

This was the shortest of all short lines. At the head of Canal at the Cemeteries, there were for many years a car and a man. Their duty was to fulfill an old franchise obligation, part of the old Bayou Bridge and City Park mule car line, which originally ran from New Basin Canal, on Metairie Road (now City Park Ave.) to Bayou St. John and the bridge leading into Esplanade Ave. With the mule car line gone, there was no end to end operation, although the Canal Belt cars turned right from Canal and covered most of the franchise to Bayou St. John, and the West End Line cars turned left and covered the 600 feet from Canal to the New Basin Canal. The franchise car would operate whenever required to cover the 600 feet between head of Canal St. and the New Basin Canal on City Park Ave. Persons desiring the service would push buttons located at each end of the "line"—the buzzer would actuate the man and the car would move. However, no one can recall ever seeing the car—or the man—in motion. Co-author Charlton saw the car and the man often, but never saw the service actually operate. The poor motorman was usually seen inside the car reading a paper or standing in the door smoking a cigarette. The car was one of the oldest models, an 1894 Brill that carried no destination sign. HOWEVER, it was the only one man electric street railway operation in New Orleans for revenue service, even if it was motionless nearly all the time.

10. CITY PARK.
    Original company: Orleans RR. Co.
    Opened: July 1, 1898.
    Closed: 1905.
    Re-opened: Dec. 24, 1910.
    Always electric.
    Buses substituted: Jan. 1, 1941.

77

Trackless trolleys: April 3, 1949.
Buses again substituted: Dec. 13, 1964.
Original route: same as original Bayou St. John and Broad from Exchange Place and Canal to Dauphine and Dumaine, then out Dumaine to City Park Ave. RETURN: Dumaine, N. Rendon, Ursulines, and same as original Bayou St. John and Broad to Exchange Place and Canal. In *1905*, City Park Line was abolished while the ex-Orleans RR.'s French Market Line was renamed "French Market-City Park" (see: route No. 24). On *December 24, 1910*, the French Market-City Park Line was extended over existing trackage to reach the downtown district: from stand at Canal and Camp, in Canal, down N. Peters, out Dumaine to City Park Ave. RETURN: Dumaine, N. Rendon, Ursulines, Decatur and North Peters, Canal to Camp. During *1919-21*, the French Market-City Park was briefly joined with Tchoupitoulas Line. In *1921*, the line was renamed "CITY PARK". In the late *1920's*, City Park was re-routed, as follows: From Canal and N. Peters, out Canal, down Bourbon, out Dumaine to City Park Ave. RETURN: Dumaine, N. Rendon, Ursulines, Decatur, N. Peters to Canal. On *Jan. 31, 1932*, the line was again re-routed to enter Canal on Royal, but going out via Bourbon as formerly.

City Park's original electric cars were American FB&D seven-window cars in red livery and cream trim, green route sign with white frosted letters. Later came Palace cars and the 800-900's. (Double truck cars assigned February 17, 1929).

11. CITY PARK RACE TRACK.
Original company: New Orleans Ry. & Lt. Co.
Opened: November 30, 1905.
Always electric.
Discontinued: July, 1908.
Original route (unchanged): from City Park Ave., out beside Orleans Ave. Drainage Canal for about one mile to Race Track. Line was double track, private right of way, catenary suspension (first 600 volt catenary in U. S. for street railway service). Line lasted until racing was outlawed in Louisiana by the Locke Bill, signed by Governor J. Y. Sanders June 24, 1908, going into effect in 30 days. Last day of betting was July 18, 1908. The car line suspended service that day, or very soon thereafter.

12. CLAIBORNE (NORTH). (Originally known as CANAL AND CLAIBORNE).
Original company: Canal & Claiborne Sts. RR. Co.
Opened: May 13, 1868.
Electrified: Oct. 10, 1896.
Buses substituted: Dec. 27, 1934.
Original route: from Canal and N. Basin, out Canal, down N. Claiborne, Elysian Fields, Urquhart, to Lafayette Ave. (later Almonaster Ave., now Franklin Ave.). RETURN: Lafayette Ave., St. Claude, Elysian Fields, Claiborne, Canal. On *May 9, 1869*, C. & C. Sts. RR. Co. opened its "Grand Trunk Route", allowing its cars to run on Canal's outside track all the way in to loop

*Louis C. Hennick Collection*
Royal and Iberville Sts., looking "down", circa 1915.

at the foot of Canal. Later listings show extensions. In *1908*, the line was running below Lafayette Ave., as follows: from Elysian Fields, down St. Claude to Poland (extension to Poland opened *1906*). RETURN: St. Claude, Lafayette, Urquhart, and through car house at Urquhart and Lafayette, then out Elysian Fields, up Claiborne, in Canal. From *1917* to *October 28, 1925* Claiborne and Jackson Lines were joined (route signs: JACKSON, and CLAIBORNE in opposite direction). After St. Claude and Gentilly Lines started in *1926*, Claiborne had this route: from loop at foot of Canal, out Canal, down Claiborne, Elysian Fields, Villere to Almonaster Ave. RETURN: same route. Claiborne Line was nearly all neutral ground operation (street running on Urquhart and later on Villere). Original electric cars were American Car Co. FB&D type (first and original design by Ford, Bacon & Davis) in olive green livery trimmed with cream. Route sign was white frosted glass with green letters. When the Line was opened in 1868, it was 5' 2½" gauge. Gauge changed to 4' 8½" when electrified, and widened to 5' 2½" on February 21, 1926.

13. CLIO. (Originally JACKSON RR. DEPOT LINE).
Original company: St. Charles St. RR. Co.
Opened: Jan. 23, 1867.
Electrified: Jan. 2, 1896.
Discontinued: Sept. 1, 1932.

Chas. L. Franck Photo

Camp St., about 1917. Looking toward Canal. Coliseum car in foreground headed for Henry Clay Ave. American Car Co. semi-convertible in background (Magazine Line).

Original route: from St. Charles and Canal, up St. Charles, Delord (now Howard Ave.), Rampart, Clio, Magnolia, Erato, Carondelet, Canal. Extended in *1874* to cross Canal as follows: down Carondelet, crossing Canal, down Bourbon, Esplanade, Decatur to Elysian Fields. RETURN: Elysian Fields, Royal, crossing Canal, up St. Charles and to Magnolia and Erato as formerly. On *September 19, 1901,* the line was extended on Magnolia from Erato to Seventh, near Louisiana.

On *September 1, 1904,* the Clio was extended from Louisiana and Magnolia terminus, up Magnolia, Napoleon, Freret, Broadway to Maple. Below Canal, line went past the old Decatur and Elysian Fields terminus, out Elysian Fields, Chartres, Louisa to Royal, and back on Royal. On *July 1, 1908,* the line was cut back to Elysian Fields. Yet a *1926* listing gives this route: from Louisiana and Broad, Broad, Napoleon, Magnolia, Erato, S. Rampart, Canal, University Place, Dryades,

Julia, S. Rampart, Clio, Magnolia, Napoleon, Broad to Louisiana. Service out Napoleon and Broad to Louisiana began *April 11, 1921*.

What little neutral ground running Clio had belonged to other lines. Track was poor to fair. Line was early nicknamed "C-L-TEN", presumably by colored people who have a long-standing reputation for providing catchy cognomina. First electric cars were single truck Pullmans, later American FB&D types. Route signs were red with white frosted letters. Last cars to run on Clio were the Prytanias in 1932.

14. COLISEUM (originally CANAL AND
COLISEUM AND UPPER MAGAZINE).
    Original company: Crescent City RR. Co.
    Opened: Sept. 1, 1881.
    Electrified: Feb. 22, 1895 .
    Discontinued: May 11, 1929.

Original route: from foot of Canal, out Canal, up Carondelet, Clio, Camp, Coliseum, Felicity, Chestnut, Louisiana, Magazine to Joseph St. (6th Dist.). Trackage in Magazine purchased in 1880 from Sixth District & Carrollton RR., had been in operation since 1864. RETURN: Magazine, Louisiana, Camp, Calliope, St. Charles, Canal. In *1884*, Coliseum was extended up Magazine to Exposition Blvd. (Upper City Park, now Audubon Park). On *September 1, 1897*, Coliseum began running up Magazine, Broadway, Maple, Carrollton, Oak to Protection Levee and Jefferson-Orleans Parish Line at Southport. By *1908*, upper terminus had slightly changed, with cars going up Oak to Protection Levee, and returning via Leake, Gen. Ogden, and Willow to Carrollton, Maple, etc. back to town. On *August 12, 1913*, Coliseum was shortened and took over part of the Henry Clay Line. New Route: from Canal and St. Charles, in Canal, up Camp, Henry Clay Ave., to Magazine. RETURN: Henry Clay Ave., Coliseum, Louisiana, Chestnut, Felicity, Camp, Howard Ave., St. Charles to Canal. Routing typical of Coliseum's *last years* as follows: from Canal and Camp, in Canal, Magazine, Poeyfarre, Camp, Henry Clay Ave. to Magazine. RETURN: Henry Clay Ave., Coliseum, Louisiana, Chestnut, Felicity, Camp, Canal.

First electric cars were the 1894 Brills with 22-E maximum traction trucks, then American semi-convertible cars in 1906, and single truck cars in 1913. Route sign was green glass with white frosted letters. Coliseum had some neutral ground operation, but mostly street running. Its twisting and circuitous route quickly inspired the nickname "The Snake Line". The line was well travelled on Saturday nights during the years 1896-1913. In those years, Southport (in the "Free State of Jefferson") had many gambling establishments. It is little changed today, it might be added.

15. DAUPHINE. (originally RAMPART AND DAU-
PHINE).
    Original company: New Orleans City RR. Co.
    Opened: July 1, 1861.
    Electrified: Nov. 22, 1894.

Name changed to "ST. CLAUDE" Feb. 21, 1926. Original route: from Clay Statue, out Canal, N. Rampart, Esplanade, Dauphine, Poland, to N. Rampart. RETURN: N. Rampart, Canal. On *December 22, 1894*, Dauphine absorbed the Barracks and Slaughter House Line and in *1898* began running all the way in Canal to loop at the foot of Canal. On *December 29, 1910*, the line was extended down N. Peters, crossing the Parish Line, into St. Bernard Parish to the American Sugar Refinery. Dauphine began using the new St. Claude Ave. bridge over Industrial Canal *March 12, 1922*. Final route before name change in *1926*: from loop at foot of Canal, out Canal, down N. Rampart, Esplanade, Dauphine, Poland, St. Claude, Reynes, Chartres, Tricou, Alhambra, Delery, N. Peters to American Sugar Refinery. RETURN: N. Peters, Delery, Dauphine, Forstall, St. Claude, Poland, N. Rampart, Canal.

This was a downtown line, with much neutral ground running in N. Rampart, St. Claude, and Canal. At one time plans were made and franchise granted to the St. Bernard Traction Co. (chartered Sept. 19, 1906 by Messrs. H. J. Kelly, H. P. Hart, and O. T. Livaudais) to build an interurban down N. Peters and private right of way deep into St. Bernard Parish, serving the Parish seat (St. Bernard) and other communities. This never materialized.

Original electrics were the 1894 Brills, light red route sign with white frosted letters. Later Dauphine got palace cars. The line was nicknamed "The Chalmette Line" due to its terminus' proximity to Chalmette. *Oct. to Dec. 1902*, Dauphine was joined with the Magazine Line, making a line from Audubon Park to Chalmette, without transfer. Upon separation, each line resumed its former operation. Most of Dauphine's trackage was divided between St. Claude and Desire in 1926.

16. DESIRE.
    Original company: New Orleans Ry. & Lt. Co.
    Opened: Oct. 17, 1920.
    Always electric.
    Last full day of service: May 29, 1948.
    Last Car: May 30, 1948.
    Buses substituted.

Original route: (at first a part of Carondelet Line— see: route No. 8, CARONDELET) from Canal and Bourbon, down Bourbon, Esplanade, Decatur, Elysian Fields, Chartres, Desire, Tonti, France, Royal to Canal. On *May 6, 1923*, the Desire Line was re-routed. from Canal and Bourbon, down Bourbon, Pauger, Dauphine, Desire, Tonti. France, Royal to Canal.

Original cars on Desire Line were single truckers, replaced by double truck cars December 6, 1924. Line eventually got arch-roof 800-900's. The Desire Line perhaps the most famous streetcar line in the world due to Tennessee Williams' hit play, "A Streetcar Named Desire". Line was all street running except for one block on Canal's outside track. Desire served the bar and nightclub section of the French Quarter along

The 500 block of Royal Street, looking toward Esplanade. Circa 1900.

Bourbon and the shop district along Royal, a densely populated residential area along lower portion of its route, and the Industrial Canal at the car line's outer terminus at Tonti and France.

17. DRYADES (originally RAMPART AND DRYADES, later DRYADES-FERRY).
    Original company: St. Charles St. RR. Co.
    Opened: Nov. 1866.
    Electrified: Jan. 14, 1896.
    Discontinued: July 2, 1929.

Original route: from St. Charles and Canal, up St. Charles, Delord (now Howard Ave.), Dryades, St. Andrew, Baronne, 8th St. to Carondelet. RETURN: 8th St., St. Denis (now S. Rampart), Philip, Dryades, St. Andrew, S. Rampart, Canal. On *July 26, 1901,* it began running down the outside track in Canal from S. Rampart to the Ferry House (just beyond the loop and across the L&N RR. tracks), returning out Canal on the outside track from the Ferry House to St. Charles. Circa *1917,* Dryades ceased running to the Ferry House and reverted to a route practically identical to its original one. Louisiana Line gave service to the Ferry House from 1917 to 1923. On *June 8, 1924,* the Dryades Line was discontinued, but re-opened *September 23, 1925* when the Peters Ave. Line was discontinued. The last routing of Dryades (including some old Peters Ave. trackage) was, as follows: From Canal and St. Charles, up St. Charles, Julia, Dryades, Philip, Danneel, 8th, Baronne, Dufossat, Peters Ave. (now Jefferson Ave.) to Tchoupitoulas. RETURN: Peters Ave., Dryades, Erato, Carondelet, Canal.

First electric cars were the Pullmans in green livery, white trim, with green route signs, white frosted letters. Dryades was an uptown line with mostly street running.

18. ESPLANADE (originally RAMPART AND ESPLANADE, also ESPLANADE AND BAYOU BRIDGE).
    Original company: New Orleans City RR. Co.
    Opened: June 1, 1861.
    Electrified: Nov. 12, 1894.
    Changed to Esplanade Belt June 1, 1901.

Original route: this was another of the splendid all neutral ground lines in New Orleans. From Clay Statue, out Canal, down N. Rampart, out Esplanade to car house. Line looped through car house yard, alongside Bayou St. John, to Esplanade, and returned via the same route. On *May 1, 1897,* an extension across Bayou St. John, out Moss and City Park Ave. to Alexander St. entrance to City Park was opened. About *1898,* Esplanade began operating in Canal all the way to the loop, in and out on the second tracks. First electric cars were 1894 Brills, then the 1899 Americans. Route sign yellow with brown letters.

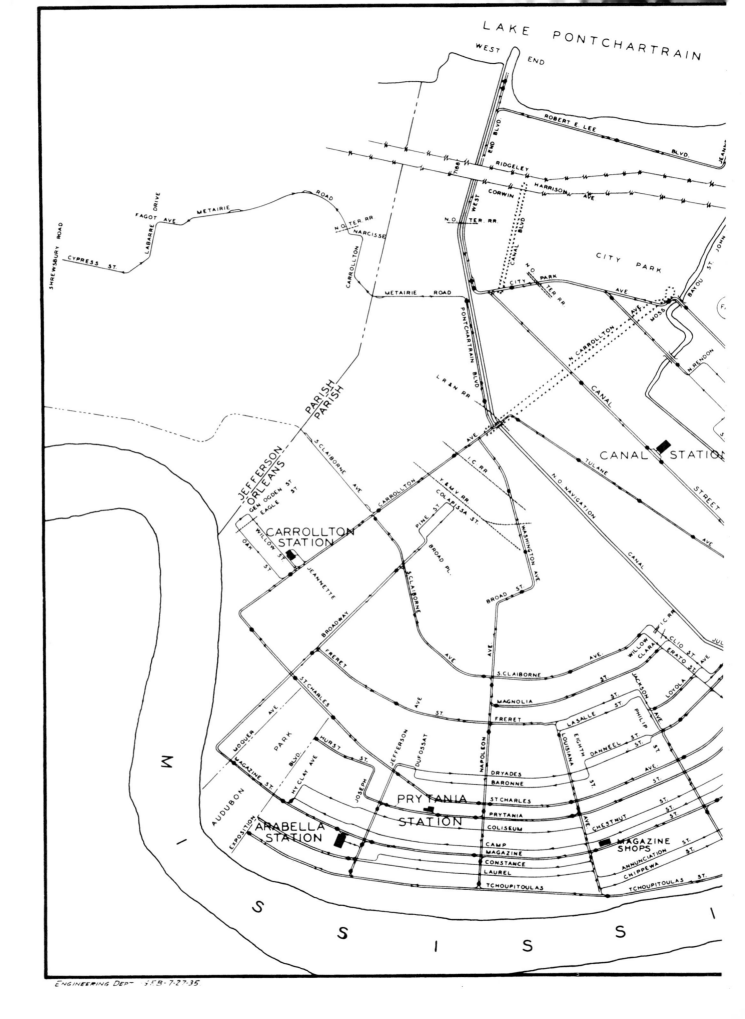

LAKE PONTCHARTRAIN

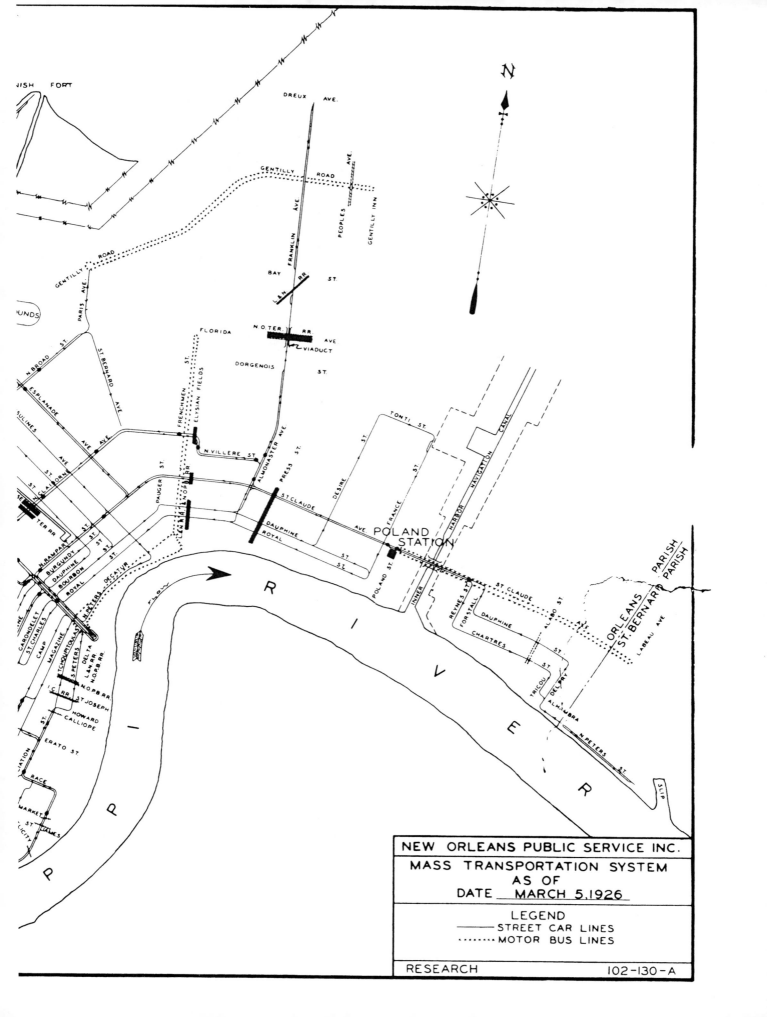

NEW ORLEANS PUBLIC SERVICE INC.

MASS TRANSPORTATION SYSTEM
AS OF
DATE   MARCH 5, 1926

LEGEND
——— STREET CAR LINES
········· MOTOR BUS LINES

RESEARCH                    102-130-A

19. ESPLANADE BELT.
   Original company: New Orleans City RR. Co.
   (second corporation).
   Opened: June 1, 1901.
   Always electric.
   Buses substituted: Dec. 27, 1934.
Original route (unchanged): from loop at foot of
Canal, out Canal, down N. Rampart, out Esplanade,
Moss St., City Park Ave., and in Canal to loop. Clearance between cars and trees on Esplanade was much
closer than one would normally see on lines in other
places. The large trees on Esplanade's neutral ground
did not allow enough space for normal track clearance
—also, citizens would not permit the trees to be touched.
If cars swayed too much on certain parts of Esplanade,
they would sometimes brush against tree limbs or even
scrape a passing streetcar! The trees were impressively
beautiful, nonetheless, and formed a perfect arch over
the tracks. Esplanade Line's scenery was the same
almost unparalleled beauty as described for the Canal
Belt.
   First cars were 1899 Americans, followed in June
of 1902 by the Palace cars (which stayed with the
line until 1934).
   In 1902, from August 28 to December 20, the
Prytania and Esplanade Belt were joined, allowing
Prytania cars to pass City Park. During this period,
the Canal Belt was not affected.

20. FERRY. This was a short-lived shuttle operation
started by N.O.P.S.I. FB&D cars, from foot of
Canal, out Canal, S. Rampart to Gravier. RETURN:
Same route. This line lasted from August 14, 1923
to August 22, 1925.

21. FRANCE.
   Original company: N.O.P.S.I.
   Always electric.
   Opened: July 7, 1923.
   Discontinued: July 26, 1931.
Original route: from Canal and Bourbon, down Bour-
bon, Pauger, Dauphine, France, and back up Royal,
Canal. This line was all street running except for one
block on Canal. FRANCE was actually a short working
of DESIRE. Service started with single truck cars.

22. FRERET.
   Original company: N.O.P.S.I.
   Opened: Sept. 7, 1924.
   Always electric.
   Buses substituted: Dec. 1, 1946.
   Trackless trolleys: Sept. 4, 1947.
   Buses again substituted: June 10, 1963.
Freret started over portions of old Carondelet Line
(discontinued Sept. 7, 1924) and segments of Clio Line
given up when that line was re-routed. The original
route was, as follows: from Canal and St. Charles, up
St. Charles, Julia, South Rampart, Clio, S. Franklin
(now Loyola), Jackson, Howard St. (now La Salle St.),

*Courtesy N.O.P.S.I.*
Testing for clearances on Esplanade Ave. Ten inch clearances at this location. Destination sign meaningless. The 605
is a Palace car with Herr fender.

Louisiana, Freret, Broadway to S. Claiborne. RETURN:
Broadway, Freret, Louisiana, Howard, Jackson, S. Frank-
lin, Erato, Carondelet, Canal to St. Charles.
   Several route changes were made in *1924-1930.* On
*September 12, 1925:* from Canal and S. Rampart, in
Canal, up University Place, Dryades, Jackson, Freret,
Broadway, Broad Place to Colapissa (line opened out
Broadway and Broad Place to Colapissa *November 7,
1924*). RETURN: Colapissa, Pine, Broad Place, Broad-
way, Freret, Louisiana, LaSalle, Jackson, Dryades, Howard Ave., S. Rampart, Canal. Route effective *October
1, 1926:* from St. Charles and Canal, up St. Charles,
Julia, Dryades, Jackson, Freret, Broadway, Broad Place
to Colapissa. RETURN: Colapissa, Pine, Broad Place,
Broadway, Freret, Louisiana, LaSalle, Jackson, Dryades,
Erato, Carondelet, Canal. *August 10, 1930,* Freret cut
back to Freret and Broadway. Remainder of Freret
operated with only minor changes until bus substitution.
   Narrow streets and congested traffic conditions characterized this line. Little neutral ground running. Line
saw both 800 and 900 type arch roof cars.

23. FRENCH MARKET (originally LEVEE AND
   ESPLANADE, also ESPLANADE AND FRENCH
   MARKET).
   Original company: New Orleans City RR. Co.
   Opened: 1874.
   Electrified: May 21, 1895.
   Discontinued: March 27, 1925.
   Carried name "NORTH PETERS" in last years.

Chas. L. Franck Photo

Esplanade Ave., looking toward Lake, near Broad. Circa 1926. In the early 1920s, about forty percent of New Orleans' Street railway mileage was in neutral ground.

Original route: from stand on middle track on Canal in front of the U.S. Custom House between Decatur and N. Peters, in Canal, down N. Peters, Decatur, N. Peters, Esplanade to Bayou St. John. RETURN: same route. This route remained effective until the Canal and Esplanade Belts started *June 1, 1901.* As of that date, French Market cars stopped at N. Villere. In *1911,* French Market Line was joined with Tchoupitoulas. This lasted until about *1917* when the lines were separated, and each returned to status before the marriage. However, instead of using designation "French Market", the line was renamed "North Peters". During *1923-25,* the Line was re-joined with Tchoupitoulas I ine.

First electric cars were 1894 Brills with 22-E maximum traction trucks. Route sign was purple with red

letters. French Market was street running except on Canal and Esplanade.

24. FRENCH MARKET - CITY PARK (originally FRENCH MARKET, *NOT* to be confused with New Orleans City RR Co.'s French Market Line).
Original company: Orleans RR. Co.
Opened: Nov. 6, 1870.
Electrified: Nov. 25, 1895.
Ceased original route: Dec. 24, 1910. Later renamed "City Park" (see route No. 10, CITY PARK).
Original route: from Decatur and Dumaine, out Dumaine, Broad to Laharpe. RETURN: Broad, Ursulines, Decatur. After *1874,* upper terminus as follows: Broad, Laharpe, Grand Route St. John, Sauvage to Fair Grounds. Return: Sauvage, Grand Route St. John, Ba-

you Road, Broad. In *April, 1896,* rerouted thusly via extension on Dumaine: from Decatur and Dumaine, out Dumaine to Alexander St. at City Park Ave. RETURN: Dumaine, N. Rendon, Ursulines, Decatur. *About 1903,* French Market was re-named "French Market-City Park". On *December 24, 1910,* line began running to Canal via Decatur, N. Peters, to Canal and stand on Canal's middle track between Camp and Magazine. For later route details, see route No. 10, CITY PARK.

Original electric cars were Brills, which stayed with the line until about 1912. Route sign "French Market-City Park" carried on dash. The line was narrow street running except for short stretches of neutral ground on Ursulines and in Canal.

25. GENTILLY (originally the Villere Line). Opened: (changed from Villere) Feb. 21, 1926 (by N. O. P. S. I.). Always electric. Buses substituted: July 17, 1948.

Original route: see: last routing for Villere, route No. 57. Route effective *October 1, 1926:* from Canal and Bourbon, down Bourbon, Pauger, Dauphine, Almonaster Ave. (now Franklin), Franklin to Dreux. RETURN: Franklin, Almonaster, Royal, Canal. Tracks in Franklin Ave. removed from street and put in neutral ground April 20-27, 1927. Neutral ground running in Canal and Franklin, street otherwise. Gentilly always had double truck cars, ending with 800-900's.

26. GIROD AND POYDRAS.
Original company: Canal & Claiborne Sts. RR. Co.
Opened: Apr. 14, 1868.
Never electrified.
Discontinued: July 1899.

Original route: from Canal and Front, up Front, Girod, S. Liberty, Poydras, S. Claiborne, Common (now Tulane) to Rocheblave. RETURN: Common, S. Claiborne, Perdido, Carroll, Poydras, Fulton, Canal, to Front. This line was 5' 2½" gauge. When C. & C. RR. Co. (formerly C. & C. Sts. RR. Co.) electrified their Canal and Common (Tulane) line October 10, 1896, changing same to 4' 8½" gauge, the Girod and Poydras Line was cut back to Tulane and S. Claiborne. Ordinance CS 15487 dated July 26, 1899, authorized the abandonment of the Girod and Poydras Line.

27. HENRY CLAY
Original company: Crescent City RR. Co. (New Orleans Traction Co.)
Opened: June 13, 1895.
Always electric.
Discontinued, divided between Coliseum, Louisiana, and Peters Ave. Lines, August 1913.

Original route: starting from stub end (double track with scissors crossover) terminus in Wells St. (just off Canal), into Canal, out Canal on second track, up Carondelet, St. Andrew, Brainard, Philip, Baronne, Louisiana, Camp, Henry Clay Ave. to Magazine. RETURN: from Henry Clay Ave. and Magazine, Henry Clay, Coliseum, Louisiana, Dryades, Julia, St. Charles, Canal and into Wells St.

The Henry Clay Line terminated at Henry Clay and Magazine, near the imposing DePaul Hospital (formerly Louisiana Retreat) that covers the blocks from Camp to Perrier on Henry Clay. The original route with minor changes was effective until *August 12, 1913,* when the Coliseum and Louisiana Lines absorbed most of it. On *August 27, 1913,* the Peters Avenue Line took over the remainder of the Henry Clay Line.

The Henry Clay was the Hart Franchise No. 1 Line, referred to by operating personnel as the "Peter Hart Line". Strange to say, the other Hart Franchise Line was officially designated Peters Avenue Line.

First cars were the 1894 Brills carrying purple route sign with white frosted letters. Line was mainly street running with some neutral ground.

28. JACKSON.
Original company: New Orleans & Carrollton RR. Co.
Opened: Jan. 13, 1835.
Electrified: Feb. 10, 1893.
Buses substituted: May 19, 1947.
Trackless trolleys substituted: Oct. 2, 1947.

Original route: from Baronne and Canal, up Baronne, Delord (now Howard Ave.), Nayades (now St. Charles), Jackson Ave. to Water St. (Gretna Ferry Landing). RETURN: same route. Effective *January 30, 1896,* Jackson began operating in Canal from Baronne to loop at foot of Canal. The only major rerouting is typified by this *October 1, 1926* listing: from Canal and University Place, up University Place, Dryades, Jackson to Tchoupitoulas. RETURN: Jackson, Dryades, Howard Ave., S. Rampart, Canal. In its final years, Jackson followed this route: same as 1926 except: From Canal and Baronne, up Baronne to Howard Ave., Howard Ave. to Dryades.

Original electric cars were the 1893 St. Louis single truck models, red route sign and white frosted letters. Later came FB&Ds, 400s and finally 800s. Route was all in neutral ground except on Dryades, Baronne, S. Rampart. From 1917 to October 28, 1925, the Jackson and Claiborne (North) Lines were combined. Both lines were standard gauge operation. The union was broken when Jackson was widened to 5' 2½" gauge on the night of October 28, 1925. The Claiborne Line was widened one year later.

29. LA COURSE STREET.
Original company: New Orleans & Carrollton RR. Co.
Opened: March-April, 1836
Never electrified.
Closed: During 1840's.

Original route: from Baronne and Canal, up Baronne, Delord (now Howard Avenue), Nayades (now St. Charles Avenue), Polymnia, across the public square between Coliseum and Camp at Polymnia, into La Course (now Race Street), and in La Course to New

French Market, North Peters St. in foreground, looking toward Canal. About 1890.          *Louis C. Hennick Collection*

Levee Street (now South Peters Street). RETURN: same route.

30. LAUREL.
Original company: New Orleans Ry. & Lt. Co.
Opened: Aug. 12, 1913.
Always electric.
Discontinued: July 5, 1939.

Original route: from Canal and S. Franklin (now LaSalle St.), in Canal, up Camp, Magazine, Peters Ave. (now Jefferson Ave.), Laurel, to Exposition Blvd. (Audubon Park). RETURN: Laurel, Louisiana, Magazine, Canal. By *1919*, the Annunciation line had been discontinued and had given a portion of its route to Laurel. New route: from Canal and Carondelet, up Carondelet, Clio, Camp, Erato, Annunciation, Louisiana, Constance, Valmont, Laurel to Exposition Blvd. (Audubon Park). RETURN: Laurel, Louisiana, Chippewa, Race, Annunciation, Erato, Camp, Canal. *1930 Routing:* from foot of Canal, out Canal, up Tchoupitoulas, Annunciation, Jefferson Ave., Laurel to Audubon Park (Exposition Blvd.). RETURN: Laurel, Louisiana, Chippewa, Race, Annunciation, Howard Ave., So. Peters, Canal. *November 11, 1932,* Laurel was cut back to Louisiana Ave. Shortened, the Laurel ended service in 1939 with this route: from loop at foot of Canal, out Canal, up Tchoupitoulas, Annunciation, Louisiana, to Magazine. RETURN: Louisiana, Chippewa, Race, Annunciation, Howard Ave., S. Peters, Canal.

Laurel had Palace cars, later the 800-900s assigned. Route sign was purple with bright green letters. Most of the route was in streets, very little neutral ground.

31. LEVEE-BARRACKS.
Original company: New Orleans City RR. Co.
Opened: May 14, 1866.
Electrified: Jan. 14, 1896.
Discontinued: Late 1918.

Original route: from middle track stand on Canal in front of U.S. Custom House (between Decatur and N. Peters), in Canal, down N. Peters, Decatur, N. Peters, Lafayette Ave. (later Almonaster Ave., now Franklin Ave.), Chartres, Poland to N. Rampart. RETURN: Poland, Royal, Lafayette, N. Peters, Decatur, N. Peters, Canal. NOTE: for first few months of service, line ended at N. Peters and Elysian Fields Ave., one block from the old Pontchartrain RR depot. Not until after electrification were there any major changes in Levee-Barracks routing.

On *September 11, 1911,* the line was extended to the American Sugar Refinery to give service (with Dauphine Line) to rapidly growing Chalmette Industrial area. New route same as formerly, except: Poland, Dauphine, Reynes, Chartres, Tricou, N. Peters to American Sugar Refinery. RETURN: N. Peters, Delery, Chartres, Reynes, Dauphine, Poland. Routing in effect at time of discontinuance *(1918):* from Canal and Camp, in Canal, down N. Peters, Decatur, N. Peters,

Lafayette Ave., Chartres, Poland, Royal, Lafayette, N. Peters, Decatur, N. Peters, Canal. When the Levee-Barracks was closed, Dauphine, Tchoupitoulas-French Market, and Clio Lines still covered most of the territory formerly served by the line.

The Levee-Barracks frequented many places of historical interest. On N. Peters, it passed the celebrated "French Market" and Jackson Square, with the St. Louis Cathedral and the Cabildo visible on Chartres, one block out. Jackson Square was the center of old New Orleans. The Cathedral was completed in 1795, just seventy-seven years after the City of New Orleans was founded. The Cabildo was the government seat of the Spanish Province of Louisiana up to the time of the Louisiana Purchase. The Cabildo, and the "Presbytere" (flanking the Cathedral, facing Chartres), are now the Louisiana State Museum. On both the North and the South sides of Jackson Square are the Pontalba Apartments (where hundreds of celebrities have stayed, including for instance, Jenny Lind in 1851). The Levee-Barracks cars allowed riders a view of the old U.S. Mint, Ursuline Convent, Holy Cross College, and the Jackson Army Barracks.

Original electric cars were 1894 Brills, with green route sign, white frosted letters. Line had more street running than neutral ground operation.

## 32. LOUISA.
Original company: New Orleans Ry. & Lt. Co.
Opened: Oct. 17, 1920.
Always electric.
Discontinued: July 7, 1923.

At first a part of Carondelet Line (see: route No. 8, CARONDELET). When made a distinct route, from Bourbon and Canal, down Bourbon, Esplanade, Decatur, Elysian Fields, Chartres, Louisa, Royal, Canal.

Service started with single truck cars. This entire route inherited from the old Carondelet Line, and an examination of the Louisa Line shows it actually to be a short working of the Desire Line.

## 33. LOUISIANA AVENUE.
Original company: New Orleans & Carrollton RR. Co.
Opened: Feb. 4, 1850.
Never electrified.
Discontinued: 1878.

Original route (unchanged): from St. Charles, in Louisiana to Tchoupitoulas. RETURN: same route. This was purely a branch operation. The Louisiana Ave. Stock Landing at Louisiana and Tchoupitoulas was perhaps the most important industry on the line. Patronage was light with usually only two cars in ordinary service. In 1877, the Chicago, St. Louis & New Orleans RR. Co. (Illinois Central) built a belt line down Louisiana Ave. The New Orleans & Carrollton RR. Co. sold its Louisiana Line trackage to the C. St. L. & N. O. RR. in 1877 and the belt line for steam railroad freight service had its inspection

trip *May 15, 1878.* Thus ended the first street railway on Louisiana Ave.

## 34. LOUISIANA.
Original company: New Orleans Ry. & Lt. Co.
Opened: Aug. 27, 1913.
Always electric.
Buses substituted: Dec. 27, 1934.

Original route: from loop at foot of Canal, out Canal, up S. Rampart, Calliope, S. Franklin (now Loyola), Jackson, Freret, Louisiana Ave. to Tchoupitoulas. RETURN: Louisiana Ave., Howard St. (now LaSalle), Jackson, S. Franklin, Calliope, Dryades, University Pl., Canal. From *1917 to Aug. 14, 1923,* line terminated at Ferry House (across L&NRR tracks from loop). In its later years, Louisiana had this route: from Canal and University Pl., up University Pl., Dryades, Julia, S. Rampart, Clio, Loyola, Jackson, Freret, Louisiana Ave. to Tchoupitoulas. RETURN: Louisiana Ave., LaSalle, Jackson, Loyola, Erato, S. Rampart, Canal.

Louisiana was an uptown line, touching back o'town. Colored people dubbed it "The Sweet Lucy" Line. Single truck cars opened service, but later the American Car Co. Semi-convertible double truck cars were assigned. Route sign was dark blue with white letters. Louisiana Line had both street and neutral ground operation.

## 35. MAGAZINE.
Original company: New Orleans City RR. Co.
Opened: June 8, 1861.
Electrified: March 15, 1895.
Buses substituted: Feb. 11, 1948.
Trackless trolleys substituted: July 7, 1948.

Original route: from Clay Statue, in Canal, up Camp, Magazine to Toledano. RETURN: Magazine, Canal. In *1883,* line was extended up Magazine to Louisiana, in Louisiana, up Laurel to Exposition Blvd. (Upper City Park, now Audubon Park). RETURN: Laurel, Valmont, Constance, Louisiana, Magazine, Canal. About *1898,* Magazine ceased running out Canal to Clay Statue, began turning at Canal and Camp, going DOWN Camp, UP Magazine. From *1901 to December 29, 1902,* Magazine and Dauphine Lines were joined, former routes resumed upon separation. On *August 12, 1913,* Magazine assumed a portion of Coliseum Line and gave up its former route above Louisiana Ave. to the newly created Laurel Line. New routing: same as formerly, except: up Magazine, Broadway, Maple, Carrollton, Oak to Leake. RETURN: Leake, Gen. Ogden, Willow, Carrollton, and same route to town. On *April 25, 1921,* Magazine was cut back to Maple and Carrollton, its upper portion assumed by the Oak St. Shuttle. On *January 8, 1923,* Magazine began running all the way out Broadway to S. Claiborne (Maple St. trackage abandoned). When the Freret Line began in 1924, the Magazine Line was pulled back to Broadway and Freret. Magazine suffered another cutback *June 15, 1930,* being shortened to a terminus in Audu-

**Looking up Metairie Road, Nov. 1927.**

*Chas. L. Franck Photo*

bon Park, at Moquer and Magazine. A shuttle car ran up Magazine from Moquer to Broadway, and out Broadway to Freret from *June 15* to *August 5, 1930.* This service was replaced by the Broadway Bus, changed to trackless trolley November 30, 1930 (and reverting back to buses on December 13, 1964). Magazine Line continued in shortened form for eighteen more years.

First electrics were open cars, soon replaced by 1894 Brills, green route sign, white letters. Semi-convertibles and Palace cars followed. 800-900s at the end.

### 36. MAGAZINE.
Original company: Jefferson City RR. Co.
Opened to Cadiz, 1864. Completed Dec. 24, 1865.
Merged into Crescent City RR. Co. before electrification.
Date of Merger: Oct. 7, 1880.

Original route: from Toledano and Magazine, up Magazine to Joseph St. (6th Dist.). RETURN: same route. Company suffered financial distress and went through several hands before merger. Crescent City RR. Co. purchased the line and joined it with its Coliseum Line (see: route No. 14, COLISEUM).

### 37. NAPOLEON (Branch operation).
Original company: New Orleans & Carrollton RR. Co.
Opened: Feb. 4, 1850.

Electrified: Feb. 10, 1893.
Merged with N. O. & P. Ry. Napoleon Line, 1906.

Original route: from St. Charles and Napoleon, in Napoleon to Tchoupitoulas. RETURN: same route. New route *effective upon electrification:* From Baronne and Canal, up Baronne, Howard Ave., St. Charles, Napoleon to Tchoupitoulas. RETURN: same route. On *January 30, 1896,* Napoleon began running in Canal from Baronne to loop at foot of Canal. When the New Orleans & Pontchartrain Ry. began running their 5' 2½" gauge line OUT Napoleon from St. Charles, the 4' 8½" New Orleans & Carrollton RR. Co.'s Napoleon Line reverted to its original operation (in Napoleon from St. Charles to Tchoupitoulas). This change took place *January 1, 1903.* In *1906,* the N. O. & C. RR. Co.'s Napoleon Line was widened to 5' 2½" gauge and absorbed by the N. O. & P. Ry.'s operation.

Original electric cars on the N. O. & C RR. Co.'s Napoleon Line were the 1893 St. Louis Car Co. single truckers, followed by the 1900 FB&D's. Route sign was yellow glass with red letters.

### 38. NAPOLEON AVENUE "ROYAL BLUE LINE".
Original company: Orleans & Jefferson Ry. Co.
(completed and put in service by New Orleans & Pontchartrain Ry. Co.).
Opened: Jan. 1, 1903.

89

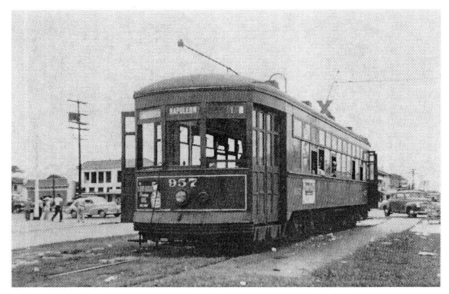

Napoleon Line terminus had been at Broad and Washington for nearly ten years when this photo was taken in August of 1951.

Always electric.

Buses substituted: Feb. 18, 1953.

Original route: from Napoleon and St. Charles, out Napoleon, Broad, Washington, S. Carrollton, Shell Road (now Pontchartrain Blvd.), to Metairie Road. This first terminus was a short walk from the Half Way House at the intersection of Canal and City Park Ave. RETURN: same route.

The intoxicating aura of Emperor Napoleon was irresistible, and the unusually wide, well groomed, and spectacular qualities of Napoleon Ave. and its neutral ground gave rise to a popular surname for the N. O. & P. Ry.'s Napoleon Line. "Royal Blue Line" quickly became part of the New Orleans vocabulary after 1903. Destination signs in Napoleon Ave. cars were of Royal Blue colored glass, white letters.

Soon after the *1903* opening, the line was extended from Shell Road and Metairie Road, out Metairie Road to the 17th St. Canal (Orleans-Jefferson Parish Line). RETURN: Same route. On *July 18, 1915*, the "Shrewsbury Extension" was completed (franchise for this extension was purchased from Orleans-Kenner Electric Ry. Co.—see page 113, Vol. I). This extension, plus the *1906* absorption of the New Orleans & Carrollton RR. Napoleon "branch", created the longest route of round trip street railway line (other than some of the married lines) in New Orleans (16.848 miles). Route, as follows: from Napoleon and Tchoupitoulas, out Napoleon, Broad, Washington, S. Carrollton, Shell Road, Metairie Road (from Metairie Road to Shrewsbury terminus, line was all dirt road or beside the road right of way), Carrollton (in Jefferson Parish, not to be confused with Carrollton Ave. in New Orleans), Narcisse, Metairie Rd., Fagot Ave., Labarre Drive, Metairie Rd., Cypress St. to Shrewsbury Road. RETURN: same route. This was the fullest extent of

the "Royal Blue Line". Cutting back began *December 27, 1934* with service in Jefferson Parish replaced by buses. On *July 5, 1937*, Napoleon was shortened to Washington and Carrollton. The next reduction was on *November 17, 1940*, when the line was snipped off at Washington and Broad. Thus it operated for thirteen more years.

The "Royal Blue Line" began in 1903 with 1894 Brills and Jackson & Sharp cars, both single truckers. Later, double truck Palace cars and finally 800-900's were assigned. Napoleon was one of the few main lines in New Orleans to have any single track with turnouts for passing on the streetcar system (the portion in Jefferson Parish was operated thusly). Napoleon Line in New Orleans had mostly neutral ground and beside the road operation with very well maintained track.

39. NORTH PETERS. (SEE route No. 23, FRENCH MARKET).

40. OAK STREET.

This was another shuttle, also known as "SOUTHPORT", which had two phases of operation.

Original company: New Orleans & Carrollton RR. Co.

Opened: As a shuttle, Feb. 19, 1900 (see: route No. 46, ST. CHARLES).

Became part of Coliseum in 1903.

Reopened: As a shuttle, Apr. 25, 1921.

Last day of car service: July 2, 1929 (car men strike). Reopened several weeks later with trackless trolleys, the first in New Orleans.

Leonidas bus line started May 14, 1934, replacing the Southport trackless trolleys.

Original route: from Carrollton and Poplar (now Willow), up Poplar, Gen. Ogden, Leake to Oak. RETURN:

St. Charles Line terminus, Carrollton and S. Claiborne Aves. December, 1964.          *Louis C. Hennick Collection*

same route. Actually, this was the outer end of the St. Charles Line until the St. Charles and Tulane Belts began in *1900*. Second phase, beginning in *1921:* only from Carrollton and Oak, up Oak and Leake to Gen. Ogden. RETURN: same route. About *1923,* a full-circuit route for Oak St. Shuttle was started, thusly: from Carrollton and Oak, up Oak, Leake, Gen. Ogden, then down Willow to Carrollton, and in Carrollton to Oak.

Line started in 1900 with 1893 St. Louis Car Co. and FB&D models, all single truckers. Oak St. had FB&D rebuilds during second phase.

### 41. PARIS AVENUE.
Original company: New Orleans Ry. & Lt. Co.
Another shuttle, later a leg of Broad.
Opened: Mar. 6, 1912.
Always electric, always single truck cars.
Buses substituted: Jan. 31, 1932.

Original route: from Broad and Laharpe, down N. Broad, out St. Bernard, Paris Ave. to Gentilly Road. RETURN: same route. In 1915, became leg of Broad. (see route No. 5, BROAD).

### 42. PETERS AVENUE.
This was the Hart Franchise No. 2.
Original company: Crescent City RR. Co.
Opened: Aug. 18, 1894.
Always electric.
Discontinued: Sept. 23, 1925 (part of line then assumed by Dryades—see route No. 17).

Original route: from stub end terminus in Wells St. (with Henry Clay Line—only the two Hart Franchise Lines used this terminus), out Canal on second track, up S. Rampart, Calliope, S. Franklin (now Loyola), Jackson, Freret, Louisiana, Dryades, Peters Ave. (now Jefferson Ave.) to Tchoupitoulas. RETURN: Peters Ave., Dryades, Dufossat, Baronne, Louisiana, Howard St., Jackson, S. Franklin, Calliope, Dryades, University Pl., Canal to Wells (NOTE: Peters Ave. Line ended at Peters Ave. and Magazine at first, soon after 1894 extended to Tchoupitoulas). After *August 27, 1913,* line reflected a slight change: from Wells St. terminus, out Canal, down Carondelet, St. Andrew, Brainard, Philip, Baronne, Dufossat, Dryades, Peters Ave. to Tchoupitoulas. RETURN: Peters Ave., Dryades, Julia, St. Charles, Canal.

91

Original cars were open models, soon giving way to the "workhorse" 1894 Brills that began electric service on so many other lines (two-hundred and twenty-six 1894 Brills were ordered!). Route sign was red with blue letters. Peters Ave. was an uptown line with good trackage and some neutral ground operation.

43. POYDRAS-MAGAZINE.
    Original company: New Orleans & Carrollton RR. Co.
    Opened: First week of January, 1835.
    Never electrified.
    Closed: March-April, 1836.

This was the second street railway in the United States and, incidentally, in the WORLD. Gauge was 4' 8½", rails were the grooved and strap type. First cars were leased from the Pontchartrain RR. followed closely by omnibus type cars on rail wheels.

Original route: from Baronne and Poydras, in Poydras, up Magazine, in La Course (now Race) St. to New Levee (now So. Peters) St. RETURN: same route. A few days after Poydras-Magazine opened, the "Lafayette" (Jackson Ave. Line opened, and presumably Poydras-Magazine cars did go down Baronne to Canal from Poydras. Trackage was planned up Magazine, in Richard, up Annunciation, and in Market to New Levee. It has not been ascertained if this trackage was built.

The city ordinance for the Poydras-Magazine Line stipulated that if property owners along any part of the route objected, that part of the route must be removed within sixty days. There were objections from property owners along Magazine St. between La Course (Race St. now) and Poydras during 1835. On *Feb. 13, 1836,* the New Orleans City Council directed that rails in Magazine between La Course and Poydras be removed. The line was gone by May of that year. Trackage in La Course St. absorbed by new La Course Street Line (see route No. 29).

44. PRYTANIA (originally CAMP AND PRYTANIA).
    Original company: New Orleans City RR. Co.
    Opened: June 8, 1861.
    Electrified: Sept. 15, 1894.
    Discontinued: Oct. 1, 1932.

Original route: from Clay Statue, in Canal, up Camp, Prytania to Toledano. RETURN: Prytania, Poeyfarre, Magazine, Canal. In 1883, extended above Toledano, as follows: Prytania, Upperline, Pitt, Joseph, Hurst to Exposition Blvd. (Upper City Park, now Audubon Park). RETURN: Hurst, Joseph, Perrier, Robert, Pitt, Prytania (and returning via Prytania and Camp to Canal). On *February 7, 1896* from Rampart and Canal, in Canal, down Camp, Prytania, Joseph, Hurst to Exposition Blvd. RETURN: same route. Prytania and Esplanade Belt were joined 1902 (see Esplanade Belt/route No 19). On *March 16, 1908,* Prytania began starting from Canal and N. Franklin (now Crozat). During

Carondelet and Canal, May 1964.     *Courtesy Otto A. Goessl*

1916-17, Prytania and Villere Lines were united (former operations resumed when separated). In 1919, route was, as follows: from Canal and Camp, up Camp, Prytania, Joseph, Hurst to Exposition Blvd. RETURN: Hurst, Joseph, Prytania, Howard Ave., St. Charles, Canal. *Final routing* quite different: from Canal and Camp, in Canal, up Magazine, Poeyfarre, Camp, Prytania, Joseph, Coliseum, Henry Clay to Camp. RETURN: Camp, Peters Ave. (now Jefferson Ave.), Prytania, Camp to Canal. This change was effected *May 12, 1929.*

Prytania was commonly known as "The Silk Stocking Line". This uptown line had mainly street running, passing through "Garden District" of fashionable and lovely homes, Louisiana and French Plantation types abounding. This was the secluded and sedate district of New Orleans' aristocracy—and still can claim this distinction. Many famous names (writers, patrons of art, wealthy old line families of banking, cotton, sugar, timber, etc.) lived up that way. However, for a line that traversed this sanctuary of "La Plus Belle" and dainty beauty, its onetime starting point at N. Franklin was indeed MOST incongrous. The cribs of not-so-

St. Charles at South Carrollton, February 1965.

dainty "Storeyville" flanked the terminus. On the other hand, this line served the renowned Touro Infirmary, founded by Judah Touro, a wealthy philanthropist of the middle nineteenth century.

Original electric cars were 1894 Brills with 22-E maximum traction trucks, carrying yellow route sign with tan letters. Later, in succession, came single truck Jackson & Sharp cars, double truck Palace cars, single truck Prytania cars, and lastly the double truck 800-900's.

### 45. ST. BERNARD.

Original company: New Orleans Ry. & Lt. Co.
Opened: July 13, 1909.
Always electric.
Buses substituted: Immediately following 1929 strike. Car service ended at beginning of strike, July 2, 1929.

Original route: from Broad and Laharpe, down Broad, in St. Bernard Ave. to N. Claiborne. RETURN: same route. In *1915*, became leg of Broad (see route No. 5). Service began with orange and yellow FB&D cars. The St. Bernard Line was all neutral ground operation.

### 46. ST. CHARLES (originally CARROLLTON).

Original company: New Orleans & Carrollton RR. Co.
Opened: Sept. 26, 1835.
Electrified: Feb. 1, 1893. STILL IN OPERATION, after one-hundred and twenty-nine years of unbroken service. This is the oldest continuous operation of any street railway in the WORLD.

Original route: from Canal and Baronne, up Baronne, in Delord (now Howard Ave.), up Nayades (now St. Charles) to First St. (now St. Charles) and Dublin St. in Carrollton (now 6th Dist. of New Orleans). RETURN: same route. Practically no change in route until *electrification*, when line was extended out Carrollton from St. Charles to Poplar (now Willow). On

February 4, 1898, St. Charles Line (named such when electrified) was extended up Poplar, Gen. Ogden, and Leake to Oak St. This segment became a shuttle operation in *1900* when the St. Charles and Tulane Belts started (see Oak St., route No. 40). On *January 30, 1896*, St. Charles Line began operating in Canal from Baronne to loop at foot of Canal. St. Charles and Tulane Belts operated from *February 19, 1900* to *January 8, 1951*. When the Belt operations ceased, St. Charles Line resumed its former line type of operation: from Canal and St. Charles, up St. Charles, around Lee Circle, on up St. Charles, out Carrollton to Dixon. RETURN: Carrollton, St. Charles, Howard Ave., Baronne (presently operating down Carondelet), and Canal. On *August 10, 1952*, line was cut back to Carrollton and S. Claiborne, and has operated the same since.

St. Charles is all neutral ground operation save ten blocks on Carondelet and St. Charles in the downtown section, between Howard Ave. and Canal. This was the first line in New Orleans to use the overhead trolley system in electric street railway operation. First electric cars were 1893 St. Louis Car Co. models carrying green destination sign with white letters. Later, St. Charles Line had 1899 FB&D's. In 1915, the 400's were put in service. When Belts were abolished in 1951, the arch roof 800-900's were in service. At the time this book goes to press, only the refurbished 900's serve on the St. Charles Line.

47. ST. CHARLES BELT.

Original company: New Orleans & Carrollton RR. Co.
Opened: Feb. 19, 1900.
Always electric.

Discontinued, reverting to line type (end to end) operation: Jan. 8, 1951.

Original route: from foot of Canal, on outside track, to Baronne, up Baronne, Howard Ave., St. Charles, Carrollton, Tulane, S. Rampart, and in Canal's outside track to the loop at the foot of Canal. All New Orleans & Carrollton RR. Co.'s lines were standard gauge, eventually widened to 5' 2½". The St. Charles Belt was widened during the night of October 2-3, 1929. In *1930*, the Belt had a different route: from Canal and Baronne, up Baronne, Howard Ave., St. Charles, Carrollton, Tulane, S. Rampart, and in Canal to Baronne (no longer running to the loop). On *March 6, 1947*, the St. Charles Belt cars began turning from Tulane into S. Liberty St. to reach Canal.

In its zenith, the St. Charles Belt provided twelve and one half miles of neutral ground operation (except for ten blocks on Baronne). There were more reasons why the line was about the best ride in New Orleans. The neutral ground operation was over one-hundred pound rail, rock ballast, and sod over the ballast, with a verdant carpet of grass fit for royalty. Scenery, sights, views—all unforgettable and most pleasing to the eye. Leaving Canal and Baronne, the St. Charles Belt passed on the left the Church of the Immaculate Conception, founded by the Order of Jesuits. Old City Library could be seen as Belt Line cars swept around Lee Circle. The Library was founded by a gift from Andrew Carnegie and opened in 1908. The Floral Trail, marked by signs, begins at St. Charles and Lee Circle. Along St. Charles Ave., a residential area unfolds, starting with antebellum homes and progressing through Victorian to modern as the Avenue nears Car-

New Basin Canal Bridge, St. Charles and Tulane Belts. August 6, 1950.      *Courtesy Otto A. Goessl*

South Claiborne and Josephine Sts., looking "down", original track installation. Changed 1927 to one track each side of drainage canal.

rollton. St. Charles Belt cars passed Loyola University, Tulane University, and St. Mary's Dominican College. Belt cars then passed Audubon Park. The Garden District (between Jackson Ave., 2100 block and Louisiana Ave., 3300 block) with its especially beautiful homes was skirted by the Belt. At Toledano Street was a statue of John Mc Donogh, one of the city's greatest philanthropists, whose name is borne by many of the public schools in New Orleans. The stately old "Orleans Club", an exclusive club for women, plus a reproduction of "Tara", the home of Scarlet O'Hara in "Gone With The Wind", are additional sights. A view of the levees which encircle the city can be seen at St. Charles and Carrollton. At Pontchartrain Blvd., Carrollton Ave crossed the New Orleans Navigation Canal (now filled in). Built in 1832 and originally extending from Lake Pontchartrain into the city, the canal was for some time used by lake and coastal vessels bringing cotton, lumber, and other products. Turning from Carrollton into Tulane, the Belt passed old Athletic Park, later Pelican Baseball Stadium. Then one of the greatest medical centers of the nation was passed—Charity Hospital with its nurses' home and adjoining buildings, Tulane University (Hutchinson Memorial) and Louisiana State University Medical Centers, all within the range of a few blocks. At this point between Tulane

and Canal, was New Orleans' "Chinatown". The next turn brought the Belt cars into S. Rampart St. for the return through the business district.

Original cars on St. Charles Belt were FB&D types. Green destination sign with white letters was carried. Later cars were the 400, 800 and 900 arch roof types.

48. ST. CLAUDE.
　　Original company: N.O.P.S.I.
　　Opened: Feb. 21, 1926.
　　Always electric.
　　Buses Substituted: Jan. 1, 1949.
　　Trackless trolleys substituted: Nov. 6, 1949.
　　Buses again substituted: July 22, 1962.

Original route: from loop at foot of Canal, out Canal, N. Rampart, Mc Shane, St. Claude (crossing Industrial Canal), Reynes, Chartres, Tricou, Alhambra, Delery, N. Peters to American Sugar Refinery. RETURN: N. Peters, Delery, Dauphine, Forstall, St. Claude, Mc Shane, N. Rampart, Canal to loop. On *January 21, 1930,* operation to Canal loop discontinued. St. Claude cars began terminating downtown thusly: up N. Rampart, in St. Peter, up Burgundy, out Canal, and back down N. Rampart. This looping terminus was abolished *November 22, 1934* with St. Claude cars going up and down N. Rampart all the way to Canal. A shelter protecting

South Claiborne at Fern shows beauty of S. Claiborne Line. April 6, 1950.　　　　*Courtesy Otto A. Goessl*

waiting passengers was built in the neutral ground of N. Rampart at Canal, where the St. Claude ended at a double track, scissors crossover terminus. Lower portion of St. Claude remained unchanged up to 1949 substitution.

The St. Claude was a downtown line mainly on neutral ground. Much of it was part of the old Dauphine Line. Line always had double truck cars, and after 1935 the long 1000 class arch roof cars were assigned.

49. SOUTH CLAIBORNE.
    Original company: New Orleans Ry. & Lt. Co.
    Opened: Feb. 22, 1915.
    Always electric.
    Buses substituted: Jan. 5, 1953.

Original route: from Canal and St. Charles, up St. Charles, Howard Ave., S. Rampart, Clio, S. Claiborne, Broadway to Maple: RETURN: Broadway, S. Claiborne, Erato, Carondelet, Canal. Broadway running discontinued *March 1, 1916* with S. Claiborne cars running all the way out S. Claiborne to Carrollton Ave. For a number of years, in the 1920's, line used Julia St. instead of Howard Ave. to reach S. Rampart on outbound trips.

The neutral ground operation beside the canal in S. Claiborne was quite spectacular (see photo, page 70). Originally, the line's double track was on the river side of the wide canal. As of *June 15, 1927*, tracks were changed to run on both sides. S. Claiborne Line had neutral ground operation on S. Claiborne, Canal, and Howard Ave.—rest of trackage in streets. Line opened with FB&D cars, later the 800-900's.

50. SOUTH CLAIBORNE SHUTTLE.
    Original company: New Orleans Ry. & Lt. Co.
    Opened: May 8, 1916.
    Buses substituted: Jan. 1, 1931.

Original route (unchanged): on S. Claiborne from Carrollton Ave. to Protection Levee (Orleans-Jefferson Parish Line). RETURN: same route. This was a standard gauge line throughout its life, for it carried the interurban cars of the Orleans-Kenner Traction Co. (see Vol. I). The shuttle operation normally was provided by one FB&D car.

51. SOUTH PETERS.
    Original company: Crescent City RR. Co.
    Opened: Apr. 26, 1890.
    Electrified: May 8, 1895.
    Discontinued: Late 1916.

Original route: from Canal and Camp, in Canal, Tchoupitoulas, Annunciation, Toledano to Tchoupitoulas. RETURN: Toledano, Chippewa, Race, Annunciation, Howard Ave, South Peters, Canal. In its last four or five years, South Peters operated in a one-direction circuit, as follows: from Canal and Tchoupitoulas, up Tchoupitoulas, Annunciation, Toledano, Chippewa, Race, Annunciation, Erato, Camp, Howard Ave., St. Charles, Canal.

First electric cars were 1894 Brills carrying red destination sign with white letters. After electrification and before one-direction circuit operation, cars terminated on Canal at stand on middle track between Camp

Train at Spanish Fort, about 1916. Three Coleman trailers behind a Barney & Smith 500-507 or an American Car Co. 509-12 was the usual consist.

and Magazine, crossing over to second track to start runs.

This was an uptown "near river front" line with all street running except in Canal and later in Howard Ave. South Peters served the poorer section of the city, passing through the "Irish Channel", a colorful section of honest but rough fighting elements. Warehouse, factories, docks, and attendant saloons, this ungraceful part of New Orleans had another dubious distinction—it WAS the only part of town where police patrolled in pairs.

## 52. SOUTH PETERS SHUTTLE.
Original company: New Orleans Ry. & Lt. Co.
Opened: 1916.
Always electric.
Discontinued: Apr. 18, 1921.

Original route (unchanged): from Erato and Annunciation, down Annunciation, Howard Ave. S. Peters to Canal and N. Peters. RETURN: Tchoupitoulas, Annunciation to Erato. Line presumably established when S. Peters Line abolished in 1916.

## 53. SPANISH FORT.
Original company: New Orleans Ry. & Lt. Co.
Opened: Mar. 26, 1911.
Always electric.
Buses substituted: Oct. 16, 1932.

This line had seasonal operations. Summer service started from S. Rampart between Canal and Tulane, out Canal to City Park Ave., left to New Basin Canal, and along the bank on private right of way to Adams Ave. (now Robert E. Lee Blvd.) and on Adams Ave. to Spanish Fort. RETURN: same route. There was a pier that extended three quarters of a mile out over Lake Pontchartrain at Spanish Fort. N. O. Ry. & L. Co. built trackage on this pier to its very end, and operated a shuttle car over this strange "line" each summer for several years (the pier was in place and tracks there as late as June of 1925). In *late 1920's*, S. Rampart terminus discontinued: New downtown terminus: In Canal, down Crozat, out Iberville, up N. Liberty, and out Canal.

Winter service on Spanish Fort Line was simply a shuttle car from West End to Spanish Fort. However, beginning June 11, 1911, Spanish Fort Line had local cars operating from the resort all the way in to the Half Way House. Duration of this service unknown, but listed in 1912 and 1913 issues of "Times-Democrat" newspapers. Local cars varied, sometimes Palace cars, sometimes single truckers. At the end, local car service provided by experimental car 288.

Original destination signs were violet with white letters. Summer service handled by car with trailers, often the Barney & Smith and American motor cars pulling three trailers, each.

Courtesy Otto A. Goessl

858 crossing New Basin Canal bridge, South Carrollton near Julia. St. Charles-Tulane Belts, August 6, 1950.

## 54. TCHOUPITOULAS.

(pronounced: "Chop-a-tool-us"). Originally known as the TCHOUPITOULAS AND NEW LEVEE LINE.
Original company: Crescent City RR. Co.
Opened: Aug. 10, 1866.
Electrified: Apr. 20, 1895.
Discontinued: July 2, 1929.

Original route: from Canal and Camp, in Canal, up Tchoupitoulas to Stock Landing at Tchoupitoulas and Louisiana Ave. RETURN: Tchoupitoulas, New Levee (now South Peters), Canal. Extended up Tchoupitoulas to Joseph St. in *1867*. On *May 26, 1876,* the line was opened further up Tchoupitoulas to Exposition Blvd. (Upper City Park, now Audubon Park). *After electrification,* line's starting point on Canal was the stand on middle track between Camp and Magazine, cars going out to second track when leaving. In *1911,* Tchoupitoulas was joined with the old New Orleans City RR. French Market Line, with cars crossing Canal from N. Peters to Tchoupitoulas and from South to North Peters. Route then continued down N. Peters, Decatur, N. Peters, and out Esplanade to N. Villere. RETURN: same route. In *1919,* the union between Tchoupitoulas and French Market Lines was severed, and the Tchoupitoulas was joined with the French Market-City Park Line from 1919-21 and from 1923-25. On *March 5, 1926,* the Tchoupitoulas Line was cut back to Louisiana Ave., following this route: from Tchoupitoulas and Canal, in Canal, up South Peters,

Howard Ave., Annunciation, Race, Tchoupitoulas to Louisiana Ave. RETURN: Tchoupitoulas, Race, Annunciation, Tchoupitoulas, Canal. On *December 17, 1927,* the Tchoupitoulas Line was further reduced and re-routed, as follows: from Canal and South Peters, up South Peters, out Howard Ave., Annunciation, Race to Tchoupitoulas. RETURN: Race, Annunciation, Tchoupitoulas, Canal. In this final meagre form, the once sprawling Tchoupitoulas Line ended service in 1929.

The Tchoupitoulas Line made its way up and down Tchoupitoulas fighting traffic as dense as any found today. The difference was that the type of vehicles encountered were the heavy cotton floats and drays which found it convenient to drive with their wheels in the grooves of the 5' 2½" gauge tram girder rail. Often, these vehicles would become wedged. Always they were much slower than the mule cars and later the electric cars. Nothing much could be done about it, although the motorman or driver would try verbally (usually with exasperated encouragement of impatient passengers) in sometimes very colorful language to induce sluggard carts and drays to move aside. This persuasion was often returned in equally masterful style by wagon and dray drivers. A rough but interesting line.

The 1894 Brills were the original electric cars on Tchoupitoulas, carrying a dark green route sign with white letters. Later, the line had FB&D cars. Tchoupitoulas was purely an uptown, river front line, long as its name and as rough to ride as it is to spell. Served warehouse, dock, factory and "Irish Channel" districts.

Viaduct over N.O.T.Co. tracks at Franklin Avenue and Florida Walk. Villere Line, 1922.      *Chas. L. Franck Photo*

**55. TULANE AVENUE.**
    (originally CANAL AND COMMON).
    Original company: Canal & Claiborne Sts. RR. Co.
    Opened: Jan. 15, 1871.
    Electrified: Oct. 10, 1896.
    Became Tulane Belt: Feb. 19, 1900.
    Reinstated with slightly longer route and trackless
      trolleys: Jan. 8, 1951.
    Buses substituted: Dec. 27, 1964.

Original route: from loop at foot of Canal, out Canal, up N. Rampart, Common (now Tulane) to Rocheblave. RETURN: Common, Basin, Canal. Extended out Tulane to Carrollton Ave. on *October 11, 1896.*

Original electric cars were 1896 FB&D's with purple route sign, white letters. In mule car days, line was 5′ 2½″ gauge, changed to 4′ 8½″ gauge when electrified.

**56. TULANE BELT.**
    Original company: New Orleans & Carrollton RR.
      Co.
    Opened: Feb. 19, 1900.
    Always electric.
    Discontinued: Jan. 8, 1951 when Tulane Line re-
      instated with trackless trolleys.

Original route: from loop at foot of Canal, out Canal, S. Rampart, Tulane, Carrollton Ave., St. Charles, Howard Ave., Baronne, Canal. When opened, the Tulane and St. Charles Belts both were 4′ 8½″ gauge. On the night of October 1-2, 1929, the Tulane Belt was widened to 5′ 2½″ (St. Charles Belt was widened the very next night). After widening, there were a few minor changes in the Tulane Belt route—such as going down Carondelet instead of Baronne from Howard Ave. to Canal (beginning about *1930*) or turning from Canal into Loyola (now S. Saratoga) to reach Tulane (effective *November 15, 1929*). Of the two belts, the Tulane was the heaviest and had tighter headways. This was one finding published in 1923 in the Beeler Report (see Chapter 1). For details on cars and scenery for the Tulane Belt, see route No. 47, ST. CHARLES BELT.

**57. VILLERE (later named GENTILLY TERRACE).**
    Original company: New Orleans City & Lake RR.
      Co.
    Opened: Oct. 15, 1895.
    Always electric.
    Name changed to Gentilly: Feb. 21, 1926.

Original route: from Canal and St. Charles, out Canal (second track), down N. Villere to Lafayette Ave. (later Almonaster Ave., now Franklin Ave.). RETURN: same

Crossing the New Orleans Terminal Co. tracks, October 3, 1949.

route. Began running to loop at foot of Canal in 1898. In *1908*, extended out Lafayette and Franklin Aves. from Villere to Grant St. (now N. Galvez), and one year later opened all the way out Franklin Ave. to St. James Ave. (now Dreux). In *1910*, litigation between the New Orleans Terminal Co. and N. O. Ry. & L. Co. caused quite an inconvenience. A grade crossing over the N. O. T. Co. tracks was restrained by court order upon the objection of N. O. T. Co. For a few months the Villere Line operated in two segments, until a trestle was built (per ordinance NCS 6445, March 9, 1910). The Villere Line began operating over the trestle "through" to Dreux on *May 15, 1910*.

During the "break" in the Villere Line, passengers had to walk across the N. O. T. Co. tracks at Florida Walk in transferring from a Villere car from town to the temporary shuttle running on the divorced segment and vice-versa. This discomfort was somewhat relieved by the Gentilly Land Development & Realty Corp., real estate interests developing land and housing at the outer terminus of the Villere Line, and the Gentilly Automobile Co. The auto company purchased a few gasoline motor coaches of the Gramm Motor Car Co. design (built by Brill) and put them in operation in January of 1910. The buses' route commenced at Gentilly Land Development & Realty Corp. offices at 216 Baronne, and ran down Baronne, out Canal, N. Claiborne, Esplanade, N. Dorgenois, Lapeyrouse, Gentilly Blvd. out to Gentilly Terrace and St. James residential areas. Fare was 10¢ and service restricted to ONLY people going to and from the new residential areas mentioned. This operation may hold the title of being the first motor buses to operate in public (street transit) service in New Orleans (although there were a few motor buses running at the same

time in railroad depot transfer and touring service). This "invasion" of the rubber tired transit vehicle was short-lived. As soon as the Villere car Line was restored to through operation, the Gentilly Automobile Co. quit the bus business. and sold the motor coaches.

Beginning *January 24, 1912*, Villere Line started a new route downtown, as follows. from foot of Canal, out Canal, down N. Rampart, out Dumaine, and down N. Villere as before to Franklin Ave. and Dreux. RETURN: same as formerly, except up N. Villere, in St. Peter, up N. Rampart, and in Canal.

For a few months in *1916-17*, Villere and Prytania Lines were joined. After separation, each returned to former routings. Just before the Villere was changed to Gentilly, routing in effect in *1925*: from Dauphine and Canal, out Canal, down Burgundy, Dumaine, N. Villere, Almonaster Ave., Franklin Ave. to Dreux. RETURN: Franklin Ave., Almonaster Ave., N. Villere, St. Peter, Dauphine, Canal.

Villere was a downtown back o' town line. First cars were the 1894 Brills with indigo route sign, red letters. Later cars were FB&D's. After the line was opened to Dreux, and during winter seasons, some of the Barney & Smith and American Car Co. 500's saw service on Villere.

58. WEST END (later CEMETERIES-WEST END).
Original company: New Orleans City RR. Co.
Opened: From Half Way House to Lake—Apr. 20, 1876. From Carondelet and Canal to Lake—June 18, 1876.

Electrified: July 17, 1898 (ceremonial run held July 16. Wires up and test run made Apr. 2, 1898. Steam service remained until double truck

The West End Line could be quite artistic—leaving Florida Ave. waiting shed, October 14, 1949.     *Courtesy Otto A. Goessl*

Near Homedale Ave., June 6, 1949.     *Courtesy Otto A. Goessl*

Inbound on private right of way beside Greenwood Cemetery, October 3, 1949.　　　　　*Courtesy Otto A. Goessl*

Barney & Smith electric cars were delivered in July).

Buses substituted: Jan. 15, 1950.

Original route (completed): from middle track stub at Carondelet and Canal, out Canal to City Park Ave., turning left to New Basin Canal at Half Way House, then out along bank of New Basin Canal to West End, on Lake Pontchartrain. RETURN: same route. When electrified in *1898*, terminus was moved out one block to Baronne and Canal. On *May 7, 1911*, the downtown terminus was moved again, this time to S. Rampart and Canal, between Canal and Tulane. The terminus at West End was under a large train shed built over the Lake and consisted of two tracks, refreshment stands, waiting rooms and a baggage room.

Route length was six and one half miles. When electrified, the line had but six stops: 1—Claiborne, 2—Galvez, 3—Broad, 4—Hagan (now Jefferson Davis Parkway), 5—Carrollton Ave., and 6—Half Way House.

Beginning about *1920*, West End began running in Canal all the way to the loop at foot of Canal. Stops were added between Half Way House and West End. One such stop was added earlier (1911)—this was Adams Ave., junction with the Spanish Fort Line. West End and Spanish Fort Lines shared common route between Adams Ave. and Canal and N. Rampart.

Original service was by steam dummy passenger train. First electric cars were Barney & Smith and American Car Co. motor (double truck) cars, twelve in number, with 36 passenger trailers and one baggage trailer. Each motor pulled three trailers. When Spanish Fort opened in 1911, these fine trains quit West End

service for Spanish Fort operation. Palace cars and Coleman trailers were operated in two car units after Spanish Fort started. In 1935, steel arch roof 800-900's took over, running until bus substitution. First route sign (1898) was white with purple letters.

59. **PONTCHARTRAIN RAILROAD COMPANY** (horse and steam only).

Opened: Apr. 23, 1831 (horse), Sept. 17, 1832 (steam).

Passenger service discontinued (last train left Milneburg at 6:25 P.M.): March 15, 1932.

Freight service closed, rails removed: 1935.

Gauge always 4' 8½".

Original route: from Elysian Fields at Decatur, out Elysian Fields to Milneburg. RETURN: same route. Extension along docks opened *July 19, 1868* from Elysian Fields and Decatur St. to Girod St. Line then had five stops: leaving Girod, stops at 1—Canal, 2—French Market, 3—old Depot, 4—N. Claiborne, 5—Gentilly Road. Next was terminus at Milneburg. Old stop at Good Children St. (now St. Claude Ave.) discontinued when Mexican Gulf RR., having its terminus there, was torn up during the Civil War. Mexican Gulf RR. rebuilt under another name in the 1880's, with the St. Claude stop presumably restored. Beginning *April 15, 1872*, trains were cut back from Girod to original depot site at Decatur and Elysian Fields (1868 extension sold to Morgan's Louisiana & Texas RR. & Steamship Co.).

In 1871, Pontchartrain RR. Co. was purchased by New Orleans Mobile & Texas RR. (yet, retained its corporate identity). Louisville & Nashville RR. ownership under the same terms began 1881. For a number

102

of years, some Pontchartrain RR. trains used the L&N station at foot of Canal. Beginning about 1920, Pontchartrain passenger service operated only from foot of Elysian Fields at Decatur (Pontchartrain Junction) to Milneburg. Popularly called "Smoky Mary", Pontchartrain RR. operated thusly until its demise.

## 60. NEW ORLEANS, SPANISH FORT & LAKE RAILROAD COMPANY (steam only, original name: CANAL STREET, CITY PARK & LAKE RAILROAD COMPANY).
Opened: Oct. 3, 1875.
Passenger service suspended: July 12, 1903.
Dismantled, officially abandoned: 1904. Gauge 5' 2½" when built, changed to 4' 8½" when company re-organized.

Original route (unchanged): from N. Basin and Customhouse (now Iberville), down N. Basin, out Bienville, Bernadotte, crossing City Park Ave., following the Orleans Drainage Canal to Lake Pontchartrain, where the railway turned right and proceeded to Spanish Fort. RETURN: same route.

## 61. NEW ORLEANS TERMINAL COMPANY
(steam only—predecessor company: New Orleans & Western RR.).
Opened: Jan. 11, 1896.
Passenger service discontinued: Dec. 26, 1920.
Gauge now 4' 8½", in 1890's reported 4' 9".

Original route: from a connection with New Orleans, Spanish Fort & Lake RR. (where present N. O. T. Co. crosses Bayou St. John), down beside Florida Ave. and Florida Walk to Alexander St., beside Alexander St. to Chalmette and the River. RETURN: same route. November, 1898 "Official Guide" gives impression N. O. & W. RR. and N. O., S. F. & L RR. were under common management with service on BOTH lines commencing at N. Basin and Customhouse. The N. O. & W. RR. operated a line from the N. O., S. F. & L. RR. junction to Shrewsbury, but for freight only. Route changed *June 1, 1908* (under N. O. T. Co. management) to run on a right of way paralleling old N. O., S. F. & L. RR. to Terminal Station (opened same day) at Canal and N. Basin. Original service: steam commuter service, several trips DAILY. After June 1, 1908, a single train, daily except Sunday, with a schedule convenient for working people.

## 62. JEFFERSON & LAKE PONTCHARTRAIN RAILWAY COMPANY (steam only, built by New Orleans & Carrollton RR Co.).
Opened: Apr. 14, 1853.
Abandoned: Nov. 24, 1864.
Always 4' 8½" gauge.

Original route: from 1st (now St. Charles) and Dublin Sts., in Carrollton, up Levee St. (now Leake Ave.), to 17th St. Canal, and out along bank of 17th St. Canal to Lakeview (later called Bucktown), on Lake Pontchartrain. RETURN: same route. Railway extended out over Lake for a few hundred feet on a pier. The J. & L. P. Ry. trains ran through to Tivoli Circle (now Lee Circle) over N. O. & C. RR. Co. for most of the eleven years, 1853 to 1864. During the Civil War, the U. S. Army maintained a military supply depot about one mile by railway spur off the J. & L. P. Ry., midway between the River and the Lake, near present Shrewsbury. It is not known if the Jefferson & Lake Pontchartrain Ry. was an actual "member" of the United States Military Railroads during the war, but regular "Government Trains" were operated from Supply Depot to junction with J. & L. P., then over J. & L. P. Ry. at Tivoli Circle until the line folded. After J. & L. P. Ry. abandonment, United States Military Railroads built a railroad from docks, out St. Joseph St. to connection with N. O. J. & G. N. RR., thence over that railroad and Military RR. trackage to the Supply Depot. Finished April, 1865, this Military RR. was dismantled in 1866.

## 63. OTHER STEAM RAILROAD COMMUTER AND SUBURBAN PASSENGER SERVICES.

The Illinois Central and Yazoo & Mississippi Valley Railroads were the outstanding examples of suburban and commuter train service in New Orleans. The I. C. RR. for many years operated such service from the Union Depot to Harahan Yard and Incline. One way mileage was 10.47 with six stations (New Orleans, Government Yard, Poydras Jn., Southport Jn., Harahan Yard, and Incline (at Incline, freight cars were transferred across the Mississippi River to the T&P and T&NO at Avondale). In 1910, this I. C. suburban service was running five daily trips each way (two daily in to the Incline) and an additional trip daily, except Sunday. This service was pulled off soon after the Orleans-Kenner Electric Ry. Co. commenced service (see Vol. I). The I. C. subsidiary, Yazoo & Mississippi Valley RR., operated a frequent service from Union Depot to Sellers, one way mileage of 23.68. Seven stations: New Orleans, Orleans Jn., Frellsen Jn., St. Rose, Destrehan, Good Hope, and Sellers. In 1923, there were three daily trips in each direction. This service, provided by motor cars at the end, did not last through 1931.

The Louisville & Nashville RR. has for years operated frequent suburban trains from New Orleans to Pass Christian and Ocean Springs, Miss. Mileage in Louisiana is 34.23, from New Orleans to Rigolets. Only one train was operating to Pass Christian (Nos. 9 and 12, daily except Sat. and Sun.) arriving in New Orleans in the morning and departing in the evening, when the service was discontinued May 6, 1964.

Over the River, the Texas & Pacific Ry. operated a Gouldsboro-Waggaman service, 11.50 miles one way, three daily trips each way in 1913. Eight stations:

Gouldsboro, Gretna, Harvey's Canal, Company's Canal, Westwego, Avondale, Waggaman. This service disappeared by 1919.

Other railroads entering New Orleans provided frequent service convenient to commuters. Notable examples were: Louisiana Southern with station at Elysian Fields and St. Claude; New Orleans, Fort Jackson & Grand Isle and Texas & New Orleans, stations in Algiers (T&NO trains were ferried across the River to New Orleans), and the New Orleans & North Eastern. The New Orleans Great Northern (later Gulf Mobile & Northern and presently Gulf Mobile & Ohio) operated local services practical to shoppers and commuters from Covington to New Orleans, via Slidell, until the 1930's. The Louisiana Ry. & Navigation Co. (now KCS-L&A Lines) even offered early morning passenger train arrival at New Orleans, late evening or afternoon departure for years.

Interior New Orleans City RR. Co. mule car 73 showing Slawson fare box.

# CHAPTER 4

# EQUIPMENT

New Orleans' passenger cars were of two basic types: the single-truck and the double-truck. Single-truck cars were retained for many years, due to the powerful faction which advocated the use of a small, light car. Double-truck adherents were strong, also, and the contest between the two groups of officials had interesting results. One example is the early replacement of all Brill 22-E "Eureka" Maximum Traction trucks by the single Brill 21-E and Lord Baltimore truck. Another is exemplified by the Prytania Line's car assignments from 1894 to 1932. This line's first electrics were the 1894 Brills with 22-E M. T. trucks. Then came single-truck Jackson & Sharp cars, soon bumped by heavy, double-truck "Palace" cars, built by St. Louis Car Co. However, 1910 saw the "Palaces" give way to St. Louis Car Co. single-truck "Prytanias". Arch-roof double-truck 800's replaced the "Prytanias" on the Prytania Line in the 1920's, remaining with the line until 1932.

New Orleans had fewer car designs in comparison with some other large cities, but its cars seemingly were wisely chosen, judging by the length of service and durability of the cars over the years.

In pre-electric days, there were many experiments in methods of propulsion. In their chronological order, these were:

Animal (horses and mules) .................................... 1831
Steam ................................................................... 1832
Walking Beam .................................................... 1866
Compressed Air .................................................. 1868
Overhead Cable .................................................. 1870
Ammonia Gas ............................................ 1871 and 1886
Thermo-Specific (condensed steam, fireless)........... 1871
Third Rail (public exhibit only) ........................ 1885
Overhead Trolley (public exhibit only) .............. 1885
Storage Battery ................................................. 1889
Overhead Trolley (revenue service) .................... 1893

New Orleans briefly experienced gasoline buses in street transit service in 1910 (see: ROUTES, Chapter 3 pages 99-100). However, N.O.P.S.I. was first rail system in the city to use them, beginning 1924 on the North Carrollton Line (never a rail line of regular service). On December 2, 1929 New Orleans' first trackless trolleys were put on the Oak Street Shuttle.

Pre-electric transit vehicles were quite interesting and deserve a word here. In New Orleans, street transportation for the public started with hackmens' cabs and carriages. The omnibus came to New Orleans in 1832, and this innovation in public transit embodied the straight fare, scheduled service, and definite route with intermediate stops and termini.

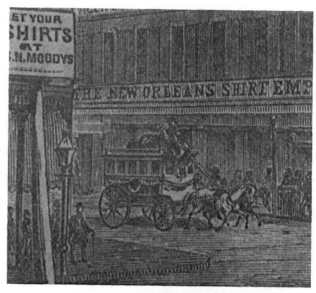

*Courtesy St. Mary's Dominican College*
From *Jewell's Crescent City Illustrated*, a circa 1860 cut by J. W. Orr of New York shows one of several types of omnibuses that operated in New Orleans.

*Courtesy N.O.P.S.I.*
Later type New Orleans & Carrollton RR. Co. double deck car, builder unknown, about 1880.

The first rail vehicles in New Orleans were the cars of the Pontchartrain RR., starting service in 1831. One of the original P. RR. Co. cars was built by the Baltimore & Ohio RR.; the balance of the P. RR.'s initial passenger rolling stock was built in Liverpool, England. All these were four wheel models. The B&O built car was little more than a box on wheels, while the English models were more elegant.

Early New Orleans & Carrollton RR. Co. double deck car, in use in the late 1850s. Baronne near Canal.

Poydras-Magazine service opened by the New Orleans & Carrollton in 1835 was handled with borrowed Pontchartrain RR. cars. Original N. O. & C. RR. horse cars were similar to the "John Mason" which opened a street railway line on New York City's Fourth Avenue. This type of equipment was merely an omnibus style body on railway wheels. Passengers entered by the rear by two or three steps up into the car body—the driver sat high up front, sometimes above the car's roof level. The first cars for N. O. & C. RR.'s Carrollton Line were "three-bodied" types built by M. P. Green of Hoboken, N. J. The late 1840's and early 1850's saw the adoption of the floor-level platform (probably in New Orleans also, although no photographic evidence could be found). The "bob tail" car appeared in New Orleans in 1861. These cars were characterized by having a front platform, but NO rear platform. Passengers used rear steps for ingress and egress.

Double deck mule cars made an appearance in New Orleans before the War Between the States. They were used by the New Orleans & Carrollton RR. Co.

The city's first electric cars for the overhead trolley system entered service in 1893 on the New Orleans &

Interior New Orleans & Carrollton RR. mule car 63 shows Slawson Farebox. Austere interior suggests the car was designed for smoking.

Carrollton RR.'s St. Charles Line (formerly Carrollton Line). Although crude mechanically, these cars obsoleted the mule car, and other New Orleans companies lost little time converting to electricity. Unfortunately, the records of those days have not survived intact, and we have attempted in the following pages to present the fragmentary pieces of information which are still available.

Although this is a history of a particular city's street railways, it is also a recording of an era that has come and gone, and it is of interest to note that human

Last mule cars delivered to New Orleans. Only ones in the city uncovered by research having true monitor deck roof. Circa 1890, builder probably St. Louis Car Co. Pedestal mount is St. Louis design.

Bombay full monitor roof, Stephenson car, date unknown. Pedestal mount. *Museum of The City of New York*

Front view of "bob tail" car 73; "Crown" truck, one of the earliest true trucks, and car built by Stephenson in New York City. Photo late 1870s.

Rear view of 73 shows more delicate and fancy art-work.

February 1, 1893. New Orleans & Carrollton RR. Co. inaugurates electric cars on St. Charles Line. First line in the city to have overhead trolley. Cars were St. Louis Car Co. models, McGuire 19F truck, Thomson-Houston motors and controls.

nature has not changed. Competition was keen then as it is now. The design of electric cars was basically the same but each manufacturer had some little thing here or there that set his product apart (even if slightly) from that of his competitors. Brill (of Philadelphia) had the knack of putting its products before the public and the traction companies by vigorous sales programs and exploitation. Brill led the field in producing street cars—advertising was the answer. Whether or not Brill cars were the best is besides the point. More of them were sold than those of any one other manufacturer.

New Orleans tried almost all of them. On the car roster at one time or another were cars by Brill, St. Louis, American, Pullman, Jackson & Sharp, McGuire-Cummings, Southern, Perley Thomas, and others—plus a respectable number of home-built cars, of which experimental single-trucker 288 was the best.

In this chapter, cars are divided into three classes: Single Truck, Double Truck (passenger); and Service. Specifications and plans were kindly provided by N.O.P.S.I. or Mr. Ed Gebhart.

Air brakes were slow in making their appearance in New Orleans. Even the first ten "Palace" cars, heavy as they were, arrived from the builder in 1902 with only hand brakes. It was quickly realized that the motorman could not make his schedules and in a few months air brakes were installed. Later "Palace" cars were equipped with air brakes at Builder's factory. The West End trains also received air brakes at this same time. Prior to 1902 these four-car trains had been controlled solely by means of hand brakes. Air brake equipment was built by Westinghouse.

## SINGLE TRUCK CARS

New Orleans had a total of twelve types of closed, single-truck passenger motors, plus about fifty cross-bench open cars and an unknown number of semi-open cars. Single truckers operated from 1893 to 1932.

Car numbers are impossible to clarify, as there were many duplications (each company had its individual numbering scheme). After consolidation, numbers were not put into any sort of master scheme, as cars were kept in their respective divisions retaining their original numbers. To cite one instance: there were THREE 240 series in service at one time. In the lower numbers there were duplications in the under 100's, the 100's, and in the 200's. In 1917-18, a general renumbering master scheme was put in effect. It applied mainly to double-truck cars. Comparatively few single-truck cars were made to conform as many were on their way to extinction at that time. The scheme was: all single-truck cars—100 through 300; all double-truck cars—400 through 1000; work and service cars—01 up.

We have compiled the following roster, correct as of June 30, 1918, showing 365 single-truck closed cars then remaining:

41—1894 Brills with 21-E truck.

1—1895 Pullman with Lord Baltimore truck.

19—Jackson & Sharp, 1898, with Lord Baltimore truck.

4—1899 American cars.

*Chas. L. Franck Photo*

Only available photo of an 1893 open car. New Orleans City & Lake RR. Co. Canal
Station, 1898. Car decorated for Employees Benefit Assn.

4—Orleans RR. Co. 1895 Brills

1—N. O. & C. RR. 1893 St. Louis car.

50—1910 "Prytania" cars, St. Louis Car. Co., with
Lord Baltimore truck.

245—Ford, Bacon & Davis type cars, all built between
1896 and 1908 by St. Louis, American, and Mc-
Guire. Lord Baltimore or McGuire truck.

As of the same date — June 30, 1918 — only 259
double-truck cars were on the roster.

To give a condensed recapitulation of single-truck
cars used in New Orleans from 1893 to their retire-
ment in 1932:

1893: Seven-window, open platforms; built by St.
Louis Car Co. with McGuire 19-F truck, for
New Orleans & Carrollton RR. Co. In 1894,
N. O. & C. RR. Co. had 70 St. Louis Car Co.
cars (including the "Atalanta") on McGuire,
Brill, and St. Louis trucks. Open cars (builder
unknown, truck unknown) built for New Orleans Traction Co.'s Hart Franchise Lines. Cars
arrived in New Orleans in 1893, but could not
be used until 1894.

1894: Seven and eight-window, open platforms; built
by Brill, with maximum traction 22-E "Eureka"
trucks, later changed to single truck (Brill 21-E
or Lord Baltimore) for New Orleans Traction
Co.

1895: Six-window, open platforms; built by Pullman
with McGuire 19-F truck for St. Charles St.
RR. Co. Six-window Brills with Lord Baltimore
truck, open platforms for Orleans RR. Co. Moni-

tor deck roof cars, builder unknown, for Annunciation Line (see photo, page 114).

1896-1901: Seven-window, FB&D, open platforms; built
by American and St. Louis Car Co.'s. All had
the Lord Baltimore truck except 30, built 1899-
1900 by St. Louis Car Co., which had McGuire
"Columbia" truck. The FB&D type cars were
first built for Canal & Claiborne RR. Co. Later,
this type of car was ordered by St. C. St. RR.
Co., O. RR. Co., N. O. & C. RR. Co. and N. O.
Ry. & L. Co.

1898: Two orders, eight-window, open platforms; Jackson & Sharp products, Lord Baltimore truck for
New Orleans City & Lake RR. Co.

1899: Eight-window, open platforms; built by American, originally with 22-E M.T. trucks, later replaced by 21-E truck, for New Orleans City RR.
Co. (second corporation).

1900: Seven-window, open platforms, similar to FB&D
types, St. Louis 8 truck, built by St. Louis Car
Co. for St. Charles St. RR. Co. (Nos. 41-50).

1908: Seven-window, FB&D type, vestibuled, built by
McGuire-Cummings, Lord Baltimore truck for
New Orleans Ry. & Lt. Co.

1910: Eight-window, vestibuled; built by St. Louis Car
Co., Lord Baltimore truck (known as "Prytania"
cars) for New Orleans Ry. & Lt. Co.

1924: Eight-window, vestibuled, experimental car No.
288, Brill 79-E-1 truck; built in New Orleans by
N.O.P.S.I.

Some semi-opens such as these were operated by Crescent City RR. Co. in 1890s. Builder unknown though appears to be St. Louis Car Co. McGuire 19 truck. Co-author Charlton remembers these cars running on Magazine and Coliseum Lines. This photo about 1900. No. 187, an 1894 Brill on St. Louis 8 truck, used as service car, hence the screening.

## ORIGINAL ELECTRIC CARS

New Orleans' first electric cars (overhead trolley system, actual revenue service) were St. Louis Car Co. models entering service February 1, 1893 on the New Orleans & Carrollton RR. Co.'s St. Charles Line. This class had 18' 6" bodies (overall length: 24' 8") mounted on the McGuire 19-F truck of 7' wheelbase. Each car had one motor of the General Electric W. P. (weather proof) type. Controls were the Thomson-Houston rheostat main circuit, or "drum", control. There was no controller box, such as the K-10, on the car platform. The "controller" consisted of a shaft with a handle on top and a sprocket wheel at the base. The sprocket engaged a chain connected to the drum control under the car body. These first cars cost $2,949.20 each. There were fifty cars in the first order (forty-nine cars were monitor deck roof models. One car, No. 50, was a Railroad Roof type, later became the private car, "Atalanta"—see: Private Cars pages 120-21).

Nearly all of these 1893 monitor deck roof models were scrapped or "salvaged", but four were sold to the Home Electric Co. (Baton Rouge, La.—see: Vol. I, pages 33 and 36), two were sold to the Brockton & Plymouth St. Ry. Co. (Mass.), and possibly four sold to a company in Biloxi, Miss. One was left in 1918 on N. O. Ry. & L. Co. rosters.

## MOTORED OPEN CARS

Unfortunately, unsuitable photos and non-existant records fail to establish exactly who built the forty open motored cars the Crescent City RR. Co. (N. O. Traction Co.) had in 1896. The cars were delivered in 1893 and saw service on the Peters Avenue Line in 1894. The Magazine Line started electric service with open cars in 1895. However, New Orleans' sudden rains made this type of equipment impractical—and unpopular. By 1899, the motored open cars were gone save one or two used for training motormen.

## THE "1894" BRILLS

Between December 11, 1893 and January 21, 1895, the New Orleans Traction Co. ordered 226 motored cars from Brill in six separate orders. These cars were

No. 50 was the first 8-window 1894 Brill for New Orleans (builders photo).    *Barney Neuburger Photo*

*Courtesy N.O.P.S.I.*

1894 Brills removed from 22-E trucks early. Car 89, circa 1903, on a McGuire A-1 Suspension truck. The 22-E truck was subject to frequent derailment.

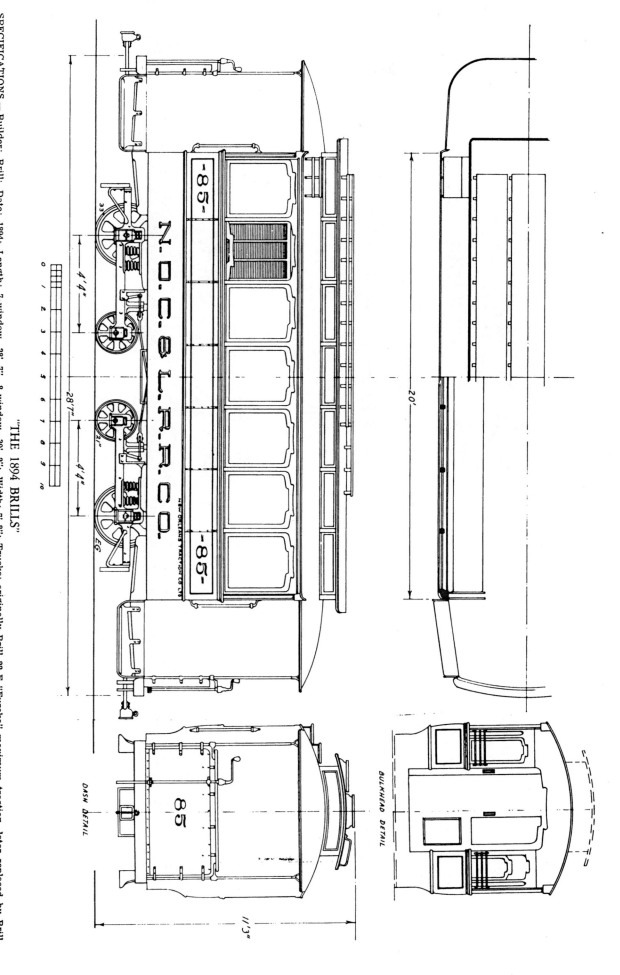

## "THE 1894 BRILLS"

SPECIFICATIONS—Builder: Brill; Date: 1894; Length: 7-window, 28' 7", 8-window, 30' 2"; Width: 7' 8"; Trucks: originally Brill 22-E "Eureka" maximum traction, later replaced by Brill 21-E, Lord Baltimore, and other types of singles; Motors: two GE 800 type (25 hp each)—with the 22-E trucks; Controls: K-10; Seats: longitudinal 7-window models seated 28, the 8-window types 32; Cost: 7-window models, $3,010.81, 8-window models, $3,050.20; Companies ordering: New Orleans City & Lake RR. Co., Crescent City RR. Co., New Orleans Traction Co. Ltd. (New Orleans Traction Co.)

N.O.C.&L.R.R.CO.

NEW ORLEANS TRACTION CO. LTD

DASH DETAIL

BULKHEAD DETAIL

-85-

85

Seven window 1894 Brill, final rebuild, circa 1916. Herr fender.

Circa 1902 view Canal, looking toward Lake, shows car 330, one of the "Annunciation" cars. Unfortunately, screen and quality of photo will not permit enlargement. Builder, date, and truck information not available.

similar in most respects, save the number of body windows. Most of the cars had seven windows to each side while some did have eight windows. All cars were at first equipped with Crawford fenders. The first 26 of these cars arrived in time to open electric service on the Canal Line in 1894. In 1894 and 1895, as batches of the 226 cars were delivered, mule cars vanished as motive power from the following lines: Canal, Coliseum, Dauphine, Esplanade, French Market, Levee-Barracks, Prytania, South Peters, and Tchoupitoulas.

The "1894" Brills were elegant cars. Windows lowered into the side panels. The car interiors were finished in cherry. Elaborate interior decor was called "Italian Finish", designed for Brill by an Italian artist. Windows and door heads on some of the 226 cars had fancy notched woodwork. All head linings, ventilator glass, etc. were carefully chosen or designed to blend with the style of the interior finish. Seating was entirely by longitudinal seats.

All cars were at first mounted on Brill 22-E "Eureka" maximum traction trucks. However, this type of truck was light and prone to derail easily on the uneven track of those early days of electric traction. The 22-E trucks were soon replaced by a single truck (Brill 21-E

or Lord Baltimore) on which these cars rolled up into the early 1920's.

Details of early numbering are hazy. Some cars had two-digit numbers, and numbers extended into the 100's and 200's. In 1918, when only six of the "1894" Brills remained, their new numbers were 310-14 and 316.

The rapid erosion of animal traction in New Orleans on the largest street railway system, the New Orleans Traction Co. (controlling New Orleans City & Lake RR. Co. and Crescent City RR. Co.) had its side effect. Comparing New Orleans with other cities, we find a remarkably small number of car body designs in the Crescent City. Houston and Atlanta, to cite but two, were much smaller than New Orleans in the heyday of the trolley, yet both had a far greater assortment of car types.

## "ANNUNCIATION" CARS

Only photographic proof exists of these cars (see: photo above). Builder, truck type are unknown (the

*Courtesy N.O.P.S.I.*

The 22-E truck was a rarity in New Orleans when this photo was taken, sometime during 1903. Most of the 1894 Brills had exchanged their 22-E trucks for a single truck, 21-E, McGuire, Lord Baltimore, or St. Louis 8. No. 135 is practically "as delivered" except for paint scheme.

*Courtesy Otto Goess'*

Bulkhead detail is clear in this builder's photo. All 1894 Brills came to New Orleans with 22-E trucks.

One of the 8-window 1894 Brills on a Brill 21C truck, circa 1900.          *Courtesy N.O.P.S.I.*

Interior original order Brills for Orleans RR. Co.          *E. Harper Charlton Collection*

Original order Brills for Orleans RR. Co., 1895. Lord Baltimore truck.

*Courtesy Historical Society of Pennsylvania*

car body exhibits Brownell Car Co. features, however). The cars were monitor deck roof models characterized by a full and wide umbrella hood, a wide dash, and a generally wider appearance than the "1894" Brills. The cars entered service on New Orleans Traction Co. (Crescent City RR. Co.) perhaps as early as 1895, disappeared in the 1900's. Co-author Charlton remembers them well as assigned to the Annunciation Line.

## BRILLS for ORLEANS RR. CO.

Orleans RR. Co. electrified in 1895 with twenty Brill cars. The cars were mounted on the Lord Baltimore truck, had 18' bodies, longitudinal seats, single sash side windows, open platforms, and the monitor deck roof. Orleans numbered the little red cars 1 to 20. The cars were priced at $2,081.61 each. Four still on the roster in 1918, scrapped very soon after.

## PULLMAN CARS

When the St. Charles St. RR. Co. commenced electrified street railway operations in early 1896, an order of 40 single truck Pullman Car Co. streetcars manned the St. Charles St. RR. Co. roster. These were small six-window closed cars costing $2,204.83 each and mounted on the McGuire 19-F truck of 7' wheelbase. Body length of these cars was 18', over all length was 23' 8". Width was 7' 4". K-10 controllers and two 25-hp GE 800 type motors per car. All these monitor deck roof cars had longitudinal seats, could seat 28 passengers. By 1918, only one Pullman car remained in service.

The first 40 St. Charles cars were numbered 1-40. In 1895, the St. Charles St. RR. ordered three more cars, one numbered 39, probably replacements for first order. Also in 1895, the Crescent City RR. Co. ordered 17 cars from Pullman, numbers, details, and photo not available.

117

Pullman car on Royal Street, about 1898. Only photo available.

Jackson & Sharp car, Lord Baltimore truck. Circa 1903.

## JACKSON & SHARP CARS

This company built 20, 21-foot body, single-truckers for the New Orleans City & Lake RR. Co. in 1898. Their original numbers were 240-259, later renumbered 100-12, 241, 244, 245, 251, 255, 256.

The Jackson & Sharps were originally closed models with open platforms, vestibuled in 1904. They were painted yellow and orange and at first entered service on the Prytania Line (hence their nickname, "Early Prytanias"). Later, in 1903, these cars inaugurated

service on the "Royal Blue" (Napoleon) Line of the New Orleans & Pontchartrain Ry. Co.

SPECIFICATIONS: Builder: Jackson & Sharp, 1898. Body length: 20′ 0″ first order, 21′ 0″ second order. Length over-all: 29′ 7″ and 30′ 7″. Trucks: Lord Baltimore. Wheelbase: 7′ 7″. Motors: two GE 1000 type, 25 hp each. Cost (longer cars): $2,633.07 each. Seats: transverse. Capacity: 28 and 32 passengers. Scrapped: unknown, but at least two cars remained in 1923.

Interior "Atalanta", New Orleans & Carrollton RR. Co. President's private car. Circa 1895.

## PRIVATE CARS

There were three private cars belonging to New Orleans' street railway systems. The "Atalanta" was the property of the New Orleans & Carrollton RR. Co. while the less magnificent "Sancho Pablo" was the pride of the New Orleans Traction Co. lines.

The "Atalanta" was a 4' 8½" gauge car built by St. Louis Car Co. and delivered as No. 50 of an order of fifty cars that commenced overhead trolley electric street railway service in New Orleans in 1893. Originally, the car had no name, was open platform, railroad roof (it was the only RR. roof car in the order for 50), and was mounted on a St. Louis type "8" truck. In 1894 the car was vestibuled and had its interior lavishly refitted and re-upholstered. The "Atalanta" was the first electric car in New Orleans to be vestibuled and was the only Railroad Roof motored car ever to operate in the city. The dignified car had a long life. As late as 1911, the car was being used for theater parties, and could be rented by the public for $15.00 per night.

The "Sancho Pablo" was the 5' 2½" gauge private car of the New Orleans Traction Co. This was actually one of the "1894" Brill cars—open platforms, closed body, 22-E trucks, monitor deck roof. The car was in no way as elaborate as the "Atalanta".

The "Palastine" was a 5' 2½" gauge car ordered May 30, 1902 from St. Louis Car Co. (order No. 302) for the New Orleans Rys. Co. No other details available.

## THE FORD, BACON & DAVIS DESIGNED CARS

The engineering firm of Ford & Bacon (later Ford, Bacon & Davis) of New York City, was retained by the Canal & Claiborne RR. Co. to make a survey of its property and to design necessary improvements to electrify and modernize the company. FB&D made many improvements to the C&C roadway and facilities, but the major contribution was the famed "FB&D Car".

The outstanding feature of this car, in the visible sense, is the huge and almost exaggerated monitor deck roof. This roof characteristic sets this type of car apart from any other design of car. Three major improvements were incorporated: The Lord Baltimore truck (soon the standard of New Orleans), rattan transverse seats (cross seats), and both steel side posts and carlines which greatly strengthened the car's body and made these cars remarkably solid.

So successful was the "FB&D" on the Canal & Claiborne RR. Co. that other companies in New Orleans placed orders for this design of car. In all, about 350 FB&D's ran in New Orleans. They were built by American, St. Louis, and McGuire-Cummings with the orders placed from 1896 to 1908.

Other cities were attracted by this design of car. Shreveport, La., Montgomery and Birmingham, Ala., Butler, Pennsylvania, and Pine Bluff, Arkansas to name but five.

120

Courtesy Baker Library, Harvard Univ.

An inspection trip over New Orleans & Carrollton RR. Co. just prior to opening regular electric service on February 1, 1893. Car 50 was only railroad roof motored car to run in New Orleans. In 1894 the car was vestibuled, became private car "Atalanta". St. Louis Car Co. built No. 50. Truck is St. Louis No. 8. Photo from Street Railway Review.

## ST. LOUIS CAR COMPANY — FORD, BACON & DAVIS DESIGN CARS
### Ordered 1899-1902

| Order No. | Amount | Description | Order Date | Car Numbers* | Company |
|---|---|---|---|---|---|
| 92 | 18 | 21' Closed | Jan. 2, 1900 | 260-277 | N. O. Tr. Co. (N. O. C. RR. Co.) |
| 144 | 15 | 20' 8" Closed | Oct. 27, 1900 | 230-244 | N. O. & C. RR. Co. |
| 232 | 30 | 20' Closed | Oct. 31, 1901 | (Not given) | St. Charles St. RR. Co. |
| 245 | 9 | 20' Closed | 1902 | (Not given) | Orleans RR. Co. |

*Note—numbering systems overlapped in New Orleans until 1918 renumbering.

The Ford & Bacon (later Ford, Bacon & Davis) design, 1896. First of its type. American Car Co., Lord Baltimore truck.

*Street Railway Journal through Rod Varney.*

121

Ford Bacon & Davis type, as delivered.  Lord Baltimore truck, American Car Co., 70 cars, nos. 160-229.  *Courtesy N.O.P.S.I.*

*Chas. L. Franck Photo*

Race and Tchoupitoulas Sts., March 25, 1925.  St. Louis Car Co 1899 FB&D type, rebuilt at New Orleans about 1917.  Lord Baltimore truck.

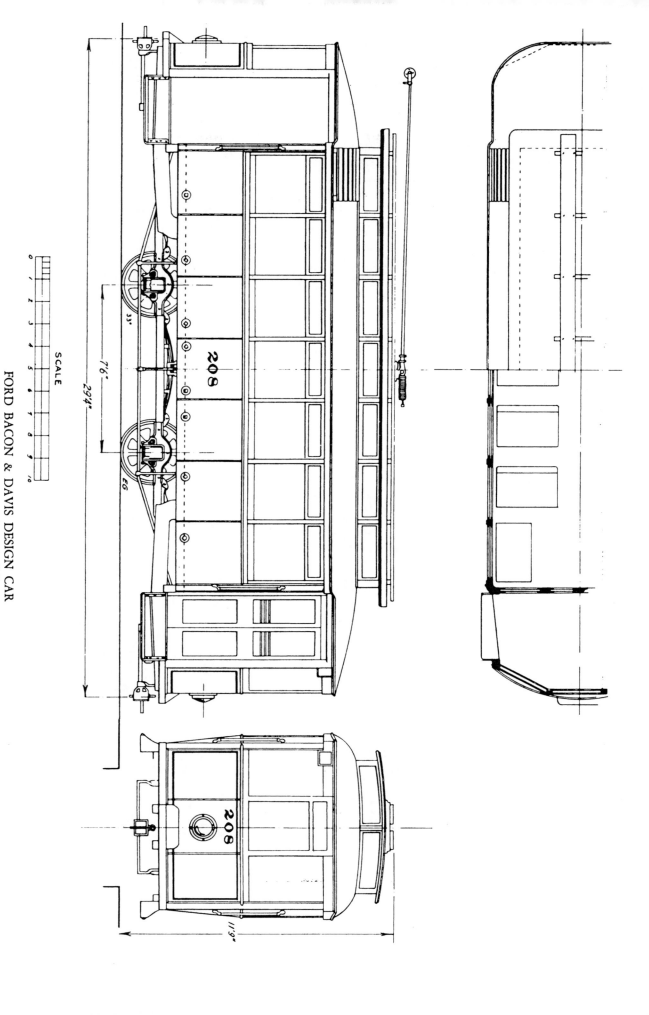

## FORD BACON & DAVIS DESIGN CAR
### (Typical N. O. Ry. & L. Co. Rebuild)

SCALE

SPECIFICATIONS — Builders: St. Louis, American, McGuire-Cummings; Type: closed, 7-window; Body Length: 20' 8''; Overall length: 29' 4''; Width: 8' 0''; Aisles: 21'' width; Truck: Lord Baltimore (McGuire on 30 cars); Motors: two GE 800 type (40 hp each); Seats: rattan cross, H&K walkover; Capacity: 28 passengers; Weight: 19,000 lbs.; Sample Costs: $2,793.66 each—St. Charles St. RR. (1897); $3,060.30—N. O. & C. RR. (1898); $3,388.55—C. & C. RR. Co. (1896); Span of service: 1896-1932.

Rebuilt McGuire-Cummings FB&D type, 1908 order, 25 cars, 20′ 8″ bodies. Arabella station, about 1917. *Wm. Vieckman Photo*

*Courtesy Rita Ann Collins*
Interior Ford, Bacon & Davis designed car No. 29, converted to rail grinder. Photo, taken 1963, illustrates the extra-wide monitor deck roof characteristic of the FB&D design.

124

The 1899 order to Brill was sublet to American Car Co. of St. Louis. Car is shown "as delivered", open platforms, Brill 22-E trucks (later replaced by the Lord Baltimore truck). Note narrow waist panel.

## THE "1899" AMERICAN CARS

In 1899, the New Orleans City RR. Co. obtained about twenty monitor deck roof cars of a definite Brill design (no order of Brill cars 1898-1901 exists for a New Orleans company on Brill records. However, orders can be diverted or changed without a notation made on the order book). These cars were characterized by a narrow waist panel and exhibited features of American Car Co. design.

SPECIFICATIONS: Builder: American Car Co., sublet by Brill, 1899. Type: closed, 8-window. Cost: $3,071.41 each. Body length: 22' 0". Over-all: 30' 2". Width: 8' 0". Trucks: Brill 22-E, later 21-E. Motors: two GE 800 (25 hp). Controls: K-10. Seats: cross. Capacity: 32 passengers. Scrapped: four running in 1918, believed all gone by 1920.

Pride of St. Charles St. RR. was this order of cars from St. Louis Car Co. Note etched glass in upper sash. Cars were painted white and canary, with brown trim. No. 45 has the St. Louis 8 truck. Three-piece rod is an anti-gallop device. Ten cars constituted this 1899 order, numbers 41-50.

## THE 41-50 CLASS

St. Louis Car Co. built ten 20' closed cars for St. Charles St. RR. Co. in 1900 (order No. 88 of Dec. 7, 1899). In many respects these cars resembled the FB&D design, but a few features (such as an arched upper sash) set them apart. The cars came with open platforms, St. Louis 8 truck. About 1917, a few of these cars were rebuilt, renumbered into the 300s in 1918. They were gone by 1926.

126

Rebuilt and renumbered 41-50 class cars, ex St. Charles St. RR. Co., 1899 St. Louis Car Co. order. Lord Baltimore truck. Car rebuilt circa 1917 by N.O. Ry. & Lt. Co.

## THE PRYTANIA CARS

The fifty "Prytania" cars were unique. For one thing, they were built somewhat late for a single-truck type of non-Birney car. Also, they were New Orleans' first Pay-as-you-enter cars which were built as such. They used the Robertson system—the windows dropped into the side panels.

St. Louis Car Co (1910 order) cars for Prytania Line. Lord Baltimore truck 8′ wheelbase.     *Electric Ry. Journal*

*John Letellier Photo, Courtesy N.O.P.S.I.*

Rebuilt "Prytania" (1910 St. Louis Car Co. product) at Broad and St. Bernard, July 15, 1932. Conductor Newton Daigle and motorman John Letellier pose on that day, the last for the Broad streetcar line.

The "Prytanias" (so called because of their almost exclusive service on that line) were of the monitor deck roof, straight side, round-end vestibule type, arranged for double-end operation and prepayment fare collection.

The bottom construction was St. Louis' Robertson steel channel (see "Palace" Cars) design. Side sills consisted of two 6-inch channels placed back to back with wrought iron spaces between to receive the posts. Subsills consisted of angle iron riveted together and bolted to all cross and end sills. The end sills and cross timbers were all of white oak. Flooring was of 13/16" yellow pine, with maple strip floor mats.

Body framing was of the straight panel type for eight windows on each side and two panels at each end. Bulkhead doors were of the double sliding type. Interior finish was mahogany with nickel plated trim.

All fifty cars entered service on the Prytania Line upon delivery and remained on that line until suc-ceeded by the 800's on September 16, 1923. Twenty-four "Prytanias" were retained for service on lighter lines. They went out of use when the Broad and Clio lines were abandoned in 1932. The twenty-four retained after 1923 were: 351, 355-58, 361, 377, 379-92, 396-398. Remaining "Prytanias" were scrapped in 1932.

The "Prytanias" were carried on the Lord Baltimore truck, as were most of the FB&D cars. This truck was used in two wheelbases: 7' 6" and 8' 0". It was the most satisfactory single-truck used in New Orleans. Cars carried on this truck required less body work than those carried on any other truck.

Originally, the "Prytanias" were equipped with other motors. Nos. 350-84 had two GE 80 motors. The remainder (15) had Westinghouse 101-B double equipments.

The fifty "Prytania" cars were ordered April 20, 1910, St. Louis Car Co. order No. 869. Initially, the cars were numbered 355-404, renumbered in 1918.

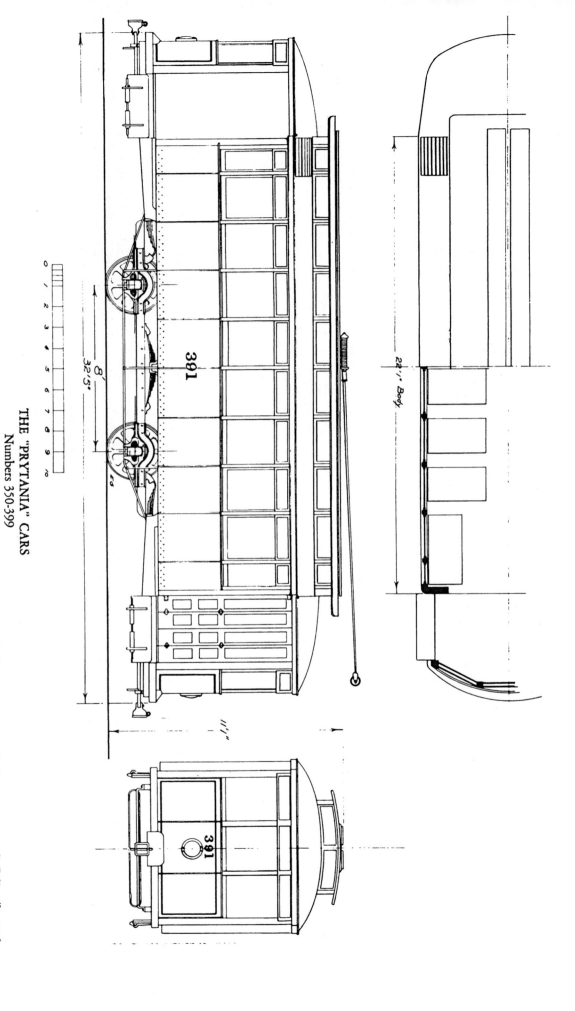

# THE "PRYTANIA" CARS
## Numbers 350-399

SPECIFICATIONS—Builder: St. Louis Car Co.; Date: 1910; Underframe: wood and steel; Side posts: wood; Vestibule posts: wood; Belt rail: wood; Car lines: wood; Roof: Monitor deck, wood and canvas; Headlining: Agasote; Floor: double wood; Motors: two GE 247-D (40 hp each); Gear ratio: 15:76; Controllers: K-11; Total seats: 32 (24 cross, 8 longitudinal); Type seats: St. Louis, rattan; Trucks: Lord Baltimore, 33" wheels; Wheelbase: 8' 0"; Axles: 4"; Journals: 3¾" by 7"; MCB; Body weight: 11,750 lbs.; Truck weight: 5,150 lbs.; Electrical equipment weight: 4,540 lbs.; Total weight: 21,440 lbs.; Curtains: Pantasote; Door operation: N. P. Manual; Headlights: Crouse-Hinds ZP; Life Guards: H. B.; Lights: 18, 36 watt; Registers: two International type R-7; Sash: bottom lowers, top (standee) fixed; Sign boxes: Hunter; Trolley base: Ohio Brass form 1; Brakes: hand, Peacock; Cost (per car): $3,637.01; Last year of service: 1932.

Experimental car 288, built Carrollton Shops 1923. Only one built. Note similarity to 400s, 800s, 900s, and 1000s. Many parts were interchangeable. Only photo available.

## EXPERIMENTAL CAR NO. 288

Car 288 was an experimental pilot model which was never duplicated. Built in 1924 at the Carrollton Shops, this car was not unlike the 800 class, many parts being interchangeable (see specifications). N.O.P.S.I.'s idea in building the 288 was to design a car which provided economical operation by a one-man or a two-man crew, but which could also handle moderately heavy traffic. In slack periods, it was planned to operate this type of car on lighter lines with a one-man crew on a fifteen minute headway (instead of the then-prevailing 30 minute service by double-truck two-man cars. In rush hours, the 288 type could be operated by two men if necessary.

The 288 was double-end with two sets of double folding doors. The front right-hand doors were controlled by the motorman's brake handle in accordance with standard safety car practice. Right-hand rear doors were manually operated. With one-man operation, passengers entered at front. With two-man crew, passengers entered at rear.

The 288 was the only single-truck passenger *motor*

car built at New Orleans, and was the LAST car built in the city. The car was first to get the Keystone roll sign in right-hand front window showing run number. Any number from one to 99 could be displayed, illuminated, and a letter (such as "X") could be substituted for the first digit. This sign was later installed in all arch-roof cars.

The city's anti one-man crew attitude prevented duplicates from being built. The 288 was relegated to the Spanish Fort shuttle run, from Spanish Fort to Pontchartrain Boulevard and Adams Avenue until that line was abandoned in 1932. The car was scrapped soon afterwards.

The struggle between the single-truck and double-truck factions of street railway officials has been mentioned elsewhere. The 288 was the final bid for power by the single-truck men. Although definitely not a Birney (note its weight), 288 confused some rail historians and is possibly the raison d'etre of persistent rumors to the effect that New Orleans once operated a Birney car. Nothing could be further from the truth.

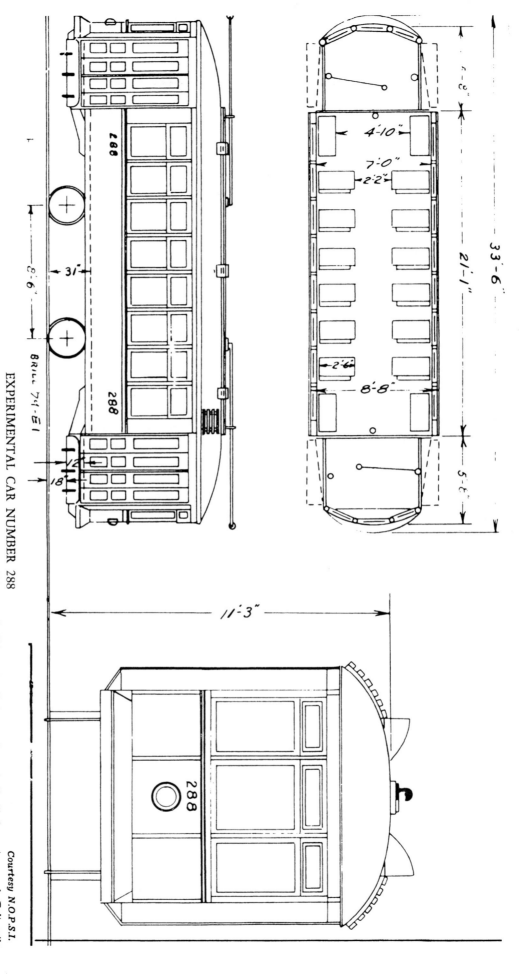

# EXPERIMENTAL CAR NUMBER 288

*Courtesy N.O.P.S.I.*

SPECIFICATIONS — Builder: N.O.P.S.I.; Date: 1924; Type body: closed, steel; Underframe: steel; Bolster: none; Sides: steel; Side posts: T, iron and wood; Vestibule posts: wood; Belt rail: wood; Car lines: T, iron and wood; Roof: wood and canvas; Headlining: Agasote; Floor: single pine; Truck: Brill 79-E1; Wheelbase: 8' 6"; Wheels: 30"; Axles: 5" Pollak; Journals: 3¾ by 7"; Controllers: two K-11; Compressor: GE CR-27; Brake valve: Westinghouse M-28; Cylinder: West. 10 by 10; Reservoirs: two 10 by 36, one 8 by 12; Hand brake: Peacock wheel; Motors: two West. 514-C (40 hp); Ratio: 15.76; Weights: body—14,815, truck—6,138, electrical mech.—4,797, brake—1,028, total—26,778 lbs.; Curtains: Pantasote; Headlight: Crouse-Hinds ZP; Fenders: H. B. West; Register: one International type R-11; Sash: bottom raised, top fixed; Seats: H&K 300-A, wood; Sign boxes: Hunter; Trolley base: Ohio Brass form 1; Trolley Lifeguards: 18, 36 watt; Register: one International type R-11; Sash: bottom raised, top fixed; Seats: H&K 300-A, wood; Sign boxes: Hunter; Trolley base: Ohio Brass form 1; Trolley catchers: Earl; Ventilators: Utility; Seating capacity: 32 (24 cross).

## CONDENSED ROSTER OF DOUBLE TRUCK CARS

| Car Nos. | Builder | Weight | Seats | Trucks | Type | Length | Width | Height | Motors | Ratio | Contr. | Comp. | Scrp'd. |
|---|---|---|---|---|---|---|---|---|---|---|---|---|---|
| 400-449 | Sou. 1914 | 34,898 | 52 | 39-E1 | A.R. | 47' 8" | 8' 7" | 11' 3½" | 2-201-I<br>2-306 | 15:71<br>14:69 | K36JR | D-16 | 1948 |
| 450-474 | Brill 1906 | 42,000 | 44 | 76-E2 | S.C.-M. | 40' 6" | 8' 4" | 11' 8" | 2-306 | 19:64 | K36JR | CP-27 | 1935 |
| 500-507 | B&S 1898 | ------ | 40 | B&S"H" | B.S.-M. | 36' 1" | 8' 5" | ------ | 4-12A | ------ | ------ | ------ | 1921-24 |
| 509-512 | Amer. 1899 | ------ | 40 | B&S"H" | M | 37' 1" | 8' 7" | ------ | 4-58 | ------ | K-10 | ------ | 1921-24 |
| 513-518 | NORys 1902 | ------ | 64 | Tay"A" | Morris-M. | 52' 0" | 8' 5" | ------ | NONE | ------ | ------ | ------ | 1921-24 |
| 519-524 | NORys 1903 | ------ | 64 | Tay"A" | Morris-M. | 52' 0" | 8' 5" | ------ | NONE | ------ | ------ | ------ | 1930-32 |
| 525-536 | NOC&L 1891 | 31,200 | 68 | 67-F | Coleman | 54' 6" | 8' 6" | 11' 2" | NONE | ------ | ------ | ------ | 1934 |
| 537-547 | NOC&L 1896 | 22,300 | 60 | W.F. | Spliced | 45' 4" | 7' 7" | 11' 4" | NONE | ------ | ------ | ------ | 1932-33 |
| 548-549 | NOR&L 1905 | 27,000 | 56 | 67-F | Rojo | 48' 3" | 8' 5" | 11' 3" | NONE | ------ | ------ | ------ | 1934 |
| 550-553 | NOR&L 1905 | 31,000 | 56 | 67-F | Rojo | 48' 3" | 8' 5" | 11' 3" | NONE | ------ | ------ | ------ | 1934 |
| 554-560 | Amer. 1894 | 22,300 | 56 | St.L. | R.R. | 43' 4" | 8' 7" | 11' 9" | NONE | ------ | ------ | ------ | 1933 |
| 600-617 | St.L. 1902 | 58,436<br>57,580 | 52 | 77-E2<br>76-E2 | Palace-M. | 48' 1½" | 8' 6" | 12' 2½" | 4-57 | 16:69 | K35JJ | DH-16<br>CP-27 | 1934-35 |
| 618-723 | St.L. 1902 | 45,000 | 52 | 23-A | Palace-M. | 46' 7" | 8' 6" | 12' 2½" | 2-263A<br>2-306<br>2-57 | 15:71<br>14:69<br>16:69 | K36JR<br>K36JR<br>K-11 | DH-16 | 1933-35 |
| 800-972 | Brill 1922<br>P-T 1922-23 | 41,148<br>42,036 | 52 | 76-E2 | A.R. | 47' 8" | 8' 4" | 11' 4¼" | 2-306<br>2-263-A | 14:69<br>15:71 | K36JR | CP-27<br>DH-16 | NOTE 1 |
| 1000-19 | P-T 1928<br>St.L. 1928 | 40,300<br>40,900 | 52 | 76-E1<br>EIB-64 | A.R. | 48' 2" | 8' 6½" | 10' 8½" | 4-265G<br>4-510E | 14:69 | K35JJ | CP-127<br>DH-20 | 1949 |

Abbreviations: Sou.—Southern
Amer.—American
NORys—New Orleans Rys.
NOC&L—New Orleans City & Lake

St.L.—St. Louis
P-T—Perley Thomas
A.R.—Arch Roof
S.C.—Semi Convertible

M.—Monitor Deck Roof

R.R.—Railroad Roof
B & S Barney & Smith
TRUCKS: By Brill: 39-E1, 76-E2, 67-F, 77-E2, 76E1.
By St. Louis: 23-A, EIB-64.

NOTE 1: All 800's scrapped by 1964. Some 900's still running.

MOTORS: By Westinghouse: 12-A (25 hp), 306 (65 hp), 510-E (35 hp). By GE: 57 (50 hp), 201-I (60 hp), 263-A (65 hp), 265-G (35 hp) 800 (25 hp). Horsepower ratings used by N.O.P.S.I.

COMPRESSORS: 16 cu. ft. capacity: GE CP-27, Westinghouse D-16 and DH-16.
20 cu. ft. capacity: GE CP-127 and Westinghouse DH-20.

There were twelve types of double truck motor and trailer cars used in New Orleans city passenger service. In addition, there was a solitary double truck baggage trailer type running in West End service. These cars are briefly listed below:

Circa 1880: Double truck (builder unknown) trailers, seats—60.

1891: The Coleman Car. These were trailers, built at the Canal Shops by the New Orleans City & Lake RR. Co. Their design was altered somewhat in later rebuilding by changing the roof ends and by removing the ventilators that sat prominently on the roof. A later rebuild saw ends vestibuled, platforms enlarged. Trucks were home-built wood-frame MCB, later replaced with Brill 67-F trucks. Seated 68.

1894: Railroad roof, wire side trailers, built by American. Cars retained original condition throughout their use. Seated 56.

1896: Spliced semi-open trailers, built from small Brill single-truck open cross bench trailers. Three Brills made one of these large trailers. Trucks were home-built wood-frame MCB's. Seated 60.

1898: Large motor cars, two types. Nos. 500-507 built by Barney & Smith, nos. 509-512 (there was no 508) built by American Car Co. Both had four motor Barney & Smith "H" type trucks. The American cars were slightly longer and wider than the B.&S. models. Cars were monitor deck roof, and originally had open platforms (vestibuled in 1904 including train door). These cars were used to pull trailers in West End service. All twelve seated 40.

1902: St. Louis Car Co. "Palace" cars. Deck roof with St. Louis 23-A MCB trucks. Seated 52.

1902-03: Morris Cars, built at Canal Shops by New Orleans Rys. Co. Some had two motors, some had four. Taylor S-B trucks. Vestibuled in 1904, later got enlarged platforms, train door eliminated. Seated 64.

1905: Rojo trailers: Looked much the same as the spliced trailers, underwent two rebuildings and emerged in two different treatments (see Plans). Originally built at Canal Shops by New Orleans Ry. & Light Co.

1906: Brill standard semi-convertibles with 27-G trucks originally, later 76-E2 trucks. Cars seated 44, later rebuilt getting "fish belly" sides.

1915: Steel, arch roof closed cars. First order (400-449) was built by Southern Car Co. with Brill 39-E trucks, seating 52. In 1922, the first of the 800-972 class appeared. This type was very similar to the 400's. In 1928, 1000-1019 were received. They, too, were an improved 400. All these types seated 52, with the same seating arrangement. All had either the Brill 76-E1 or 76-E2 trucks except the 1010, which had St. Louis EIB-64 trucks.

*Courtesy N.O.P.S.I.*

Spanish Fort, about 1916. New Orleans Ry. & Lt. Co. operation. Motor car one of the American Car Co. 509-512 series built 1899. Barney & Smith trucks, Coleman trailers.

View of Canal Station, circa 1900. Car 500 is one of the 1898 Barney & Smith cars in the 500-507 series. Only photo that could be found of this series.

## CARS 500-512

These large motor cars were primarily famed as the motive power of the West End trains for many years. They came in two lots, from two builders. Nos. 500-507 were built by Barney & Smith and were delivered in 1898. Nos. 509-512 (there was never a 508) were American Car Co. products, ordered in 1898 but delivered in 1899. Both batches were somewhat similar. Certain minor differences were: The 509-512 group were slightly longer, wider, had a wider clerestory deck, and windows at corner posts were wider.

These cars were never renumbered. Indeed, their original numbers formed the framework upon which the renumbering of all other cars was based. All twelve cars were scrapped between 1921 and 1924.

## MORRIS CARS

The Morris Car was named after Master Mechanic E. J. Morris of the Canal Shops, where twelve cars of this design were built 1902-03.

It is the authors' opinion that the Morris Car design was influenced by the Barney & Smith 500-507 series, then in use hauling West End trains. Car body, roof, side window and side panel placement, width of car bodies, and other features were very much alike.

The Morris Cars were originally numbered from 046 to 057, in numerical sequence with the "Palace" cars. In 1917, they were renumbered 513 to 524. The cars originally had open platforms, were vestibuled in 1904, with train doors in the vestibule. In 1918, cars 519-524 were de-motorized and thereafter ran as trailers on the Canal-Cemeteries Line, pulled by motors 513-518. The only visible difference was lack of trolleys on the trailers. Later, all twelve had platforms enlarged, with air operated doors and folding steps. The Morris Cars were scrapped as follows: 513-517, from 1921-24; 518 in 1931; 519-522 in 1932; 523 and 524 in 1930.

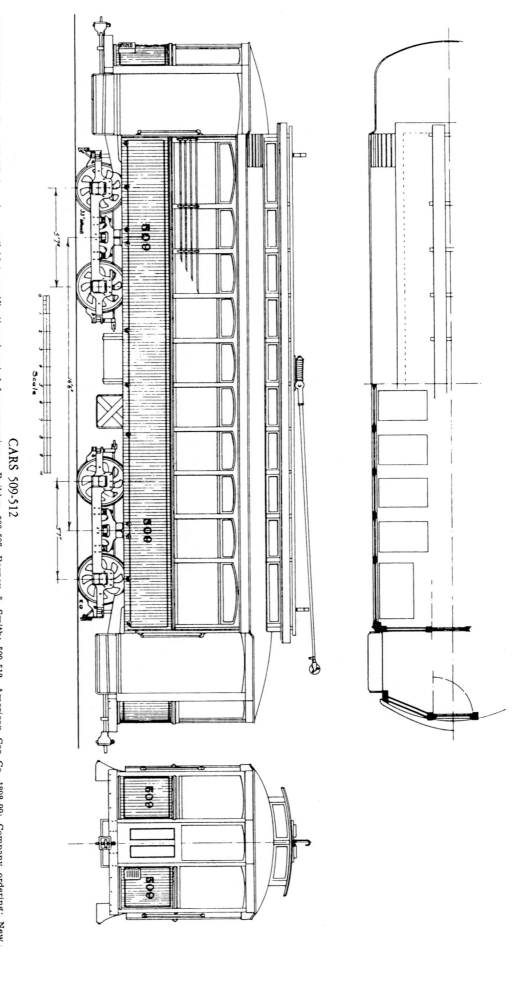

## CARS 509-512

SPECIFICATIONS — Cars 500-507 (no plan available) specifications inserted for comparison — Builder: 500-507, Barney & Smith; 509-512, American Car Co. 1898-99; Company ordering: New Orleans City & Lake RR. Co.; Type: Monitor deck roof, closed; Body length: 500-507, 28' 1''; 509-512, 29' 1''; Over-all length: 500-507, 36' 1''; 509-512, 37' 1''; Width: 500-507, 8' 5''; 509-512, 8' 7''; Trucks: Barney & Smith "H", 33" wheels; Motors: four Westinghouse 12A and four GE 58; Cost: 500-507, $4,864.17; 509-512, $4,833.86; Seates: 40 passengers, cross seats; Last year of service: 1924.

Morris Car. Nos. 046 - 057 built Canal Station 1901-02. Taylor Trucks.

Courtesy N.O.P.S.I.

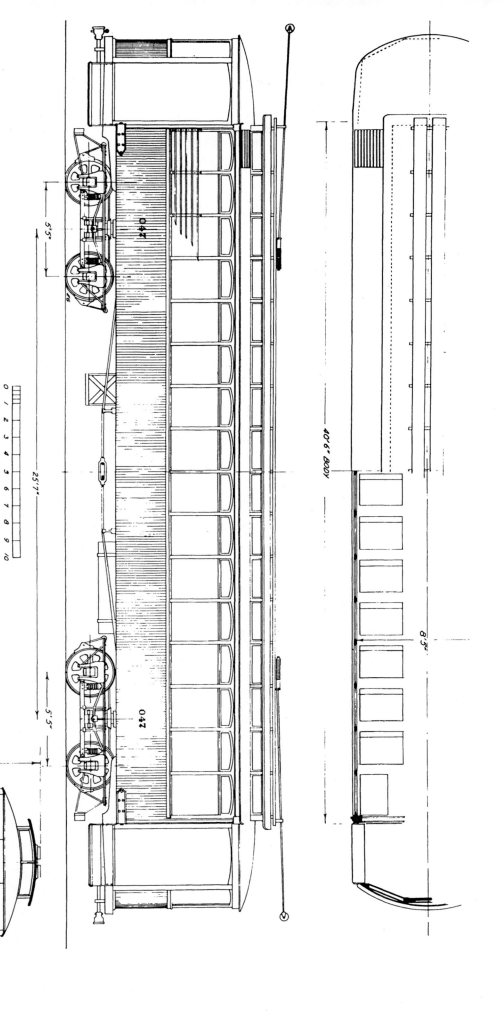

THE MORRIS CARS . . NUMBERS 046-057

SPECIFICATIONS — Builder: N. O. Rys. Co.; Date: 1902; Trucks: Taylor Hi Speed "A"; Wheels: 33"; Motors: four GE 800 (25 hp); Length: 52' 0"; Width: 8' 5"; Length of body: 40' 6"; Number of seats: 64; Type seats: cross; Cost, each car: $5,440.87.

For straight city service there has never been designed a more comfortable and handsome car than the type New Orleans called "Palace". The era wherein this car was designed was a prosperous one. There was much progress, but there had not died that charm of certain leisure and courteous manners that is indeed a pleasure to remember.

In all, New Orleans purchased 125 of these cars from St. Louis Car Co. between 1902 and 1905. Originally numbered 01 to 0137 (with twelve numbers omitted to accommodate the twelve Morris Cars), the "Palace" Cars were later renumbered into the 600-723 series.

St. Louis Car Co. order numbers, dates, and car numbers, as follows: cars 01-020, order No. 257, January 30, 1902; cars 021-045, order No. 301, May 15, 1902; cars 058-0107, order No. 321, July 31, 1902; and cars 0108-0137, order No. 606, November 24, 1905.

This was indeed a comfortable car. The "Palace" was a semi-convertible, yet distinctly different from other semi-convertible types. This type was built according to "The Robertson Semi-Convertible System". Mr. Robertson was with the Third Avenue Railway (New York City) when he designed this principle. His pilot model was built by Brill, but immediately afterwards he left New York to go into the employ of the St. Louis Car Co., where he further developed his ideas. St. Louis Car Co. delivered 100 cars to Third Ave. Ry. built on the basic design of the first car, Robertson's pilot model.

The basic difference between the Brill semi-convertible and the New Orleans "Palace" Car was as follows: The Brill car's upper and lower sash raised into the roof, while the New Orleans model's main sash lowered into the side pocket and its upper sash raised into the hip of the roof (some of Robertson's cars did have both sashes lowering into side panel, but NOT the "Palace" Cars). The "Palace" had a steel body sill of "U" section that permitted the sash to descend lower than was possible with most models. A splendid feature in connection with this was a hinged cover about four inches wide that opened inward and permitted the sash to lower. When the sash was down, the cover closed over the sash, affording a wide, smooth arm rest at a comfortable level. The interior lines of the car were far more handsome than the Brills, not having the "squeezed" look so many Brills had in their upper portion.

With beveled plate glass mirrors set in its foot-wide stanchions between the wide windows, with seats three feet wide (standard seat width in many places was 31"), with wide, large platforms, wide bulkhead doors, handsome interior lines and other special features intended to afford comfort—the "Palace" Cars were striking, splendid, and magnificent pieces of equipment.

No wonder the "Palace" type car was selected to operate on the grounds of the Louisiana Purchase Exposition in St. Louis in 1904. This giant of expositions featured a ten-mile long intramural railway circling within the Fair's grounds.

New Orleans first placed these elegant cars in service on the Canal Belt, and when enough had been delivered, on the Esplanade "side" of the Belt operation. Then in turn, the Dauphine, Magazine, and Prytania Lines were given their share. In later years, the "Palace" Cars saw service on other lines. For many years, the "Royal Blue Line" (Napoleon Avenue) had them. The Palace Cars served New Orleans until the last of them was scrapped in 1935.

Electrical equipment for the whole series, 600-723, was as follows: Three sets were employed. Nos. 618-662, 684-686, 692-695, and 697-707: Two GE 263-A 65 hp motors, K36-JR controllers, 71:15 gear ratio, weight of 8,008 lbs. Nos. 663-669, 671, 672, and 708-718: Two Westinghouse 306-CV4 65 hp motors, K36-JR controllers, 69:14 gear ratio, weight of 7,120 lbs. Nos 670, 673-678, 680-683, 688-691, and 719-723: Two GE 57 motors of 50 hp each, K-11 controllers, 69:16 gear ratio, weight of 7,818 lbs.

In 1923, eighteen Palace cars were rebuilt for two-unit rush hour service hauling rebuilt Coleman trailers on Canal Street. These Palace cars had sides sheathed with steel, losing from view their distinctive St. Louis sill; platforms were enlarged; 76-E2 or 77-E2 four motor type trucks were used; and the appearance of the rebuilt cars was heavy and cumbersome. The eighteen cars rebuilt were numbered 600 to 617.

SPECIFICATIONS FOR PALACE CARS 600-617, REBUILT 1923

Weight: 58,436 (Nos. 600-607, 610) and 57,580( Nos. 608, 609, 611-617)

Trucks: Brill 77-E2, 6' 4" wheelbase, 14,000 lbs.
   Brill 76-E2, 4' 10" wheelbase, 13,144 lbs.

Couplers: Tomlinson    Door operation: Pneumatic

Brake Valve: Westinghouse 12" by 12"

Reservoirs: 2-16" by 36",
   2-8" by 12", 1-12" by 33"

Emergency valve: West. M-2-A

Slack adjuster: Amer. Brake type X

Motors: Four GE 57 (50 hp)    Gear ratio: 69:16

Controllers: K-35-JJ Compressor: West. DH-16 (Nos. 600-602) GE CP-27 (Nos. 603-617)

Governor: West. S-6-A (Nos. 600-602) GE Type ML (Nos. 603-617)

All other specifications unchanged in rebuilding.

138

"Palace" Cars as delivered to New Orleans City RR. Co. in 1901. St. Louis MCB 23 trucks.    *Courtesy N.O.P.S.I.*

*Courtesy N.O.P.S.I.*
Palace car in 1916, showing rebuild with steel side sheathing, air operated doors, Herr fender, before 1918 renumbering. Note Prytania cars alongside the 012.

Turning off Esplanade into Rampart, August 20, 1929.  62E2 Trucks.                    *Teunisson Photo*

Next to final modification "Palace" Cars, 76E trucks. Mid 1930s, Foot of Canal.        *H. B. Olsen photo*

Evening peak hour, North Rampart and Canal. August 17, 1929. *Teunisson Photo*

*Courtesy N.O.P.S.I.*

Final "Place" Car modification — standard vestibules, air operated doors, Tomlinson couplers, 77E2 trucks, four motors (for trailer service).

Second modification "Palace" cars, No. 630 at City Park. St. Louis MCB 23 trucks, Herr Fender. Photo circa 1915.

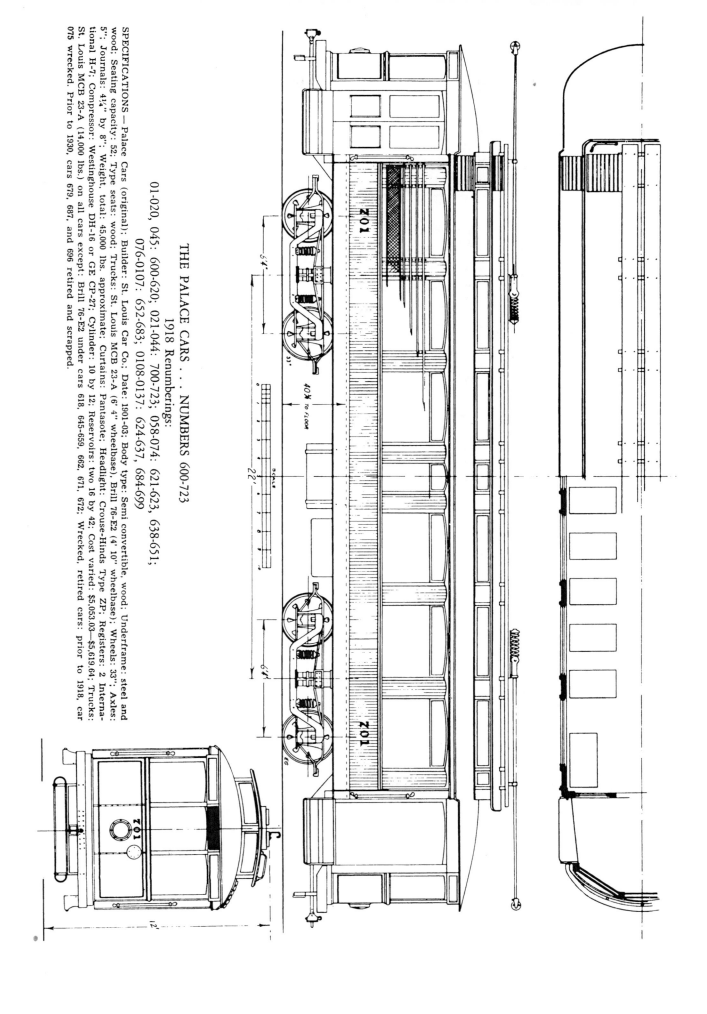

# THE PALACE CARS . . . NUMBERS 600-723

## 1918 Renumberings:

01-020, 045; 600-620, 021-044; 700-723; 058-074; 621-623, 638-651; 076-0107; 652-683; 0108-0137; 624-637, 684-699

SPECIFICATIONS — Palace Cars (original): Builder: St. Louis Car Co.; Date: 1901-03; Body type: Semi convertible, wood; Underframe: steel and wood; Seating capacity: 52; Type seats: wood; Trucks: St. Louis MCB 23-A (6' 4" wheelbase), Brill 76-E2 (4' 10" wheelbase); Wheels: 33"; Axles: 5"; Journals: 4¼" by 8"; Weight, total: 45,000 lbs. approximate; Curtains: Pantasote; Headlight: Crouse-Hinds Type ZP; Registers: 2 International H-7; Compressor: Westinghouse DH-16 or GE CP-27; Cylinder: 10 by 12; Reservoirs: two 16 by 42; Cost varied: $5,053.03—$5,619.64; Trucks: St. Louis MCB 23-A (14,000 lbs.) on all cars except: Brill 76-E2 under cars 618, 645-659, 662, 671, 672; Wrecked, retired cars: prior to 1918, car 075 wrecked. Prior to 1930, cars 679, 687, and 696 retired and scrapped.

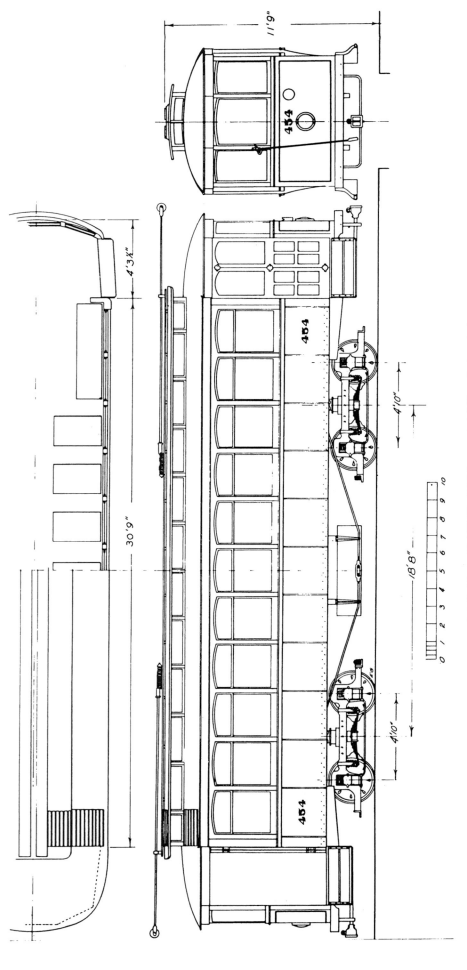

## SEMI-CONVERTIBLE CARS . . . NUMBERS 450-474

(originally 300-324)

SPECIFICATIONS — Builder: American Car Co.; Date: 1906; Cost: $4,945.97; Trucks: originally 27-G, with two GE 57 motors (50 hp), wheelbase—4' 6''; reequipped 1923 with Brill 76-E2 trucks, wheelbase—4' 10'', wheels—30'', axles—5'', journals—4¼'' by 8'', truck centers—18' 8''; Body type: Brill semi-convertible; Underframe: steel and wood; Body: wood; Weight: with 27-G trucks, 37,100 lbs.—with 76-E2 trucks, 42,000 lbs., approx.; Lights: 18, 36 watt; Seats: 44 (28 cross, 16 longitudinal); Type seats: Brill wooden "Winner"; Roof: wood and canvas; Head-lining: ¼'' Agasote; Floor: 13/16'' yellow pine, single; Motors: two West. 306-CV-4 (65 hp); Gear ratio: 64:19; Controllers: West. K-36-JR; Circuit breakers: GE MR-12-D; line breaker; West. 801-E; Brake valve: GE type S; Brake cylinder: 8'' by 12''; Reservoirs: one—16'' by 60''; Hand brakes: Dayton drop handle; Doors: pneumatic, folding; Headlights: Crouse-Hinds type ZP; Life Guards: Providence H. B.; Registers: two International R-7; Sash: bottom, raised—top, fixed; Trolley base: Ohio Brass form 1; Compressor: GE CP-27, 15 cu. in.

New Orleans owned and operated 25 Brill type semi-convertible cars. Though following strict Brill plans, the cars were built by the American Car Co. of St. Louis, a Brill subsidiary.

The Semis were numbered 300-324, received in 1906, and assigned at first to the Coliseum Line. Later, these cars saw service on other lines, the Louisiana Line being one. In 1917, the cars were renumbered 450-474.

When delivered, the cars had the usual concave-convex sides. All were rebuilt beginning 1917, getting "fishbelly" side panels and new trucks and motors (see Specifications). The Brill Semis had a service life of 29 years, being retired in 1935. One Semi, No. 453, has been retained by N.O.P.S.I. as a training car (see photo, page 146).

*Courtesy Rita Ann Collins*
Interior, semi-convertible car No. 453.

*Courtesy N.O.P.S.I.*
The Brill type (built by American Car Co.) semi-convertibles originally had 27-G trucks. 457 has early 39-E trucks. Photo circa 1916. Motorman Howard Shaw, standing in vestibule, donated this shot. Conductor not identified.

First rebuild semi-convertibles, 1917. Panel sides removed, upper sash fixed. Brill 27-G trucks.  *Courtesy N.O.P.S.I.*

*Courtesy Otto A. Goessl*

Only semi-convertible left, used as instructor's car at Napoleon Station. Car is in "A-1" condition. **76E2 trucks.** Photo taken 1960.

A new conception of car type appeared in New Orleans in 1915—the arch roof steel motor passenger car. This type, of which the first were 400-449, became the standard car of N.O.P.S.I. Two improved versions were subsequently added to the car fleet, the 800--900 and the 1000 classes. In all, there were 243 steel arch roof motors represented by the three classes.

The 400 Class was a steel car, as the only wood used was in the floor, roof and belt rail. Underframe, side posts, side panels, vestibule posts, letter-board, car lines and general bracing were all steel. IN FACT— the 400's contained a higher percentage of steel components than did the later 800-900 and 1000 classes!

Features of this class were Brill 39-E maximum traction trucks, folding steps and sliding door at front. The Southern Car Co. (later Perley Thomas) of High Point, N. C., built all fifty of the 400's. Dark cherry interior finish with a light green headlining (to cut down summer heat) was more conservative than earlier cars in

New Orleans. Outside livery was an olive green scheme, unadorned save car numbers and an aluminum stripe around the edge of the dash. Window posts were, however, a light cream, giving some contrast.

Performance standards of the 400's were: schedule speed—10.8 mph; rate of acceleration and breaking— 1.5 mph/s. Total weight of the car, fully equipped and ready to run—36,100 lbs. (694 lbs per seat). Cost $5,116.15.

It may be of interest to note that the Southern Car Co. was formed from the old and honorable Briggs Carriage Works (Car Company) of Amesbury, Mass. Briggs built many streetcars through the years, both horse and electric. Perusal of Eastern, and especially New England, street railway rosters will reveal Briggs cars with Bemis, Taylor, and other trucks.

The 400's ran from 1915 to 1948. They were ordinarily assigned to the St. Charles and Tulane Belts and the Jackson Line.

*Courtesy Otto A. Goessl*

**Foot of Canal Street, about 1939. The 400s stuck pretty well to St. Charles-Tulane Belts and the Jackson Line. 39E trucks.**

Carrollton Station, 425 with standard gauge 39E trucks. Note sliding door, right hand side each vestibule.

Chas. L. Franck Photo

## ARCH ROOF CARS . . . NUMBERS 400-449

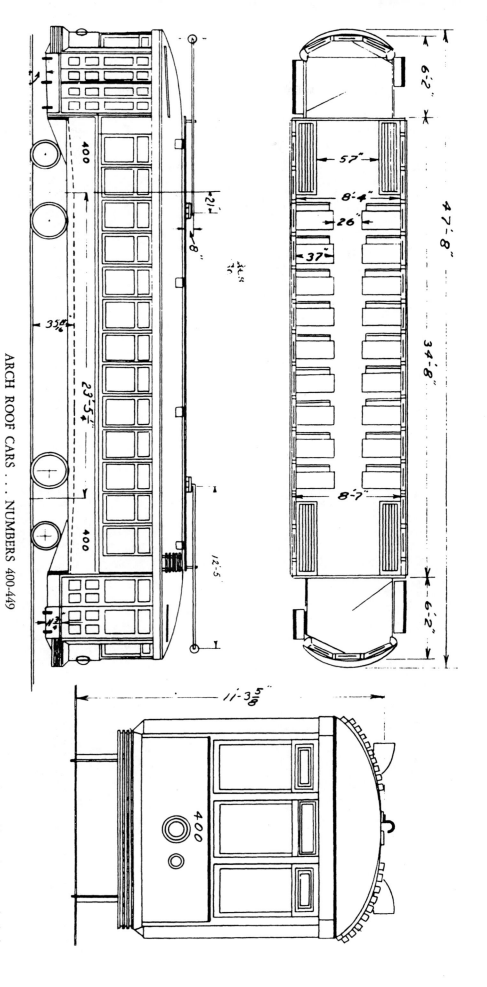

SPECIFICATIONS — Builder: Southern Car Co.; Date: 1914; Body: steel; Weight: 34,898 lbs. Underframe: steel; Bolster: steel; Side panels: steel #12 gauge; Side posts: pressed steel; Vestibule posts: pressed steel; Belt rail: wood; Car lines: pressed steel; Roof: wood and canvas; Headlining Agasote; Floor: single pine, tongue and groove; Trucks: Brill 39-E; Wheelbase: 4' 10"; Driver wheels: 30"; Idlers: 21"; Driver axles: 5"; Idler axles: 4"; Motors: two GE 201-I (60 hp) except two West. 306-CV4 on car 449; Gear ratio: 15:71—400-448 and 14:69—449; Controllers: K-36-JR; Cylinders: 10 by 12; Reservoir: one 16 by 60; Brake valve: P. V. 3; Compressor: West. D-16 (16 cu. ft.); Seats: 52 (36 cross, 16 longitudinal); Type seats: H&K #300-A wooden; Curtains: Pantasote; Door operation: manual; Headlights: Crouse-Hinds type Z; Life Guards: H. B.; Lights: 22, 36 watt; Registers: one International R-5; Sash: bottom—raised, top—fixed; Trolley base: Ohio Brass form 1; Cost, each car: $5,166.15.

When the 400s were delivered in 1915, they sported Herr Fenders. All 400s were designed by Mr. Perley A. Thomas and built by Southern Car. Co.

Light colored roof color scheme in use during late 1930s—sharp photo of the first in the 800s series brings out body detail. 76E2 trucks.

Rounding Lee Circle, 1961. Car 821 built by Brill.

*Courtesy Wilbur T. Golson*

## ARCH ROOFS

### 800-972

Very similar in appearance to the 400's were the 800's and 900's. The particular body style was designed by Mr. Perley A. Thomas as were the earlier 400's and later the 1000's, Brill and Perley Thomas Car Companies built the cars during 1922-24, with Thomas building 97 cars and Brill 76. A glance at the car plans and attendant specifications reveal the order of cars to be modern and very well constructed. Although all 800's have been scrapped (a few sold to museums), some of the 900's are still running today on the St. Charles Line. These are last "conventional" streetcars in regular service in the United States. Cars still running number thirty-five, as follows:

900, 903, 904, 905, 906, and 907.
910, 911, 914, and 915.
920, 921, 922, 923, and 926.
930, 932, 933, 934, and 937.
940, 945, 947, and 948.
951, 953, and 954.

961, 962, 963, 965, 968, and 969.
971, and 972.

*Four-Motor Experiment:* During Mr. Walter Rainville's tenure as N.O.P.S.I. Equipment Engineer in the 1930's, certain experiments to determine the feasibility of making the 800's four-motor cars were conducted. Mr. Rainville, now the Director of Research of the American Transit Association, has kindly presented to us his recollection of this experiment which is presented herewith in his own words:

"The experiments which were carried out during my time as Equipment Engineer involved cars of the 800-900 vintage, with Brill 76-E-2 trucks, both axles having 33" wheels. The experiments covered various combinations of GE and Westinghouse controls. I believe the GE job was called PCM controls and the Westinghouse "VA" or "variable automatic" control. All experiments involved doubling up the motors, either four GE-263-A's, or four WH 306-CV 4's, depending upon the

St. Charles Avenue at Jeanette, 1962. The 850 was built by Perley A. Thomas. Thomas built 25 of the 100 cars 800-899, yet designed the class himself.

manufacturer, instead of the customary two motors per car of these types.

"With these experimental changes also went an attempt at improvements in braking performance to offset the increased accelerating rates expected of the four motors and modern automatic controls. Braking ratios were boosted to 125 or 150% of the light weight of the car instead of the customary 100%. Brake levers and pull rods were proportioned accordingly, and trucks were provided with new pedestal-way wear plates, etc.

"Tests were made for the most part along the West End and Spanish Fort tracks, with recording voltmeter, ammeter, and speed indicator. Acceleration, braking, and free running speed rates were determined. Theoretical speed-time curves were constructed and checked against the test results.

"If my recollection of these matters is correct, we found some improvement in the speed-time cycle due to increased acceleration and braking rates; frequency of stops characteristic of New Orleans in those days

prevented much from being gained from the higher free-running speeds. The increased schedule speeds resulting from the application of the traditional motors and modern controls were not sufficient, however, to permit the maintenance of off-peak headways by dropping a vehicle out of the schedule and saving platform labor hours on most lines. The increased performance could, for the most part, be merely put into a slightly better headway. Unless a substantial platform labor saving could have resulted, the increased investment, maintenance and power costs inherent in the doubled motors and new controls would not have been justified. The equipments were, therefore, removed from the cars.

"Simultaneous experiments with the electric trolley coach, as you know, showed the advantages under conditions obtaining in New Orleans, of this vehicle in combination with the motor bus as a means of modernizing the property, and a program of improvements in cooperation with the City of New Orleans has recently been completed."

*Courtesy Otto A. Goessl*

Windshield wipers and safety screens were a temporary feature on some 800s. Photo taken October 3, 1949.

*Courtesy Otto A. Goessl*

Canal Line cars terminated here at Canal and City Park Avenue. Photo January, 1960. Perley A. Thomas designed and built all of the 900s 1923-24. 905 has 76E2 trucks.

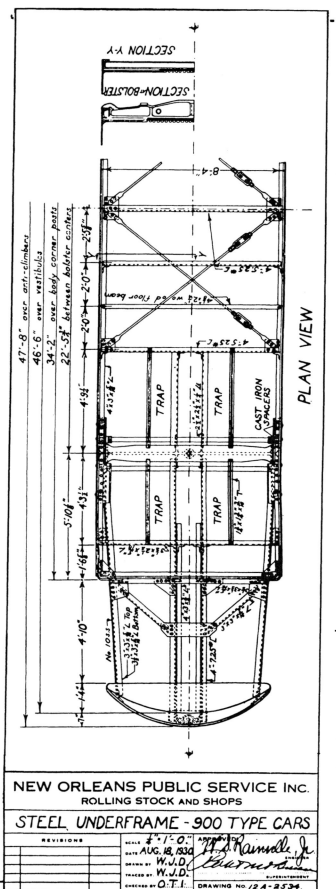

SECTION Y-Y

SECTION of BOLSTER

PLAN VIEW

TRAP

TRAP

TRAP

TRAP

CAST IRON SPACERS

**NEW ORLEANS PUBLIC SERVICE** INC.
ROLLING STOCK AND SHOPS

*STEEL UNDERFRAME - 900 TYPE CARS*

| REVISIONS | |
|---|---|

SCALE ¾"·1'·0"    APPROVED
DATE AUG. 18, 1930
DRAWN BY W.J.D.
TRACED BY W.J.D.
CHECKED BY O.T.I.    DRAWING NO. *12A-2534.*

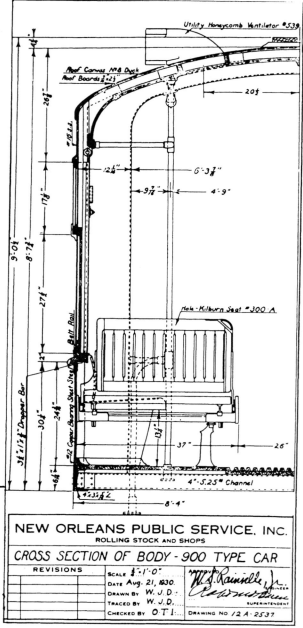

Utility Honeycomb Ventilator #539

Roof Canvas No.8 Duck
Roof Boards ⅞×2¼

Hale-Kilburn Seat #300-A

Belt Rail

4"-5.25# Channel

**NEW ORLEANS PUBLIC SERVICE**, INC.
ROLLING STOCK AND SHOPS

*CROSS SECTION OF BODY - 900 TYPE CAR*

| REVISIONS | |
|---|---|

SCALE ¾"·1'·0"    APPROVED
DATE Aug. 21, 1930.
DRAWN BY W.J.D.
TRACED BY W.J.D.
CHECKED BY O.T.I.    DRAWING NO. *12A-2537*

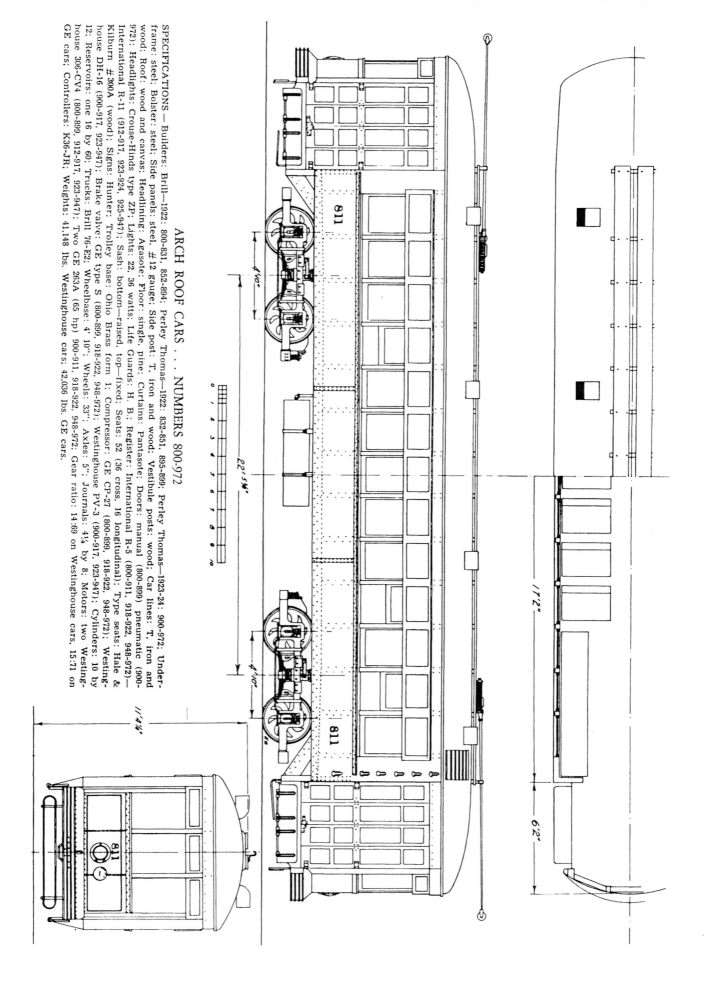

# ARCH ROOF CARS . . . NUMBERS 800-972

SPECIFICATIONS — Builders: Brill—1922: 800-831, 852-894; Perley Thomas—1922: 832-851, 895-899; Perley Thomas—1923-24: 900-972; Underframe: steel; Bolster: steel; Side panels: steel, #12 gauge; Side post: T, iron and wood; Vestibule posts: wood; Car lines: T, iron and wood; Roof: wood and canvas; Headlining: Agasote; Floor: single, pine; Curtains: Pantasote; Doors: manual (800-899) pneumatic (900-972); Headlights: Crouse-Hinds type ZP; Lights: 22, 36 watts; Life Guards: H. B.; Register: International R-5 (800-911, 918-922, 948-972)—International R-11 (912-917, 923-924, 925-947); Sash: bottom—raised, top—fixed; Seats: 52 (36 cross, 16 longitudinal); Type seats: Hale & Kilburn #300A (wood); Signs: Hunter; Trolley base: Ohio Brass form 1; Compressor: GE CP-27 (800-899, 948-972); Westinghouse DH-16 (900-917, 923-947); Brake valve: GE type S (800-899, 918-922, 948-972); Westinghouse PV-3 (900-917, 923-947); Westinghouse 306-CV4 (800-899, 912-917, 923-947); Two GE 263A (65 hp) 900-911, 918-922, 948-972; Gear ratio: 14:69 on Westinghouse cars, 15:71 on GE cars; Controllers: K36-JR; Weights: 41,148 lbs. Westinghouse cars, 42,036 lbs. GE cars.

One of the Brill built 800s at Canal Station, about 1927. 76E2 truck.

February 1965, the last conventional streetcars in the United States. The thirty five remaining cars in the 900 class have been thusly and so well refurbished, inside and out. Scene is beside Loyola University on St. Charles Ave.

*Louis C. Hennick Collection*

157

View of 904 shows safety device to prevent passengers' tripping—few cars had them. Cemeteries end of Canal Line, circa 1960.

1961 rebuild of some 900s had ventilator louvers but small standee windows. Photo, foot of Canal.

One of the Perley A. Thomas built 1000 class, circa 1935. 76E2 trucks.          *Chas. L. Franck Photo*

## ARCH ROOFS
### 1000-1019

The 1000 class was the third and final modification of the New Orleans arch roof steel (composite) car. In appearance, the 1000s were generally similar to the 400s and 800-900s, but were lower, had no drop platforms, were slightly wider, and somewhat faster. The cars' floor had a graduated ramp (almost imperceptible) from low platform level up into the car. Brass sash gave this type a lighter presence. The 1000s' 26" wheels allowed the cars to hug the rails more appreciably than other New Orleans cars.

The 1000s were ordered in September of 1927, ten from St. Louis and ten from the Perley A. Thomas Car Co. The interesting combination of Brill trucks with St. Louis bodies resulted from this. Car 1010 was unique in that it had the St. Louis EIB-64 cast-steel trucks.

Intending one man operation of the 1000s, N.O.P.S.I. possibly wished to order additional cars of this type. However, city fathers again refused to sanction one man operation! The 1000s were withheld from service

a few years after delivery in 1928. Eventually they were converted to the two-man crew operation and after serving some lines, entered service on the St. Claude Line on April 21, 1935. There they remained in service until 1949. Their numbers were too small to provide base service, yet they saw considerable use in owl service. Their speed made it possible for them to meet owl schedules with fewer units.

When the St. Claude Line was converted to trackless trolley in 1949, all twenty 1000s were scrapped. Thus, the most modern cars that New Orleans owned performed less service than any other type ever used in that city. Possible re-sale was darkened by the tremendous pace of street railway to rubber tired or PCC vehicles conversion prevailing in 1949.

The 1000s were quite modern, the highlight, almost, of the "conventional" (or pre-PCC) type streetcar. All steel framing, steel bulkheads, four step treadles (two on each platform), with usual safety devices, and high-speed motors, made these cars perform and appear proudly.

159

Interior, car 1000.

*Courtesy N.O.P.S.I.*

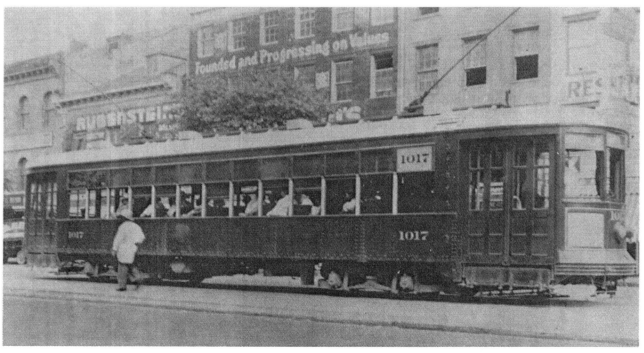

*Collection of H. B. Olsen*

One of the 1000 class built by St. Louis, taken at St. Claude terminus on North Rampart at Canal, July 31, 1937.

## ARCH ROOF CARS . . . NUMBERS 1000-1019

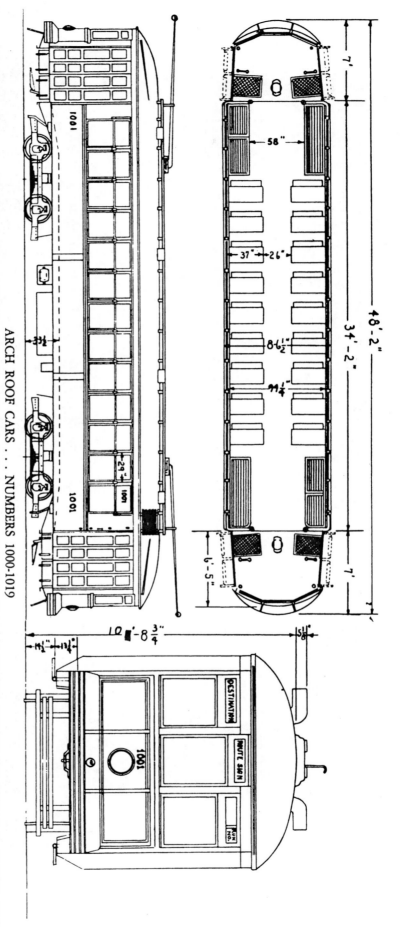

SPECIFICATIONS—Builder: 1000-1009; Perley A. Thomas Car Co.—Date: 1928; 1010-1019; St. Louis Car Co.—Date: 1928; Motors: 4 GE 265G (1000-1009, 1010, 1011), 4 Westinghouse 510-E (1012-1019) 35 hp each; Gear ratio: 14:69; Controls: L-35-JJ; Trolley base: Ohio Brass form 1; Compressor: GE CP-127B (1000-1009)—Westinghouse DH-20 (1010-1019); Brake valve: GE M-28 (1000-1009)—Westinghouse M-28 (1010-1019); Cylinders: 10 by 12; Reservoirs: Two 14 by 42; Sash: Side top, A&W Brass, stationary; Side bottom, A&W Brass, raise; Vestibule, A&W Brass, lower; Trucks: Brill 76-E1 (1000-1009, 1011-1019), St. Louis E1B-64 (1010—5' 4" wheelbase); Wheels: 26"; Axles: 4¼"; Journals: 3¾" by 7"; Underframe: steel; Sides #12 gauge steel; Side posts: T, iron and yellow pine; Vestibule posts white oak; Belt rail: Car lines: T, iron and yellow pine; Roof: arch, wood and canvas; Headlining: ¼" Agasote; Floor: yellow pine, single; Bolster: cast steel; Seats: H&K #300, wood slat, (36 cross, 16 longitudinal); Doors & treadle equipment: National Pneumatic Co.; Curtains: Pantasote; Lights: 32, 36 watt; Life Guards: Providence H. B.; Registers: International R-11, electric; Signs: Hunter, illuminated; Weight: 40,300 lbs. (1000-1009), 40,900 (1010-1019); All cars scrapped: 1949.

*Dept. Archives and Manuscripts, LSU Library*

First double truck trailers on West End Line in steam days, used circa 1880-1891. Builder unknown. Photo at Canal and Carondelet about 1890.

*Barney Neuburger Photo*

Brill open trailer, one of 30 built 1893 for New Orleans Traction Co. Later rebuilt into spliced trailers.

# TRAILERS

Trailer operation in New Orleans embraced both single and double truck cars. In this summary we deal with all types — single and double truck and the long trailers. Long trailers were confined originally to the West End and Spanish Fort Lines. Large crowds attracted to these resorts demanded their use. Good weather saw four-car trains (including motor car), while Winter and inclement weather called for two-car trains, and one-car for 'owl' service.

It is interesting to note that rarely were different types of trailers run in the same train. Officials were particular in the appearance of their trains to a degree seldom encountered elsewhere.

One four-car train could handle a tremendous crowd. Motor cars seated forty passengers (the Barney & Smith cars) and each trailer seated up to sixty-eight people (the Colemans). Thus, one of these trains could seat 244 people. A single motor car would carry its train at a speed of about thirty miles per hour.

The end came for West End and Spanish Fort excursion traffic in the early 1920s. Trailers then entered the field of rush hour traffic only. Eighteen of the thirty six long trailers were rebuilt in 1923 for two-car operation on Canal-Cemeteries and West End lines. The eighteen chosen were the best — the Colemans and Rojos. All but two of these were entirely enclosed, while all got Tomlinson couplers, vestibules, air operated doors and folding steps.

From October 19, 1919 to March 3, 1934, the two-car trains were often seen on Canal Street. Rebuilt "Palace" cars performed as motors. In the following notes, each type of trailer is briefly described. On following pages, plans for nearly every class of trailer are shown.

*Single Truck Trailers:* In 1876, the New Orleans City RR. Co. built a number of single truck trailers for West End steam dummy line service. Exact number built is unknown, but it is certain these cars were turned out at the Canal Shops (Station) at a cost of $700 each. Cars were double end, with reversible seats for twenty-eight passengers per car, and sported blinds to combat New Orleans' oppressive heat. These cars were gone by the late 1890s.

Another single truck trailer operation was the order of Brill open trailers, built in 1893 for service on West End Line. These later became the spliced cars in 1896.

A third trailer operation was put in service on St. Charles and Tulane Belts in 1912. Some FB&D cars were converted to trailers for two unit operation. Trailing FB&D car had hose connections for air brakes but no motive power. This experiment was short lived, as the double truck 400s went in service in 1915.

*Early Double Truckers:* In the early 1880s, the New Orleans City RR. Co. purchased an unknown number of small double truck trailers for West End Service. Cars appear to be Jackson & Sharp models, but this is not certain. Only photographic proof of their existence is available — no records could be found. They disappeared when the Colemans were built in 1891.

*519-524:* These were the six Morris Cars demotorized in 1917 and relegated to trailer service. The six were used in two-train service with the other six motored Morris Cars for rush hour service on Canal-Cemeteries. The trailers were rebuilt in 1917, having platforms lengthened with air operated doors and folding steps installed. Other than those refinements, there was little or no difference between the six trailers and the remaining six motored Morris Cars. By 1932, all six trailers had been retired.

*525-536:* These were the Coleman Cars, built in 1891 at the Canal Shops, and the first double truck cars built there. Master Mechanic Dudley Coleman directed their construction (hence the trailers' name). The Colemans were the first of the long trailers, and were used with steam dummies in New Orleans City & Lake RR. Co. service to West End. All twelve had two rebuilds, always as trailers. One would have difficulty in recognizing the Coleman car of 1891 and the same after the second rebuild. The number of windows (seventeen) remained the same, but the roof, platforms, and trucks were changed. Originally, the cars had a "butt" end shallow arch roof, with ventilators of unique design (one at each end near the point over the third and fourth windows). Carmen of the old days called them "turtle backs". The roof did not suggest the

## SUMMARY OF LONG TRAILERS
### After 1924

| Numbers | Nickname | Builder | Date | Rebuilt | Weight | Length | Width | Height | Seats | Closed |
|---|---|---|---|---|---|---|---|---|---|---|
| 519-524 | Morris | NOC&LRR | 1891 | 1923 | 31,200 | 24' 6" | 8' 5" | -------- | 64 | Yes |
| 525-536 | Coleman | N. O. Rys. | 1903 | 1917 | ---------- | 52' 0" | 8' 6" | 11' 2" | 68 | Yes |
| 537-547 | Spliced | NOC&LRR | 1896 | 1899 | 22,300 | 45' 4" | 7' 7" | 11' 4" | 60 | No |
| 548-549 | Rojo | N. O. Rys. | 1905 | 1923 | 27,000 | 48' 3" | 8' 5" | 11' 3" | 57 | No |
| 550-553 | Rojo | N. O. Rys. | 1905 | 1923 | 31,000 | 48' 3" | 8' 5" | 11' 3" | 56 | Yes |
| 554-560 | American | American | 1894 | ------- | 22,300 | 43' 4" | 8' 7" | 11' 9" | 56 | No |

First modification Coleman trailers, 1900. Butt-end umbrella hoods without posts replaced with graceful umbrella hoods, posts added. Note unusual ventilators. Trucks built at New Orleans by NOC&LRR.

later Stone & Webster "turtle back" roof, but since most car roofs in New Orleans were monitor deck, it was a handy description.

The 1902 (first) rebuild removed ventilators with a more conventional arch roof design substituted (which survived the 1923 rebuild).

Rebuilding the cars in 1923 (second) gave them the "new look". The Colemans' platforms were extended and fully enclosed, air operated doors and folding steps were applied, along with Brill 67-F trailer trucks. The early trucks were home-made wood frame types, best described as early MCB design.

The Colemans saw service on both the West End and Spanish Fort Lines. After the 1923 rebuild, they served as trailers behind "Palace" Cars in the Canal-Cemeteries Line rush hour service. All Colemans were scrapped in 1934.

*537-547:* To look at the photo of the little Brill single truck open trailer No. 214, one would be hard put to associate it with cars 537-547 — yet, the little Brills are there.

In 1896, the Canal Shop of the New Orleans City & Lake RR. Co. built trailers 537-547 by splicing three small Brill opens to make each large trailer. To rebuild included eliminating the running boards, closing sides to half solid-half wire type, a vastly stronger underframe, and much imagination. The back to back seating was retained. In 1899, all eleven spliced cars

were fitted with cross seats and had window spacing changed (see plans). These cars retained their deck roofs throughout their lives and were never enclosed nor did they have platforms altered. Spliced cars were used in West End and Spanish Fort service until 1923 — then came rush hour duty. All were scrapped in 1932-33.

*548-553:* The Spliced Cars' good looks inspired duplication. In 1905, cars 548-353 were built from the sill up in Canal Shops. These trailers were shorter by one window than their Spliced Car brethren, yet were wider by eight inches and did not have platforms tapering from corner posts to bumpers. These six cars were the Rojo trailers, named for Master Mechanic Frank Rojo who guided their construction. They subsequently went through two rebuilds.

Nos. 548 and 549 had platforms lengthened and enclosed, with air operated doors and folding steps added. Seating was changed at ends of the bodies, but their bodies remained the same semi-open types, as built. This work was done in 1923. This year saw Nos. 550-553 undergo a complete rebuild — cars were enclosed, both body and platforms. Nos. 548-553 saw years of use on the West End and Spanish Fort Lines, and after 1923 as rush hour trailers on Canal-Cemeteries Line behind "Palace" Cars. They were retired in 1934.

*554-560:* These were the American Car Co. RR roof trailers built in 1894 for the West End Line. The cars remained unchanged until scrapping in 1933.

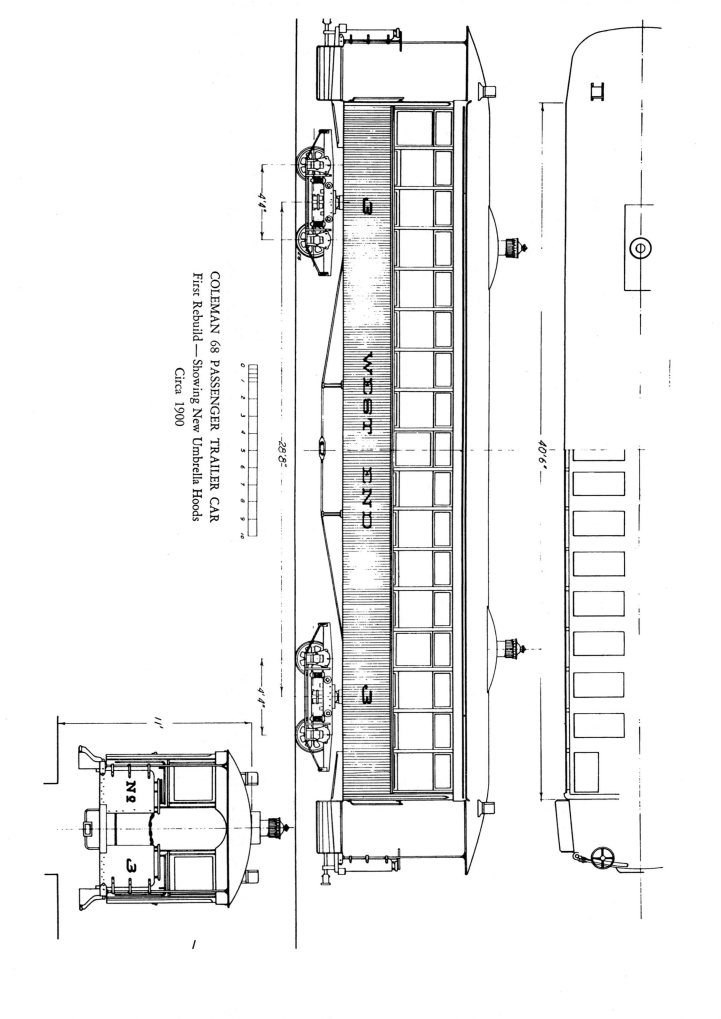

COLEMAN 68 PASSENGER TRAILER CAR
First Rebuild—Showing New Umbrella Hoods
Circa 1900

Final Coleman trailer rebuild for 2-unit rush hour operation on Canal Street.  Circa 1931.  Brill 67-F trucks.

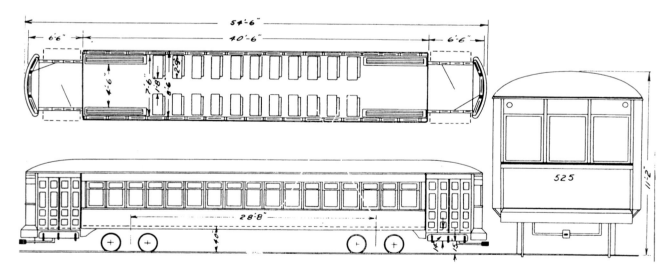

## COLEMAN 68 PASSENGER TRAILER CAR . . . NUMBERS 525-536   *Courtesy N.O.P.S.I.*
### (Rebuilt 1923)

SPECIFICATIONS — Builder: New Orleans City & Lake RR. Co.; Date: 1891; Underframe: steel and wood; Weight: 31,200 lbs.; Trucks: Brill 67-F (4' 4" wheelbase); Wheels: 24"; Brakes: Westinghouse; Sash: top fixed—bottom, lowered; Curtains: Pantasote; Lights: 17, 36 watt; Seats: 44 cross and 24 longitudinal; Registers: two International R-7; Doors: air; Couplers: Tomlinson.

*Courtesy Mrs. Edward J. Morris, Jr.*

West End Dummy train at Canal and Carondelet, about 1894. Note Brill single truck open trailers with canvas shades.

*Street Railway Journal*

Two unit operation in 1912 on St. Charles Belt Line with FB&Ds. First car a motored McGuire-Cummings, Lord Baltimore truck, built 1908. Second car, non-motored but with air brake equipment.

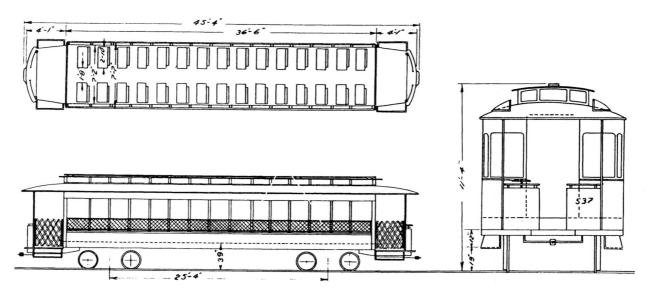

## "THE SPLICED TRAILERS"
### 60 PASSENGER TRAILER CAR . . . NUMBERS 537-547

SPECIFICATIONS — Builder: New Orleans City & Lake RR. Co.; Date: 1896; Weight: 22,300 lbs.; Trucks: wood frame, built by N. O. C. & L. RR. Co.; Wheels: 24"; Brakes: Westinghouse; Curtains: canvas; Lights: 17, 36 watt; Seats: 60 cross, wood; Couplers: link and pin; Registers: 2 International R-7.

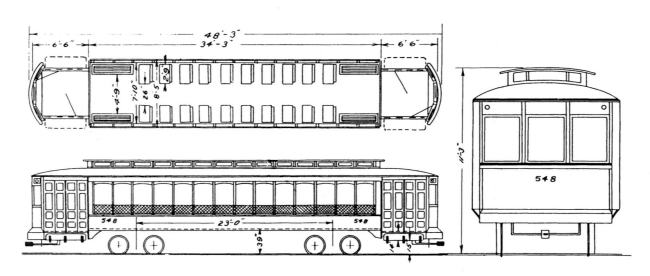

### 56 PASSENGER ROJO TRAILER CAR . . . NUMBERS 548-549
#### (Rebuilt 1923)

SPECIFICATIONS — Underframe: wood and steel; Weight: 27,000 lbs. Trucks: Brill 67-F; Wheels: 24"; Brakes: Westinghouse; Curtains: canvas; Lights: 17, 36 watt; Seats: 40 cross, 17 longitudinal; Couplers: Tomlinson; Registers: two International R-7; Doors: air.

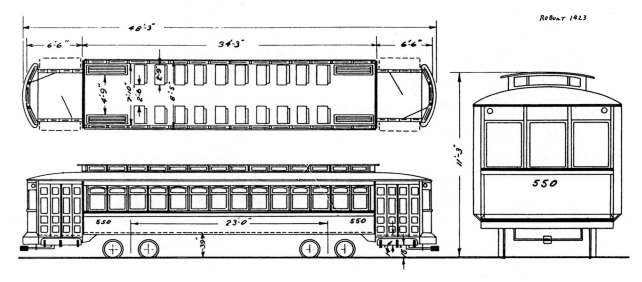

## 56 PASSENGER ROJO TRAILER CAR . . . NUMBERS 550-553
### (Rebuilt 1923)

SPECIFICATIONS — Builder: New Orleans Ry. & Lt. Co.; Date: 1905; Weight: 31,000 lbs.; Underframe: wood and steel; Trucks: Brill 67-F; Wheels: 24"; Brakes: Westinghouse; Sash: top, fixed—bottom, lowered; Curtains: Pantasote; Lights: 17, 36 watt; Seats: 40 cross, 16 longitudinal; Registers: two International R-7; Doors: air; Couplers: Tomlinson.

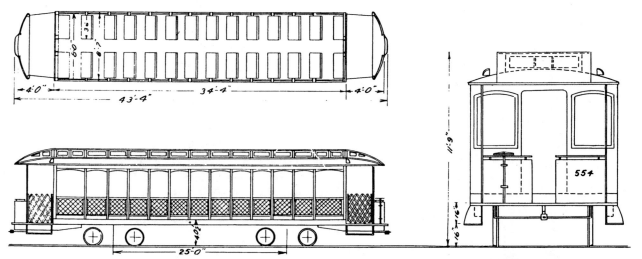

## 56 PASSENGER TRAILER CAR . . . NUMBERS 554-560

SPECIFICATIONS — Builder: American Car Co.; Date: 1894; Underframe: wood and steel; Weight: 22,300 lbs.; Trucks: St. Louis Trailer; Wheels: 24"; Brakes: Westinghouse; Curtains: canvas; Lights: 17, 36 watt; Seats: 56 wood cross; Couplers: link and pin; Registers: two International type R-7.

Baggage car, built 1894 by Brill after original one was destroyed by fire. Above 57D trucks not used. Car fitted with original MCB trucks in New Orleans. Number, not visible, should be "1" or "B-1". Baggage car used on both West End and Spanish Fort Lines.

*BAGGAGE CAR:* In 1894, Brill built a double truck baggage car for N.O.C. & L. RR. Co. (similar to one built by N.O.C.RR.Co. at the Canal Shops). It had a RR roof, center door, one small window midway between baggage door and each end, and was never motorized. Trucks were home-built wood frame MCB design. The car was 30' 10" long (over body), and 37' 0" overall, with a width of 8' 7". It was used on both the West End and Spanish Fort Lines.

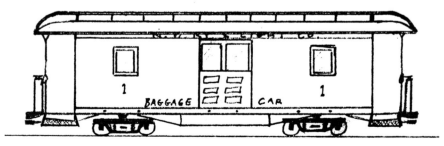

Brill Baggage car drawn 1954 by Charlton—from memory—eight years before photo was discovered at Historical Society of Pennsylvania in Philadelphia.

170

# SERVICE CARS

Service cars in New Orleans reached their peak in 1918 with a total of 69 units in service. Compare this figure with 41 in 1910, 17 in 1944, and 1 in 1955.

Most of the service cars were company built, mostly from the older single truck cars. The only service cars bought from outside builders were the dump cars and the Brown Hoist. As a result of this free-wheeling building, a number of odd designs resulted. A glance at Sand Car 021 or the plans of the grass cutting car, or the construction cars substantiates this statement.

Today, only one car remains, rail grinder 29 (formerly a sand car, and before that a wrecker). During Hurricane Hilda in 1964, No. 29 saw service once again

as a sand car. Leaves blown from trees made rails dangerously slick.

The demise of the rail service car is attributable to the rubber tire, or off-rail, vehicle. Yet, off track vehicles were used early. Tower wagons, drawn bv two horses, were in use fifty years ago. A tower truck was brought into service as early as the middle twenties. With the introduction of good roads, there was no point on the rail network (except the West End and Spanish Fort Lines in earlier days) which could not be reached by rubber tired service equipment.

Two rosters, 1918 and 1931, of service equipment are available. These are official N.O.P.S.I. records, yet contradictions exist that cannot be explained.

Arabella Yard, Supt. of Roadway Estill in 051's cab. About 1925.                    *Courtesy N.O.P.S.I.*

## ROSTER OF SERVICE CARS — NEW ORLEANS RAILWAY & LIGHT COMPANY June 30, 1918

| Type Car | No. | Numbers | Length | Motors | Builder | Year | Trucks |
|---|---|---|---|---|---|---|---|
| Wreckers | 8 | 19, 22, 38, 21, 24, 179, 170, 149 | 20' 0" | 2 GE 800 | Brill | 1895 | Brill 21-E |
| Sprinklers | 1 | 102 | 18' 0" | 2 GE 800 | N.O.C.RR. | 1900 | Lord Baltimore |
|  | 8 | 1 - 8 | 13' 0" | 1 GE 800 | N.O.C.RR. | 1900 | Lord Baltimore |
| Fire Car | 1 | 200 | 30' 0" | 2 GE 800 | N. O. Rys. | 1910 | N.O.Rys. |
| Sand Cars | 5 | 9, 10, 14, 23, 26 | 20' 0" | 2 GE 800 | N.O.C.RR. | 1898 | McGuire |
|  | 1 | 23 | 18' 0" | 1 W. 20 | Pullman | 1896 | McGuire |
| Freight Cars | 1 | 2 | 20' 0" | 2 GE 800 | N.O.C.RR. | 1895 | Brill 21-C |
|  | 1 | 2 | 20' 0" | 2 GE 800 | Brill | 1898 | Brill 21-E |
|  | 1 | 101 | 18' 0" | Trailer | N.O.C.RR. | 1896 | Lord Baltimore |
| Flat Cars | 28 | 101-08 110-13 | 20' 0" | Trailers | NOC&L | 1898 | St. Louis |
|  |  | 51-62, 4* | 30' 9" | Trailers | NOR&L | 1905 | Brill 27-G |
| Construction | 8 | 10-18 | 20' 0" | 2 GE 800 | NOC&L | 1898 | NOC&L |
|  | 1 | 30 | 20' 0" | 2 GE 800 | NOC&L | 1898 | Lord Baltimore |
| Tower Cars | 1 | 2 | 20' 0" | 2 GE 800 | NOC&L | 1898 | Brill 21-E |
|  | 1 | 3 | 20' 0" | 2 GE 800 | NOC&L | 1898 | Lord Baltimore |
| Hoist | 1 | None | 43' 2" | 4 GE 203 | Brown Hoi. | 1913 | Brill 50 AB |
| Side Dump | 1 | 1 | 20' 0" | Trailer | N.O.Rys. | ? | McGuire |

*Recapitulation:* There were 68 service cars as of 6/30/18.
*Abbreviations:* GE - General Electric. W - Westinghouse. Hoi. - Hoist. N.O., also NO - New Orleans.
 * 4 cars, no numbers.

## ROSTER OF SERVICE CARS — NEW ORLEANS PUBLIC SERVICE INC. as of 1931

| Type Car | No. | Numbers | Length | Width | Height | Weight | Motors | Builder | Year | Trucks |
|---|---|---|---|---|---|---|---|---|---|---|
| Side Dump | 4 | 050-053 | 40' 6" | 8' 3" | 10' 9" | 55,000 | 4-236A | Differ | 1923 | Diff. AB |
|  | 4 | 030-033 | 40' 0" | 8' 3" | 6' 4" | 36,000 | None | " | " | " |
| Ctr. Dump | 1 | 054 | 40' 6" | 8' 3" | 10' 9" | 52,000 | 4-263A | Differ. | 1924 | Diff. AB |
|  | 1 | 034 | 40' 9" | 8' 3" | 6'10" | 32,000 | None | " | " | " |
| Brown Hoist | 1 | None | 43' 2" | 8' 6" | 14' 6" | 103,190 | 4-201H | Brown | 1913 | Brill 50 |
| Wrecker | 6 | 24-26 28-30* | 29' 4" | 7' 7" | 11' 9" | 19,600 | 2-80 | Rebuilt | ........ | Lord Balt. |
| Sprinkler | 7 | 020-025, 044 | 20' 6" | 6' 9" | 11' 2" | 20,060 | 2-80 | Various | 1899 | Br. 21-E |
| Constr. | 9 | 037-042, 044-046 | 20' 3" | 8' 0" | 11' 9" | 21,500 | 2-80 | NOR&L | 1906 | Lord Balt. |
| Tower | 1 | 055 | 21' 1" | 7' 8" | 14' 7" | 16,670 | 2-80 | NOR&L | 1908 | Lord Balt. |
| Sand | 1 | 021 | --------- | ------- | ------- | ---------- | ------- | Rebuilt | ------ | Lord Balt. |
| Flat | 12 | 50-61 | 30' 9" | 8' 3" | 4'1½" | 11,000 | None | NOR&L | 1905 | Br. 27-G |

*Recapitulation:* There were 47 work cars as of 12/15/31, 30 of which were motors.
*Scrapping:* NOPSI has not provided exact scrapping dates for above cars except to say that the last remaining five work cars "went to their just reward" in January of 1953. Today, off-track equipment does all the work. One car exists today — No. 29, but is retained for an emergency only.
*Abbreviations:* Differ., and Diff. - Differential. AB - Arch bar.
NOR&L - New Orleans Ry. & Lt. Br. - Brill. Lord Balt. - Lord Baltimore. Ctr. - Center.
 * (note) No 30 was a sand car.

172

Ford, Bacon & Davis type car now used occasionally as rail grinder and sand car. No. 29 built 1899 by St. Louis Car Co., originally had McGuire "Columbian" truck. Now has 21-E truck. This is the only FB&D car in existence.

Construction car with work train, Laurel St. below Henry Clay. Jan. 10, 1917.

Differential dump, January 1950.  Greenwood Cemetery, near site of old Half Way House.

*William B. Harry Photo*

Tchoupitoulas at Milan, April 12, 1950.  Train is about to enter Napoleon storage yard.

*Courtesy Otto A. Goessl*

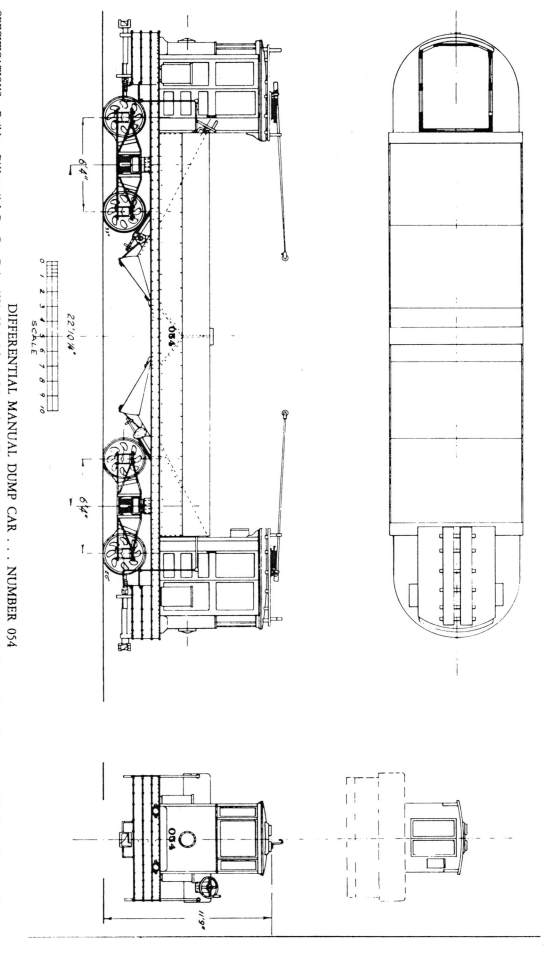

**DIFFERENTIAL MANUAL DUMP CAR . . . NUMBER 054**

SPECIFICATIONS — Builder: Differential Car Co.; Date: 1924; Material: steel (wood car lines, roof, floor); Trucks: Differential, 6′ 4″ wheelbase; Motors: four GE 263-A (65 hp each); Controls: K-35-JJ; Weight: 52,000 lbs.; Trolley base: Ohio Brass form 2; Brakes: Westinghouse air, DH-24 compressor; Total load capacity: 20 cubic yards; Dump operation: manual.

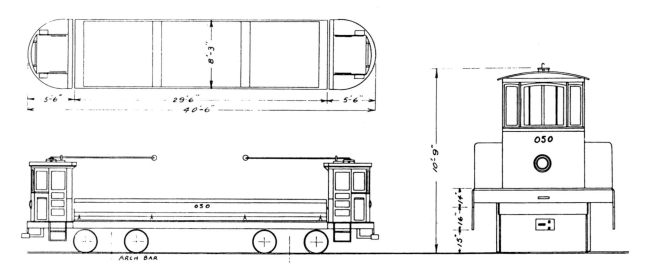

### SIDE DUMP CAR . . . NUMBERS 050-053

*Courtesy N.O.P.S.I.*

SPECIFICATIONS — Builder: Differential Car Co.; Date: 1923; Material: steel (wood car lines, roof, floor); Trucks: Differential (6' 3" wheelbase); Motors: four GE 263-A (65 hp); Controllers: K-35-JJ; Weight: 55,000 lbs.; Trolley base: Ohio Brass form 2; Brakes: Westinghouse air, DH-25 compressor; Total load capacity: 18 cubic yards; Dump operation: pneumatic.

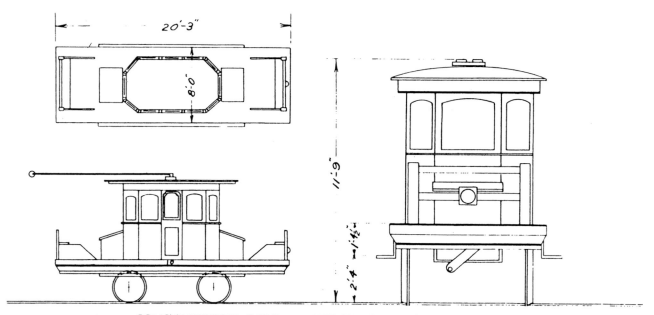

### CONSTRUCTION CARS . . . NUMBERS 037-042 AND 044-046

*Courtesy N.O.P.S.I.*

SPECIFICATIONS — Builder: N. O. Ry. & L. Co.; Date: 1906; Material: wood body, composite underframe; Truck: Lord Baltimore; Motors; two GE 80 (40 hp); Controllers: K-11; Weight: 21,500 lbs.; Trolley base: Ohio Brass form 1; Brakes: hand.

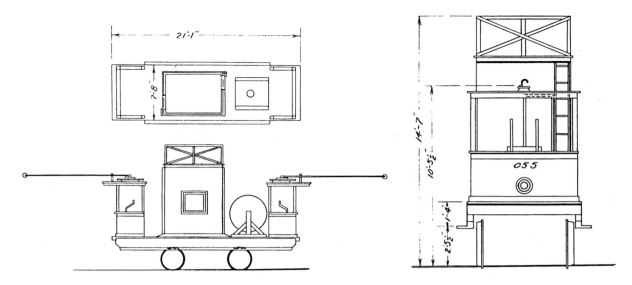

## TOWER CAR . . . NUMBER 055 *Courtesy N.O.P.S.I.*

SPECIFICATIONS — Builder: N. O. Ry. & L. Co.; Date: 1908; Material: wood throughout; Truck: Lord Baltimore (7' 6" wheelbase); Motors: two GE 80 (40 hp); Controllers: K-11; Weight: 16,670 lbs.; Trolley base: Ohio Brass from 1; Brakes: hand.

Tower Car, Lord Baltimore truck.                    *Courtesy Wilbur T. Golson*

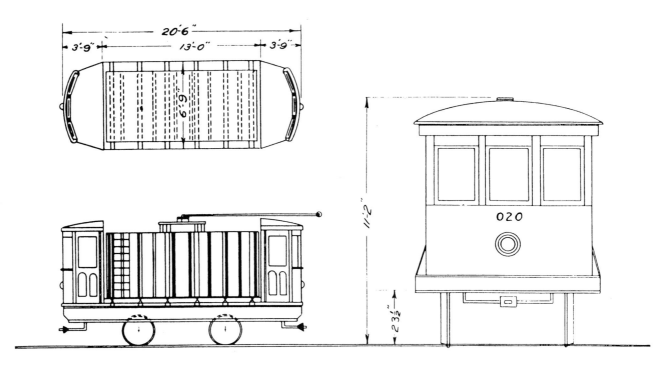

## SPRINKLER CARS . . . NUMBERS 020-025 AND 044

SPECIFICATIONS — Builder: N. O. & C. RR. Co.; Date: 1899; Material: wood throughout; Truck: Brill 21-E (7' 6'' wheelbase); Motors: two GE 80 (40 hp); Controllers: K-11; Weight: 20,060 lbs.; Trolley base: Ohio Brass form 2; Brakes: hand; Tank capacity: 2,500 gals.

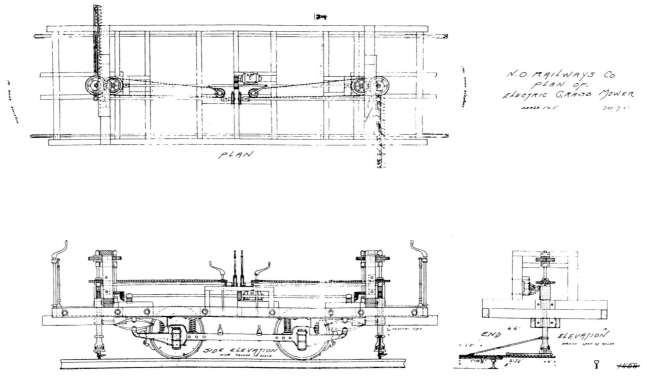

*Courtesy N.O.P.S.I.*

No photo could be found of the grass cutter car, only these plans. Today grass on the neutral ground about street railway tracks is cut by City of New Orleans, Parkway and Park Comission. At end of each year, N.O.P.S.I. pays the city for work done.

178

Brown Hoist, as delivered, at work in Laurel Street. Circa 1917. Brill 50 trucks.

History of sand car 021 is clouded. Perhaps it was a rebuild of sand car 23 shown in 1918 roster. The sand cars would operate during wet days. Sandwiched between regular cars, these odd contraptions would sand one rail as they went along (sanding both rails would have interfered with the electrical circuit).

179

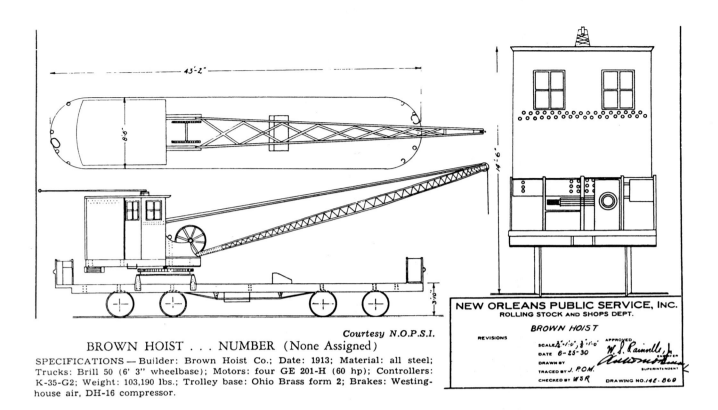

## BROWN HOIST . . . NUMBER (None Assigned)

SPECIFICATIONS — Builder: Brown Hoist Co.; Date: 1913; Material: all steel;
Trucks: Brill 50 (6' 3" wheelbase); Motors: four GE 201-H (60 hp); Controllers:
K-35-G2; Weight: 103,190 lbs.; Trolley base: Ohio Brass form 2; Brakes: Westing-
house air, DH-16 compressor.

NEW ORLEANS PUBLIC SERVICE, INC.
ROLLING STOCK AND SHOPS DEPT.

BROWN HOIST

REVISIONS

SCALE ½"=1'-0", ¾"=1'-0"
DATE 6-25-30
DRAWN BY
TRACED BY J. P.O.M.
CHECKED BY W S R

APPROVED
W. S. Painville, Jr.
ENGINEER
SUPERINTENDENT

DRAWING NO. 14 C - 860

Brown Hoist working in Napoleon Yard, April 12, 1950. Hoist is powered by extension cable, visible lower center.

180

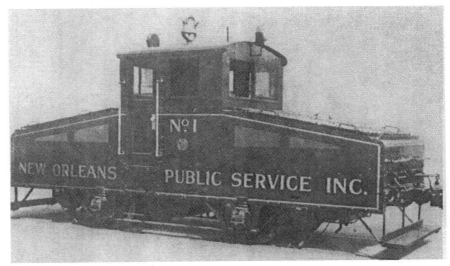

*Courtesy Wilbur T. Golson*

Atlas storage battery locomotive, used at Market Street power plant.

*BATTERY LOCOMOTIVE*: In 1926, N.O.P.S.I. purchased one battery operated, single-truck steel locomotive from the Atlas Car & Mfg. Co. of Cleveland, Ohio. This locomotive was put in service at the Market Street Power Plant where it worked a segment of track about two blocks long connecting the plant with the New Orleans Public Belt RR. on the River front. Gondolas loaded with coal were picked up, hauled to the plant, and empties returned to the Belt connection. The locomotice was a steeple cab type. Tractive effort was 12,500 lbs. — sustained tractive effort was 9,000 lbs. at five miles per hour.

*General Comments:* Rolling stock was well maintained and shop practices were good. Average on pull-ins was lowest of any city for the period 1923-30. In 1923, the figure on pull-ins was extraordinary: 217,723 car miles per pull-in. (A chargeable pull-in was any failure *not* due to outside factors, such as collisions and storms). Incidentally, the accident rate in 1923 showed New Orleans with 323 accidents per million car miles (average of the sixteen biggest U. S. cities was 447).

In 1904, the Louisiana Legislature passed a law requiring the vestibuling of all motor cars (open cars and trailers excepted), both passenger and work. New Orleans Railways Co. complied to the nth degree. No portable or hang-on type of vestibule was considered —cars were vestibuled in solid, permanent manner. The conventional three-window front, semi-oval radius, was the standard adopted. One car, No. 088, had a three segment angular vestibule of the Boston - Pittsburgh type briefly, for comparative purposes. It was soon removed and the regular semi-oval form installed. Deviations were Morris and West End motor cars which had train doors, as did their trailers (no trailer as used in West End service was ever vestibuled—but those which later were rebuilt for two-unit rush hour service on Canal Street were vestibuled with air operated doors

and folding steps, but no train doors). Cars, when first vestibuled, were equipped with the "X" type compressible folding (also termed "pantograph") gate and had doors as well. These doors were closed only during gusty storms and cold weather, and then had to be closed by hand (no lever controls). In 1914, the manually operated lever control appeared, and in 1923 air operated doors and folding steps came into use.

New Orleans never had a "single end" car or a "blind-side" type. All could be entered from either end and both sides. Three reasons for this were: most outer route termini were stub; cars on Canal Street's outside tracks were entered and left from the right side (but on inner tracks the left side, or both sides were used); and cars using the middle track on Canal Street turned trolleys at the stand with passengers using all four doors.

It was the practice on the Belts to turn cars at the barn after a day's use so the other end would be used the next days. Belt cars used only one end during their service day.

New Orleans had one-man operation in ONLY ONE instance on electric streetcars (Cemeteries Franchise Car). The 1000's were built for one-man crew but the city fathers prohibited it. These cars were revamped for two-man crews. Experimental car 288 was another abortive attempt to initiate the one-man crew in regular service (yet, city fathers approved the one-man bus!?).

As of today (1964), the last remaining car line operates with two-man crews, ten cents fare!

No PCC or Birney cars were ever operated in New Orleans.

Only one steam hood (railroad) roof motor ever ran in New Orleans, the private car "Atalanta". There were eight RR. roof trailers (554-60 and the baggage car). Until 1914, all other cars were monitor deck roofs. The arch-roof motor car appeared with the 400's in 1915. No deck roofs were ever changed to arch

# LATE 1920s RUBBER TIRED VEHICLES

**New Orleans' first trackless trolley, Oak St. Shuttle. ACF-Brill model, 1929.**

An early N.O.P.S.I. bus used in late 1920s. Buses had little improved in size or looks.

roofs. The only rebuilding of roofs took place with the Coleman trailers' original roof, with ventilators, and low arch butt end over platforms. These were changed to the more or less conventional arch roof with ventilators removed and butt ends changed to the umbrella hoods over platforms.

As was seen in section on single-truck cars, the 1896 FB&D cars with cross seats fanned a flame of protest against longitudinal seats. By early 1902, those cars which had longitudinal seats had been shopped and cross seats substituted. Aside from the fact that the belt rail was a little high in some cases, cars were more pleasant than when they had longitudinal seats.

No cars in New Orleans ever had the irritating feature that prevailed in many cars elsewhere—sashes so arranged that they had to be raised, and when raised the lower member of the sash was exactly at eye level. Another bad feature encountered elsewhere (but NOT in New Orleans) was cars with no arm rest at belt rail, only the sharp molding where the main sash fitted when lowered. Design could be "functional" and yet be comfortable and pleasing. Irritating designs were poor and no excuse can be offered for building that way. New Orleans had NO such cars.

It is interesting to note the life of some of the cars. Although all but one type were rebuilt at some time or other, or certain repairs were made to replace worn or damaged sections, much of the original handiwork would remain and at least as such we must recognize the car as we would an individual who, say, had been

First motor bus in New Orleans for public transit, built by Brill of Philadelphia. Vehicle operated for only about six months. in 1910.

to war, patched up, and lived to a ripe old age. For instance:

| | | | |
|---|---|---|---|
| Coleman Cars | 1891-1934 | 43 | years |
| Palace Cars | 1901-1935 | 43 | " |
| The 400's | 1915-1948 | 33 | " |
| Spliced Cars | 1896-1933 | 37 | " |
| R.R. Roofs | 1894-1933 | 39 | " |
| Brill Semi-Convertibles | 1906-1936 | 29 | " |
| The 800's | 1922-1964 | 42 | " |
| The 900's (some still running) 1923- | | 41 | " |

Thus, much rolling stock proved its worth—operating years after full financial depreciation had accumulated. Exquisite maintenance standards were mainly responsible. Co-author Charlton can recall no double-truck cars with sagging platforms or shabby bodies, and but few of the old single-truckers with a "humped" body or droopy platform.

Both authors have ridden the St. Charles and Canal Lines in 1964 in well cared for cars—the fact cannot be glossed over: The relaxed feeling experienced riding the cars over smooth neutral ground track with little noise, vibration, or motion except the easy forward glide, is indeed an ideal method of city transportation.

*Fenders:* There were four types used at various periods. Best photos are, as follows: (1) Crawford Fender: Brill 1894 car No. 50, circa 1894-1908, page 256. (2) Wire Guard "Apron" Fender: FB&D car No. 50, circa 1896-1908, page 265. (3) FB&D car No. 208,

the "Herr" Fender, from 1908 to 1914, page 266. (4) Providence H.B. Lifeguards appeared in 1915, and by 1922 most cars in New Orleans had them.

*Fare Registers:* Two International fare registers were carried on most cars in the early days. One recorded cash fares, the other transfers. West End and Spanish Fort trains neither issued nor accepted transfers, thus second register tallied round trip tickets. These registers were hand operated.

Steel arch roof cars, including 288, carried one register—on the 400's and many 800-900's, it was a hand operated International R-5, on the rest of the 800-900's and the 1000's, as well as 288, it was an electric International R-11.

*Journals:* Standard friction bearings were universal except on one car. The 1010 had St. Louis EIB-64 trucks with roller bearings. During the past two years, the remaining thirty-five 900's have been fitted with roller bearings in their old Brill 76-E1 trucks.

*Fare Boxes:* In electric operation, fare boxes first appeared on the Palace cars in 1911. Soon these manually operated fare boxes were installed on all cars. However, N.O.P.S.I. later made a complete return to the hand collection system.

*Markers:* West End and Spanish Fort trains displayed rear marker lights. Regulation trainmens' lanterns were affixed to a clip in a half box section on roof (see plans, cars 537 and 554). Such markers were standard

183

# LATEST TRACKLESS TROLLEYS

Last day for Freret trolley coach, June 9, 1963. Coach is a 1947 Marmon-Herrington. All trolley coaches in this series were retired in 1964.

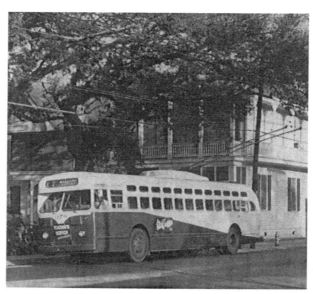

St. Louis model trackless trolley. This is only type still in service. Feb. 1965, Magazine and Exposition Blvd., at Audubon Park.

---

on these two, but no other, New Orleans lines. No front markers were used.

*Couplers:* (1) Draw bar—a bar with pierced head, holding pin and link. This was standard on all trains to West End, Spanish Fort, and on all city cars. Trains had air connection with standard air hose coupling. (2) Tomlinson automatic couplers were installed in 1923 on rebuildings of "Palace", Morris, and trailer cars for two unit rush hour operation. This coupling

also was installed on work cars, such as the Differential dump cars. (3) Standard MCB knuckle radial type couplings were used on Orleans-Kenner Traction Co. equipment (see Vol. I).

There was never any Multiple Unit train operation in New Orleans.

*Trolley Parties:* The 1893-1910 period, roughly, saw about as extensive a use of cars for trolley parties in New Orleans as anywhere in the nation. All cities availed themselves of the facilities offered by street railways in this respect, but New Orleans, with its great love of pleasure, found the streetcar to be a jolly, convivial vehicle for making whoopee. Research even uncovered public complaints and letters to the editor indignantly asking why don't the wooers stay in the parks. Joyriding on the streetcar often was a method to beat the heat in pre-aircooling and pre-airconditioning days. Picnic parties used trolleys—and still today it is a custom in New Orleans for parents to charter a car for their child's birthday party, usually decorating the car with bunting and streamers. Colored light decorations embellished the cars on such occasions in the old days.

*Maximum traction trucks:* For those who have doubts as to the original placement of wheels in installing the maximum traction truck, here are the facts:

Brill patented a Pony Wheel Maximum traction truck in 1890, as far as any record shows. The truck was quickly copied by other builders. Photos of cars from 1891 show the traction (large) wheels LEADING. Car bodies were lowered in later years, and for this and other reasons (heavier truck frames), trucks of this type began appearing with pony (small) wheels leading. Why did the large wheel lead at first? Cars were lighter in the old days—truck frames were light—and when the small wheel led, derailments were a nuisance. Even with pony wheels trailing, New Orleans found the Brill 22-E "Eureka" maximum traction truck prone to derail. Thus the 22-E trucks were replaced by single trucks.

*Streamlining:* No company in New Orleans at any time streamlined, or dressed out cars in skirts or fantastic paint schemes. Lately some 900's have received new rounded side windows and some have been fitted with bus type upper sashes and ventilation louvers. However, the only "way out" paint scheme applied at any time was during the last war's bond drive when car 832 received a patriotic livery in stars and the old red, white and blue.

*Seats:* The first electric cars (1893 St. Louis closed, open platforms for New Orleans & Carrollton RR. Co.) in New Orleans used a longitudinal rattan seat. The next year, the Brills arrived with wooden longitudinal seats. In 1896, the FB&D cars came with rattan cross seats. So popular were these, no more longitudinal seat cars were purchased. All single-truck cars after this order (except car No. 288) came with rattan cross seats. It is interesting to note that all double-truck cars from the 400's (1915) onward used wooden cross seats. Almost all the 1894 Brills had longitudinal seats removed and cross seats installed.

*Vestibules:* Prior to 1904, all cars had open platforms (except N. O. & C. RR. private car "Atalanta"). In that year, the city followed a ruling by the Louisiana Legislature requiring all motored and closed cars to be vestibuled. Vestibules were affixed in a thorough-going

program and afterwards new cars were vestibuled by builders.

*Trucks:* The following trucks were used under New Orleans' single-truck cars:

St. Louis 8—under "Atalanta", some St. C. St. RR. Co. cars.

McGuire 19-F—first (1893) electric cars for N. O. & C. RR. Co.

McGuire "All Steel Columbian"—30 under St. Louis 1899-1900 FB&D's.

Brill 21-E—under many of the 226 cars of 1894 original Brill Order, and the 1899 Brills, replacing 22-E "Eureka" maximum traction trucks.

Brill 79-E-1—under only one car, experimental No. 288.

Lord Baltimore—the standard single truck of New Orleans, used on all but 30 FB&D cars, on the "Prytanias", Jackson & Sharp, and under many 1894 Brills.

*Destination Signs:* The very first electric cars had their route destinations painted on the front and sides, continuing the mule car practice. Roof destination boards were tried, but by all means the most distinctive route signs were those carried in the front lights of the clerestory. These multi-hued glass signs, introduced in 1893, were a familiar part of the New Orleans scene until about 1913, when the first roll signs appeared.

The background of the clerestory signs was a solid translucent (not transparent) color, on which was superimposed the frosted glass lettering. Such signs were very easily read, and, as they occupied the full space of the front transom, were quite large. They were especially easy to read at night, when the cars' interior lights shone through the various combinations of colors, which were distinctive for each line. The color scheme was derived mainly from the traditional mule cars' body and night light colors, as seen by perusing the chart on page 218.

Later, as glass transoms were broken and the cost of replacing them became more expensive, the combinations of colors were painted on glass. No matter how carefully the work was done, the effect was never the same.

Then came the roller destination signs. New Orleans had the roof roll sign only in one case, the Orleans RR. Co. in late 1890's. The roll was otherwise placed in the front vestibule window (first a sign in the middle window, then a sign in each of the three vestibule windows for destination, route, and run number).

Insofar as research could determine, letter or numeric route designation symbols were never used in car service in New Orleans.

Typical West End steam dummy operation opposite Canal Station, about 1895. Trailers built by American Car Co. in 1894.

# STEAM LOCOMOTIVES

Steam locomotives of many builders have seen street railway and suburban railroad service in New Orleans, 1832 to the 1950s. Street railways that used such motive power were the following: New Orleans & Carrollton RR. Co., Crescent City RR. Co., New Orleans City & Lake RR. Co. (originally New Orleans City RR. Co.). Rosters are available for all but the Crescent City RR. Co. Steam railroad suburban service was provided by the Pontchartrain RR. Co., New Orleans Spanish Fort & Lake RR. (originally Canal Street City Park & Lake RR. Co.), Jefferson & Lake Pontchartrain Ry. Co., the New Orleans Terminal Co. (originally the New Orleans & Western RR. Co., late the New Orleans Belt & Terminal Co.) and several trunk lines entering New Orleans (see: Routes, chapter 3). Rosters exist for all these except the Jefferson & Lake Pontchartrain Ry. Co. However, since the J. & L.P. Ry. was owned by the New Orleans & Carrollton from the start, it is probable the road was served by N. O. & C. RR. engines. Rosters appear below, street railways first.

The photograph of N. O. & C. RR. steam engines on page 16 taken from reverse side of photo owned by Mr. Roger N. Conger and obtained by Mr. Avery Von Blon.

"Description of Dummies"

|  | Perpendicular | Horizontal |
|---|---|---|
| Weight, when ready for use | 8,000 lbs. | 8,000 lbs. |
| Track gauge of wheels | 4'8½" | 4'8½" |
| Wheel base | 5' | 5'7" |
| Length of boiler | 6'8" | 8'6" |
| Diameter of boiler | 36" | 32" |
| Fire Box size (Dahmers Pat. Water Grate Bars) | 20 by 30 | 20 by 30 |
| Number of tube flues | 32 | 32 |
| Size of tube flues | 1¾" by 3' by 6" | 1¾" by 5' by 8" |
| Size of steam dome | 18" by 24" | 20" by 30" |
| Size of cylinders | 4½ by 8 | 4½ by 10 |
| Size of drivers | 30" | 30" |
| Size of forward wheels | none | 22" |
| Height of dummy from rail to top of smoke stack | 10'4" | 10'4" |
| Capacity of water trank | 72 gals. | 70 gals. |

## NEW ORLEANS & CARROLLTON RR. CO.
### STEAM LOCOMOTIVES

| Name | Builder | Gauge | Wh. Arr. | Dr. | Cyls. | Date Bought |
|------|---------|-------|----------|-----|-------|-------------|
| "New Orleans" | Benj. Hicks & Co. | 4' 8½" | ? | ---------- | ? | 1835 |
| "Carrollton" | Benj. Hicks & Co. | 4' 8½" | ? | ---------- | ? | 1835 |
| "Enterprise" | Wm. Norris | 4' 8½" | 4-2-0 | 48" | 10½x18 | 1836 |
| "Industry" | Wm. Norris | 4' 8½" | 4-2-0 | 48" | 10½x18 | 1836 |
| "Lafayette" | Wm. Norris | 4' 8½" | 4-2-0 | 48" | 9x18 | 1837 |
| "Washington" | Wm. Norris | 4' 8½" | 4-2-0 | 48" | 9x18 | 1837 |
| "New Orleans" | Benj. Hicks & Co. | 4' 8½" | ? | ? | ? | 1838 |
| "Pelican" | N.O.&C.RR. | 4' 8½" | ? | ? | ? | 1850 |

NOTES: Disposition dates, scrapping dates unknown except in the case of the 1938 Hicks engine "New Orleans" which was destroyed in car house fire October 3, 1838 and the 1835 engines, sold 1837 (buyer or buyers unknown). In 1850-51, the New Orleans & Carrollton received three new engines. "Daily Picayune" failed to reval builder or any other details.

Other New Orleans & Carrollton RR. Co. locomotive data: In 1873-74, ten Lamm Thermo-Specific locomotives were received, but soon converted to steam operation. In 1883, the N. O. & C. RR. was running fifteen "dummies". A company listing of 1888 gives the following information: TOTAL ENGINES: 18.

RUNNING: 13. UNDER REPAIRS: 1. (four unexplained probably for sale). Twelve engines had vertical boilers and six had horizontal boilers. This information is from 1888 New Orleans & Carrollton RR. annual report. All steam locomotives were withdrawn from service May 1, 1889.

## NEW ORLEANS CITY RAILROAD COMPANY
### (later . . . New Orleans City & Lake Railroad Company)

The first engines received for service on the West End Line numbered four, were built by Porter and Baldwin (the first three Porter engines' data is not available because a fire destroyed some of that builder's early records). N. O. C. RR. Co. engines were all dummy types and were in the low numbers, probably beginning at "1".

| Builder and Builder Number | | Cyls. | Wh. Arr. | Gauge | Date Bought | Company | Number |
|------|------|-------|----------|-------|-------------|---------|--------|
| Baldwin | 3875 | 8 by 12 | 2-4-0 | 5'2½" | Apr. '76 | NOCRR | ? |
| Porter | 254 | 7 by 12 | ? | " | Aug. '76 | " | ? |
| Porter | 255 | " | ? | " | " | " | ? |
| Baldwin | 4098 | 8 by 12 | 2-4-0 | " | June '77 | " | ? |
| Porter | 312 | 8 by 16 | " | " | July '78 | " | ? |
| " | 313 | " | " | " | May '79 | " | ? |
| " | 373 | " | 2-4-2 | " | May '80 | " | ? |
| " | 434 | " | " | " | May '81 | " | ? |
| " | 435 | " | " | " | " | " | ? |
| " | 825 | " | 0-4-2 | " | Aug. '87 | NOC&LRR | ? |
| " | 826 | " | " | " | " | " | ? |
| " | 827 | " | " | " | " | " | ? |
| " | 828 | " | " | " | Apr. '87 | " | ? |
| " | 829 | " | " | " | " | " | ? |
| " | 830 | " | " | " | " | " | ? |

NOTE: Porter records do not list number assigned by companies to their engines. Steam engines were retired from service in July of 1898 when the West End Line was electrified. A few engines were sold to logging roads in Louisiana—disposition details, however, are not to be had. One old dummy was found in the swamps on the North Shore of Lake Pontchartrain by Mr. Wilbur T. Golson in 1962.

New Orleans & Western RR. and New Orleans Terminal Co. engines used in passenger service were probably 1895 Rogers 2-6-0's and 1905 Baldwin 2-6-0's. The 101, an 1895 Rogers 2-6-0, was involved in a minor passenger train accident in 1911, confirming this to that extent. However, it is possible that there were some actual passenger engines of the N. O. & W. RR. and N. O. T. Co. that have escaped locomotive historians' research.

This Rogers built engine was used in New Orleans Terminal Co. passenger service.
Photo taken February, 1917.

## CANAL STREET CITY PARK & LAKE RAILROAD COMPANY
(later . . . New Orleans Spanish Fort & Lake Railroad Company)

| Builder and Builder Number | | Cyls. | Wh. Arr. | Gauge | Date Bought | Company | Number |
|---|---|---|---|---|---|---|---|
| Porter | 298 | 8 by 16 | 2-4-0 | 5'2½" | Apr. '78 | CSCP&LRR | ? |
| " | 299 | " | " | " | " | " | ? |
| " | 312 | " | " | " | July '78 | " | ? |
| " | 313 | " | " | " | May '79 | " | ? |
| " | 364 | " | " | 36" | May '80 | NOSF&LRR | ? |

NOTE: Original 1871 order locos unknown. There has been no substantiation from any source as to early gauge of this road. Locomotive records must be regarded as the only source prior to 1889 (the '80 Porter order could be in error with the gauge incorrectly transcribed). Later sources are explicit when gauge is mentioned. Poor's Railroads Manuals of 1889, 1890, and 1891 list the N. O. S. F. & L. RR. with a 4' 8½" gauge, as did the 1899, 1900, and 1901 Official Guides. There is no data available for the standard gauge engines, although Poors credits the road with six dummies and 27 passenger cars 1889-91.

## PONTCHARTRAIN RAILROAD COMPANY
### Locomotive Data

| Name | Wh. Arr. | Dr. | Wt. | Cyls. | Builder | Year Bought | Notes |
|---|---|---|---|---|---|---|---|
| "Shields" | ? | ? | ? | ? | John Shields | 1832 | 1 |
| "Pontchartrain" | 2-2-0 | 60" | ? | 10 by 11 | Rothwell No. 2 | 1832 | |
| "Creole" | 0-4-0 | 54" | ? | 11 by 18 | Edward Bury No. 2 | 1834 | |
| "Fulton" | ? | ? | ? | ? | Benj. Hicks & Son | 1834 | |
| "(New) Orleans" | 0-4-0 | 63" | ? | 12½ by 20 | Edward Bury No. 40 | 1836 | |
| "Liberty" | 4-4-0 | 48" | 12Tt | 14¼ by 18 | Baldwin | 1849* | 2 |
| "Peter Conery, Jr." | 4-4-0 | 60" | 12Tt | 11½ by 20 | " | 1851* | 3 |
| "Union" | 4-4-0 | 60" | 17T | 11½ by 20 | " | 1851* | 4 |
| "Wm. H. Avery" | 4-4-0 | 54" | 20T | 12 by 22 | " | 1859* | 5 |
| "J. M. Lapeyre" | 4-4-0 | 60" | 21T | 12½ by 22 | " | 1861* | 5 |
| "Geo. Pandely" | 4-4-0 | 60" | 21T | 12½ by 22 | " | 1866* | 5 |
| "Charles Morgan" | 4-4-0 | 60¾" | 16½Tt | 12 by 24 | " | 1869 | |

* Engines listed in 1867 P. RR. annual report. t weight, exclusive of tender.

NOTES: 1. Unsuccessful (reason unknown), used as stationary boiler.
2. Condemned in 1867.
3. Condemned in 1867.
4. Rebuilt 1865, full stroke valve motion.
5. Engine has link motion.

This roster is not complete. No doubt there were other engines purchased between 1836 and 1849. After L&N control, 4-4-0's of that railroad performed Pontchartrain RR. passenger service until the end of P. RR. passenger train service in 1932.

Track construction at foot of Canal for 1930 beautification. Liberty Monument clearly visible.          *Courtesy N.O.P.S.I.*

# CHAPTER 5

# TRACK, PAVING AND OVERHEAD

Reference to neutral ground running has been frequent in this book—it could not be otherwise. New Orleans had the highest mileage of any city in this respect. When the maximum mileage of the rail system was 225 miles (1922), NINETY miles were on neutral ground.

Twenty-two avenues had neutral ground with cars running down their grassy central strips, with no contact or interference with general vehicular traffic, other than the crossings at each intersection. The operation was quiet, the track smooth and free from dust. Track maintenance was reduced to a minimum, and it can be said with absolute certainty that the most nearly perfect track was that of the neutral ground.

The extremes in track could be found in New Orleans as late as the early Twenties. The St. Charles-Tulane Belts, operating over 100-lb. rail on ballast with a grass carpet on the surface, compared with the old

tram girder rail to be found on Tchoupitoulas and South Peters Streets (plus the surface conditions on these two streets) was the absolute in extremes—note accompanying photos.

The following list is a partial one of avenues having rails on their neutral grounds, giving in nearly round figures their widths (as some figures come to fractions of inches); likewise, in some instances, widths vary slightly, as in the case of Carrollton Avenue. Most of this avenue is 150' 8" wide, but a portion is 138' 8". These figures are the average, generally speaking, and are measured from property line to property line:

Claiborne Avenue (North and South) ............191' 0"
Canal Street .........................................170' 6"
Carrollton Avenue ..................................150' 0"
Napoleon Avenue ...................................150' 0"
Franklin Avenue .....................................129' 0"
St. Claude Avenue ..................................127' 0"

Deterioration of cobblestones, South Peters St., 1921.

Howard Avenue ........................................................123' 0"
Broad Street ..........................................................121' 0"
St. Charles Avenue ...................................................120' 0"
Louisiana Avenue .....................................................116' 0"
North Rampart Street .................................................106' 6"
Tulane Avenue ........................................................106' 6"
La Salle Street (formerly Howard Street) ......... 96' 0"
Dryades Street ....................................................... 91' 0"
City Park Avenue ..................................................... 88' 0"
Peters Avenue (now Jefferson) ...................... 86' 9"
Jackson Avenue ...................................................... 85' 3"
Broadway ............................................................. 74' 0"

Just for contrast—consider Royal Street's narrow 38' 4" width from property line to property line.

In listing the streets with neutral ground, Elysian Fields Avenue was not included. Its middle was largely occupied by the Louisville & Nashville RR.'s tracks, including those of the Pontchartrain RR. Street railway tracks used the lower side of this Avenue for their passage from Claiborne Avenue to St. Claude Avenue. The width of Elysian Fields Avenue varies from 135' 10" to 163' 1". The neutral ground of Elysian Fields Avenue was not pleasing, occupied as it was with bare railroad tracks instead of verdant grass and trees.

Many of the streets with neutral ground once sufficiently wide enough to permit two railway tracks have been widened, at the expense of the grass-carpeted central strip. One example is Tulane Avenue which now has a neutral ground 4' 6" wide on which are placed traffic signs and light standards. Some streets have had neutral ground removed entirely and are paved unbroken from curb to curb.

Improper drainage made the task of track upkeep a major problem on streets in older parts of New Orleans, and in the dock and warehouse sections. Track gangs no more than finished work on many of these streets (such as South Peters) when it was necessary to return and do the job all over again. Until the city had installed a drainage system, little could be done to keep track properly maintained on many streets where streetcars and general traffic shared the right of way.

The drainage problem in New Orleans, before the system of pumping stations and canals was in operation, was manifest in several ways. Cemeteries, such as St. Louis No. 1 and other old ones, have row upon row of burial vaults placed above the ground. This was absolutely necessary, as one actually struck water with a hand shovel. An article during 1897 in the *Street Railway Journal* spoke of waterproofing problems connected with building car inspection and work pits for the Canal & Claiborne RR. Co. It was necessary not only to insure against water tightness, but also against the strong upward pressure of the water in the soil. The article cited an instance particularly illuminating, quote: "The persistency of this pressure is more clearly realized when it is stated that a large safety deposit vault in New Orleans of steel construction, which was duly placed in the excavation prepared for it, without, however, proper anchorage, was found floating at grade on the surface of the water filled excavation the next morning".

The general practice of laying street railway track in New Orleans in the late 1890's was: a trench approximately nine feet wide and three feet deep was dug to support each track. Planking (usually of water grown and water resistant Cypress timber) 1½" by 8" by 12" was laid lengthwise in the direction of the track, covering the trench's bottom from side to side. Roseta gravel (obtained from the Parishes across the lake) was spread level to a depth of about 12", on which a layer of sand was spread. On this were laid large paving stones called "Ballast Blocks" (or sand was laid to whatever depth and level required for Belgian Blocks or asphalt surfacing).

Hot tar, and in later years hot asphalt, was put in the crevices between paving blocks. Afterwards, sand

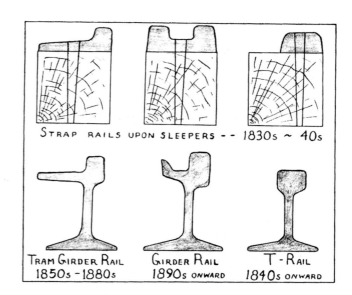

STRAP RAILS UPON SLEEPERS -- 1830s ~ 40s

TRAM GIRDER RAIL 1850s - 1880s    GIRDER RAIL 1890s ONWARD    T - RAIL 1840s ONWARD

was spread on top of the hot surface, giving a surprisingly tough surface that withstood the wear of ordinary traffic conditions while remaining fairly smooth.

Neutral ground construction practice was basically the same: Planking as a base, with crushed rock and then sod which produced the lovely green carpet of grass the cars rolled over. Ties were laid on two-foot centers.

On streets where Belgian Block paving was used for the usual border and between the rails, creosoted fillers were placed on either side of the web of the rails to prevent blocks from working in under the head of the rail.

There was less vitrified brick than asphalt used in New Orleans to pave about rails. On streets where as-

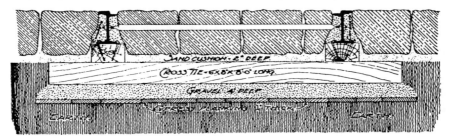

Track laying techniques of the 1890's in New Orleans. Note tram girder rail. This crossection provided by Orleans RR. Co.

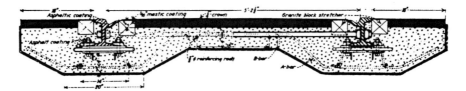

Track as laid in Canal Street neutral ground, North Claiborne to Loop, during 1930 beautification.

Magazine St., looking uptown toward Jackson Ave. Note ballast blocks. 1920.                    *Courtesy N.O.P.S.I.*

phalt was used entirely, there was of course a layer of concrete beneath the asphalt and the gravel.

The accompanying photo of Magazine Street shows clearly the paving known as "Ballast Block", and also shows old tram girder rail in use for about forty years (and the original paving blocks which were laid even earlier). The photo was taken in 1919, just before the street was repaved with asphalt.

The very worst condition is illustrated by the photo of South Peters Street. Drainage was being installed at the time (1921), and what street conditions existed in the dock and warehouse sections before full drainage and later paving was installed are evident.

The photo of Annunciation Street shows what existed in the poorer sections of the city. Cobblestones, parts of Ballast Block, broken pieces of Belgian Block, crushed oyster shells, and even pieces of asphalt taken from debris of street repair work were used to provide some kind of surface in preference to plain dirt, which obviously was mud most of the time.

As the paving of a street involved both the railway

company and the city, with the city setting the grade and the necessary tie-in with the over-all city wide drainage project, many streets waited a long time before receiving asphalt or bitulithic surfacing. However, sections which had struggled through mud and over rough sections of cutting from repairs elsewhere were improved during the 1920's.

New Orleans never used "T" rails in streets—only on neutral ground. Whenever the old streets were paved or repaved with Belgian Block, bitulithic, or asphalt, the standard girder rail replaced the old tram girder rail.

Many early day streets in New Orleans were paved from gutter to gutter with heavy planking. Many streets had crushed oyster shells or gravel as their surfacing. Any of the above had the old tram girder rail, and many a car trailed behind a string of wagons using the tracks as a roadway.

The "Ballast Block" was distinctive of New Orleans. It was a large granite block approximately 15" by 15" by 12" brought from overseas in vessels as ballast, then sold to the city for paving.

Cobblestone mixture, Annunciation St., 1921. Good example here of tram girder rail.

Belgian Block was a smaller stone, worked to a more or less uniform cut of about 6" by 6" by 10" and used extensively in many cities throughout the world. Few streets in New Orleans were paved from curb to curb with this type of paving, it being used mainly for the right of way the street railways had to maintain in the streets. This differed in no way from the general practice in other cities.

Cobblestones were irregularly rounded stones of various sizes, usually within three to five inches across without worked or truly level surfaces. New Orleans streets paved with them were always so paved from gutter to gutter. The gutters ran alongside the curb—in the dry season they held green scum, and during the rainy season they were rushing tracts of water. Streets paved thusly: Dumaine, St. Peter, North Peters, and lower Dauphine, to name a few.

In 1899, an extensive track reconstruction program was undertaken by Ford, Bacon & Davis, then in charge of the general improvements contracted for by the New Orleans & Carrollton RR. Co. (which had merged with the Canal & Claiborne RR. Co.). Speaking of the im-provement program, the *Street Railway Journal* of April, 1899, said, in part:

"The company is laying 100-lb. rail on St. Charles and Carrollton Avenues. The rail which is of A.S.C.E. section, is 5¾" high, rolled by the Pennsylvania Steel Company, in sixty-foot lengths. It is the heaviest rail in use on any street railway to date. The standard "T" rail is being laid on reserved or 'Neutral' ground, with girder rail on other portions in streets. The construction of roadbed is: creosoted planking, Roseta gravel, crushed stone ballast, and sod. Ties are 6" by 8" by 6', and are creosoted. The neutral ground is a raised portion six inches above the roadways of each side, and has trees bordering the tracks."

All revenue trackage in New Orleans was double track, or, in the case of streets with a single track, its mate could be found "one block over". The only exceptions were: over the river in Algiers, Gretna, and Marrero (see Vol. I); Napoleon Line in Jefferson Parish (the "Shrewsbury" Extension); the South Claiborne Shuttle and the Orleans-Kenner Traction Co. in Jefferson Parish (see Vol. I)—all of which were single track with turnouts.

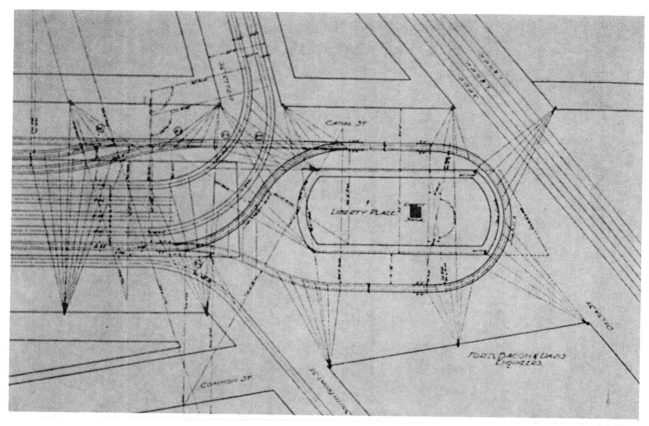

*From Street Railway Journal*

Before Ford, Bacon & Davis completed the impressive loop and layover terminus at the foot of Canal Street, the mule car trackage out of South Front Street was abandoned. The remainder of the track as shown was laid and finished by 1900. This plan remained in effect until 1930.

# THE MULTI-TRACK LAYOVER TERMINAL
## AT FOOT OF CANAL STREET

In 1899 one of the outstanding installations made by Ford, Bacon & Davis was the eight track layout at the foot of Canal Street, extending from Wells Street to North Peters. In no city was there a more interesting street railway spectacle presented than this terminal, as one viewed it from the old Louisville & Nashville RR. station, looking out Canal Street toward the lake.

As can be seen from the plan presented herewith, nine tracks were envisioned. There were eight tracks in the layover area (ninth track into Fulton Street—the Girod and Poydras mule car line—was removed in 1899, never electrified). From North Peters, proceeding for a distance of twelve blocks, then four tracks for three blocks, and two tracks for the balance of the

distance out to City Park Avenue (at the Cemeteries, where Canal Street proper ends).

The cars of twenty lines could be seen at the layover terminus, and as none of these lines had a greater headway than five minutes, the mass of cars there congregated inticed the imagination.

The eight tracks remained through the years from their installation until 1930, when the general "beautification" program of Canal Street took place. The layover area was at that time reduced to four tracks, which remained until the Canal Line was discontinued in 1964. Details on the operation at the layover terminal in the last days can be seen in Chapter 2.

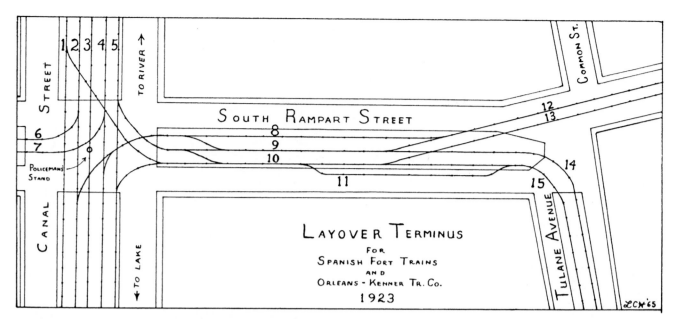

The layover termini for N.O.P.S.I.'s Spanish Fort Line trains and the Orleans-Kenner Traction Co. was built in 1911 (the O-K Line came in 1915) and lasted until about 1929. Spanish Fort trains inbound on track 4, into track 8. Motors uncoupled, proceeded to track 12, switched poles, returned via tracks 12 and 9 to get their trains for outbound journey, track 8 to 2. Until changed to terminate at the foot of Canal Street, West End Line runs likewise used the layover terminus, track 8, following same maneuvers as did the Spanish Fort trains. The Orleans-Kenner cars and trains inbound on track 14 to track 9, then backing from track 9 to track 10, then into the O-K layover track, number 11. O-K cars and trains outbound, track 11 to track 15. Track 3 was not a regular service track in 1923, did not go all the way in to the river, was used for termini of some car lines further in town, also for emergency turnbacks, work equipment. Tracks 1, 2, 4, 5, 6, 7, 9, 10, 12, 13, 14, and 15 used by streetcar lines.

## FOUR TRACK SYSTEM ON SOUTH RAMPART STREET

Another complex track layout with attendant intense utilization was to be found from 1911 to 1929 in the long block on South Rampart Street from Canal to Tulane. This was a four track section, and a busy one, as Spanish Fort four car trains terminated there, as did the Orleans-Kenner Traction Co. interurbans (see Vol. I). Add to these trains the six streetcar lines which used the two center tracks and one gets one of the most intensively used short stretches of track to be found anywhere. Headways on the O-K Traction Co. varied between one hour and 30 minutes (see Vol. I for time-table); West End-Spanish Fort headway was from 20 minutes to 3½ minutes—and the streetcars were on a 1½ to 5 minute average headway.

The intersection of Canal and South Rampart in the highlight of the trolley's era was indeed full of action. A glance at the map on this page gives details of the operation, showing a network of track that indicates just about what one would expect to see in activity. Fourteen lines crossed there from every direction

feeding in and leaving the five tracks of Canal Street, plus the four tracks on South Rampart and the two tracks on North Rampart.

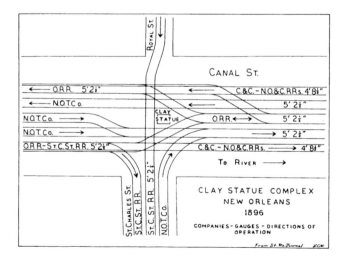

195

Differential dumps at work on Baronne Street beside DeSoto Hotel, about 1935.

*Courtesy N.O.P.S.I.*

## TRACK GAUGE WIDENING

In 1925, when track mileage was 221.26, some 28.48 miles were 4' 8½" (standard) gauge, while the balance was 5' 2½" gauge. The company planned to convert all mileage to the wide gauge. Although this plan was on the books for many years, for one reason or another it was delayed until 1925-29. As this change was considered inevitable, truck frames and wheel seats on axles of all cars 4' 8½" gauge from the 400 Class up were of sufficient width to permit practicable conversion to wide gauge (5' 2½").

There were five standard gauge lines in 1925; Claiborne (North), Jackson, St. Charles and Tulane Belts, and South Claiborne Shuttle. On the night of October 28, 1925, some 4,762 feet of double track on the Jackson Avenue Line was changed from standard to broad gauge. Service on this line was cut at nine o'clock in the evening and track laborers (200 men, 10 foremen), acetylene cutters, a Universal crane on an electric truck, the Brown hoist, and a number of Differential bottom-dump trains for handling slag were engaged in the job. Service resumed at 2:15 A.M. the next morning.

This was a spectacular "hurry-up" job, and it warrants further attention. The reason for the rush on the Jackson Line was due to rerouting of portions of this line (see: Chapter 3, ROUTES) over existing 5' 2½" gauge trackage. The section of the Jackson Line requiring widening was from St. Charles to the River.

Crossing and similar work were, as follows: Two double track crossings, four single crossings, two turnouts, and one crossover were installed, along with the straightaway involving 4,762 feet of double track. Light clusters were hung from trolley wires along the entire line of work.

In like manner, the Claiborne Line was widened February 21, 1926. The Tulane Belt Line was converted October 1-2, 1929 followed by St. Charles Belt Line October 2-3, 1929.

The conversion of trucks and axles was not so urgent, as several pairs of trucks were, of course, prepared in advance. Furthermore, since there was much broad gauge rolling stock, work could progress without the extreme pressure exerted for the track alteration.

Thus, 1929 saw the entire system almost completely flexible as to rolling stock operation without any car assignment restrictions. Only the South Claiborne Shuttle remained standard gauge, the few FB&D cars necessary to service the line kept at Carrollton Barn.

Stringing trolley wire on West End Line, 1898. *Street Railway Gazette*

*Street Railway Journal*

City Park Race Track Extension terminal showing 600 volt DC Catenary, first in U.S.A. for street railway use.

## OVERHEAD CONSTRUCTION

Standard overhead trolley construction practices in the sense as applied to street railway operation were used in New Orleans. Wire was 00 gauge. One departure was the City Park Race Track Extension, built 1905. This one mile long double track line was the very first in the U. S. to use 600 volt DC catenary. Trolley wire was No. 0000 grooved trolley, messenger wire was half-inch galvanized steel strand, supported by ten-foot steel tube brackets attached to center poles by regulation wall brackets.

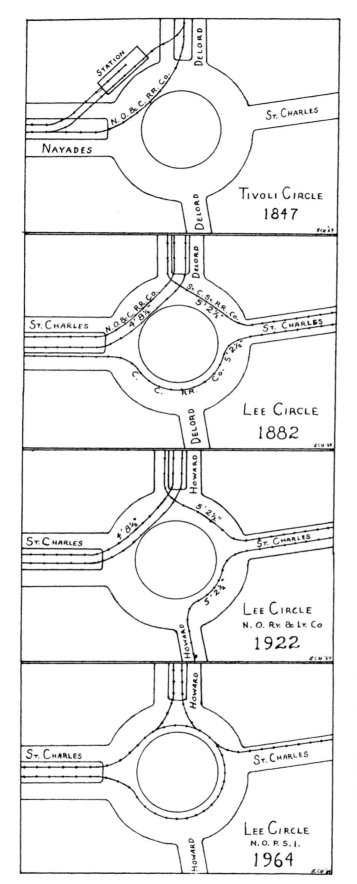

## PASSENGER SHELTERS

These conveniences saw scattered use in the old days as well as by N.O.P.S.I. Shelters were at each end of the St. Claude Line while the Jackson Line had one at its River end, near the Gretna Ferry landing. There were shelters at Half Way House and at some stops between there and West End train shed on the West End Line. Spanish Fort had a waiting station. The N. O. & C. RR. in the 1870's had shelters at Napoleon and St. Charles, Louisiana and St. Charles, and at Dublin and St. Charles. There were others at various terminals and transfer points. However, there were none on Canal Street, yet one on North Rampart at Canal for the St. Claude Line.

SAFETY ZONES: All neutral ground operation had paved strips at car stops one car length long. Passengers entered from rear of cars, left by front or rear. Raised islands in streets not having neutral ground were never built. All zones in streets were painted, as streets without neutral ground were too narrow to allow space for concrete islands.

## SWITCHES

Switch tenders were employed on Canal Street on the five track section until 1910, when gradual conversion to current-impulse automatic switch operation began. Tenders continued at the multi-track layover terminal at the foot of Canal for many years and also at other important points.

Switch rods were carried on front of dash on cars and required motormen to lean out the front window to throw switches. There were no holes in platforms for this operation as could be found in some cities.

Typical movable-tongue street railway switches were in general use in New Orleans while the West End Line outer end had railroad type double point, ground lever thrown switches.

Market Street power plant, 1926. Atlas battery powered locomotive at work.    *Courtesy N.O.P.S.I.*

CHAPTER 6

# POWERHOUSES AND SUBSTATIONS

MARKET STREET STEAM-ELECTRIC GENERAT-
ING STATION: This is the main plant for the 600
volt DC trolley system, and has been for some time.
The station as originally constructed at this site in the
1880's no longer exists. The present station's first section was constructed in 1901. Three vertical engine-
generator units totaling 6,000 kw. were installed in
1901-04. Five vertical turbo-generator units totaling
15,500 kw. were installed in 1906-09. One horizontal
turbo-generator unit of 15,500 kw. capacity was put in
use in 1916. These old units have been replaced by
larger units. In 1955, the capacity of the station was
200,000 kw., consisting of the following units:

| | | | | Year | kw. |
|---|---|---|---|---|---|
| 1 | Horizontal turbo-generator | | | 1918 | 11,500 |
| 1 | " | " | " | 1922 | 23,900 |
| 1 | " | " | " | 1924 | 24,900 |
| 1 | " | " | " | 1927 | 31,600 |
| 1 | " | " | " | 1938 | 36,400 |
| 1 | " | " | " | 1943 | 38,200 |
| 1 | " | " | " | 1952 | 33,500 |

All of the above generate three-phase alternating current at 13,800 volts except the 1918 unit which gener-
ates at 6,900 volts.

Claiborne power plant, Elysian Fields and Decatur Streets, about 1923.

*Courtesy N.O.P.S.I.*

A. B. PATERSON STEAM-ELECTRIC GENERATING STATION: This plant was built in 1947, was originally named the Industrial Canal Station. In November of 1952 its name was changed to honor the memory of N.O.P.S.I.'s deceased President, Mr. A. B. Paterson who had died that year.

The station's present capacity is 215,000 kw. This output was attained when a new 82,000 kw. unit was installed in 1954. The plant's four units are all horizontal turbo-generators ranging in power from 41,000 to 82,000 kw. and range in age from 17 to 10 years. Three phase AC power at 13,000 v. is generated.

CLAIBORNE STEAM-ELECTRIC GENERATING PLANT AND SUBSTATION: This electric generating station, located on the River front at Elysian Fields and North Peters, was built in 1895-96. The plant, housed in a steel frame and brick structure, used coal for fuel. Circulating water was piped from the River. This station was built to supply 600 volt direct current for street railway service and was operated until 1922. The generating equipment consisted of two 300, one 800, and two 1,200 kw. 600 volt DC generators, all directly connected to horizontal Corliss engines.

The following substation equipment was also housed in this plant:

3  1,000 kw. 600 volt convertors
1   500 kw. 600 volt generator
3   500 kw. 600/2300 volt transformers

In addition, this station included 22 mercury arc rectifier units for DC street lights and four constant current transformers for AC street lights.

The substation equipment was supplied with current from three 6,600 volt overhead feeders. Three 2,300 volt, three phase AC commercial circuits were fed from this substation.

OTHER ELECTRIC GENERATING PLANTS: From 1909 to 1915, the city was served by the Market Street

Plant, Claiborne Plant, Edison Plant, and the Consumers Power & Light Company Plant. The Merchants Plant at Julia and Genois Streets, and the Orleans RR. Co. Plant at Carondelet Walk (now Lafitte Avenue) and Prieur Street were both closed in 1903.

The St. Charles St. RR. Co. Plant at Decatur and Marigny and the Napoleon Avenue Power House were shut down in 1908. The St. Charles RR. Co. Plant was maintained for standby service through 1909.

The Edison Steam-Electric Generating Station and Substation supplied current to the business district and was last operated in 1923. It was housed in a steel frame brick building located on Union Street between Baronne and Dryades Streets (site of present N.O.P.S.I. office building along with the frontage on Baronne Street). Coal was trucked to this station to be used for fuel, and circulating water was obtained through long pipe lines from the New Basin Canal (which was at South Rampart and Howard Avenue and no longer exists), a distance from the plant of about 3,100 feet. This station was built to supply energy to the direct current Edison three wire system, which served the business section of New Orleans. At one time there were seven vertical engine-driven units ranging in capacity from 400 kw. to 1,000 kw., with a total capacity of 3,900 kw. Steam was generated at about 150 lbs. pressure in a boiler room fronting on Union Street. This plant also housed substation equipment, as follows:
2 1,000 kw. 125/250 volt DC motor generators
1 1,500 kw. 125/250 volt DC rotary convertor

The Consumers Electric Light & Power Co. Plant was completed in 1906, with a capacity of 3,500 kw. and was last operated in 1915. Afterwards, power was purchased from N. O. Ry. & Lt. Co. and later N.O.P.S.I.

The Citizens Power & Light Co. Plant had two 750 hp diesel engines, driving two 500 kw. generators originally. Another 500 kw. generator was later added. After this company consolidated with N.O.P.S.I. in 1925, these generating facilities were maintained for standby purposes until sold in 1929.

NOTES AND COMMENTS: For several years beginning 1907 (exact dates covering span of years not available), electricity was sold to lighting and street railway interests over the River in Algiers (for more details, see Chapter I, Volume I).

New Orleans street railway power is 600 volts DC and street lighting cables carry 2,300 volts AC.

Today Market Street and Paterson Plants supply all power for rail and trolley coach lines and street lighting in New Orleans, providing a total of 415,000 kw. Five substations distribute power for the last remaining rail line (St. Charles) and the two remaining trackless trolley lines (Jackson and Magazine). These substations are: Arabella, Bourbon, Lowerline, Polymnia, and Valence.

The City of New Orleans owns its own power plant, which furnishes power for the needs of the Sewerage & Water Board, for the purposes of drainage and sewerage.

A bay of Magazine Shops, circa 1917. FB&D type cars being rebuilt.

*Courtesy N.O.P.S.I.*

# CHAPTER 7

# BARNS AND SHOPS

In 1882, there were fifteen "stations" in use serving the six street railways in New Orleans. This was purely for the mule cars and mules, although West End Line dummies and cars were kept at Canal Station (Barn) of the New Orleans City RR. That company had four barns in service in 1882—CANAL: bounded by Canal, Bienville, White, and Dupre; ESPLANADE: located on Esplanade near Moss, across from the St. Louis Cemetery. MAGAZINE: bounded by Magazine, Camp, Toledano, and Pleasant; and POLAND: bounded by Poland, St. Claude, Rampart, and Lesseps. An 1875 annual report of the N. O. C. RR. lists a CAMP BARN, but the location of this station has not been discovered. It is possible the reference was made to the Camp Street entrance to the Magazine Barn. Magazine Barn (also called Shops) was a large affair including several buildings.

CANAL & CLAIBORNE STS. RR. CO. had two barns in 1882: COMMON: bounded by Common (now Tulane Avenue), Tonti, Rocheblave, and Banks; and URQUHART: bounded by Urquhart, Marais, Music, and Arts.

CRESCENT CITY RR. CO. operated three stations in 1882: MAGAZINE: on River side of Magazine, between Octavia and Peters Avenue (the old Magazine St. RR. Co. barn); TCHOUPITOULAS: bounded by Tchoupitoulas, Rousseau, Philip, and Jackson Avenue; and another barn on TCHOUPITOULAS bounded by Tchoupitoulas, Front, Louisiana, and Toledano.

In 1882 there were three stations serving the NEW ORLEANS & CARROLLTON RR. These were: ST. CHARLES: bounded by St. Charles, Hampson, Dublin, and another barn on ST. CHARLES: bounded by St. Charles, Pitt, Napoleon, and Berlin (now Gen. Pershing); and FELICITY: bounded by Felicity, Polymnia, Carondelet, and St. Charles.

ORLEANS RR. had but one barn in 1882—WHITE: bounded by White, Laharpe, Gentilly Boulevard and North Dupre.

ST. CHARLES ST. RR. CO had two barns in 1882: MAGNOLIA: bounded by Clio, Magnolia, Locust (now Robertson), and Erato; and 8TH STREET: bounded by 8th Street, Carondelet, 7th Street, and Baronne.

Many of the barns used during the era of animal traction survived the conversion to electric traction. Bearing testimony to that fact is the following list of barns KNOWN to have served electric cars in New Orleans. Incidentally, three of the below were major shops (after 1904)—Canal, Carrollton, and Magazine. Prior to 1904, each barn did its own repair work.

ARABELLA: At Magazine, Joseph, and Arabella Streets (see plan). Established by the Crescent City RR. Co. in 1880's after the opening of the Canal and Coliseum and Upper Magazine Line (later Coliseum Line). Still in use, but for rubber tried vehicles only. Gauge 5' 2½". Rails removed 1948. One of the three largest barns, this facility served cars for over 60 years.

CANAL: Canal and White Streets (see plan). Established 1861 by New Orleans City RR. Co. closed (to rail vehicles) 1964, after serving streetcars for one hundred and three years. Serves rubber tired vehicles only. Gauge 5' 2½"—one of three largest barns.

Considerable car building was done at Canal prior to 1905. Major body repair was done until about 1910, when Magazine Shops took over. Cars were maintained and painted until the Canal Line was converted to buses in 1964, but no heavy construction since 1910.

CARROLLTON: Dublin, Poplar (now Willow), Madison (now Dante), Streets (see plan). Established 1893 by New Orleans & Carrollton RR. Co., succeeding that company's three stations. Gauge 4' 8½" originally, converted to 5' 2½" in 1929. Double gauge installed in 1920.

This barn was the main shop for standard gauge cars and experimental car 288 was built here. Today it houses New Orleans' last streetcar line (ST. CHARLES) and also buses. Cars are rebuilt here, as well as serviced, repaired, and repainted. Carrollton Barn was closed, cars transferred to Canal Barn on December 28, 1934. The barn was reopened March 1, 1943, and has remained in service ever since.

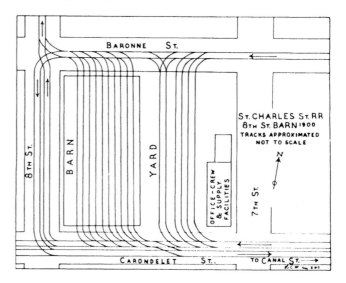

Arabella Station storage yard, 1920.

Arabella Station, about 1923.

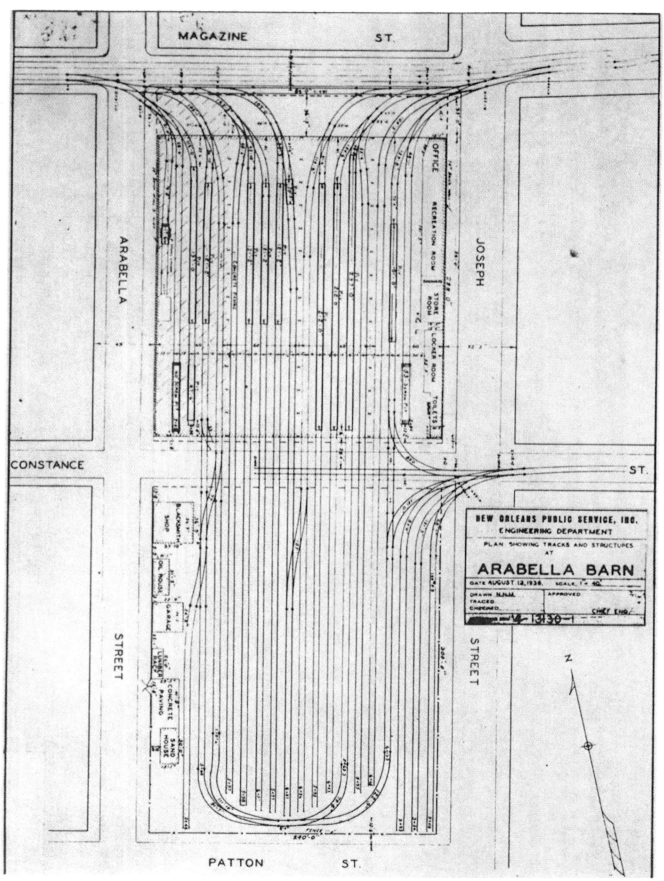

MAGAZINE ST.

ARABELLA

CONSTANCE

STREET

JOSEPH

OFFICE
RECREATION ROOM
STORE ROOM | LOCKER ROOM
TOILETS

ST.

BLACKSMITH SHOP
OIL HOUSE
GARAGE
LUMBER
CONCRETE PAVING
SAND HOUSE

STREET

NEW ORLEANS PUBLIC SERVICE, INC.
ENGINEERING DEPARTMENT

PLAN SHOWING TRACKS AND STRUCTURES
AT

ARABELLA BARN

DATE AUGUST 12, 1936.  SCALE 1" = 40'

DRAWN  N.N.M.
TRACED
CHECKED  CHIEF ENG.

13 30 1

PATTON ST.

206

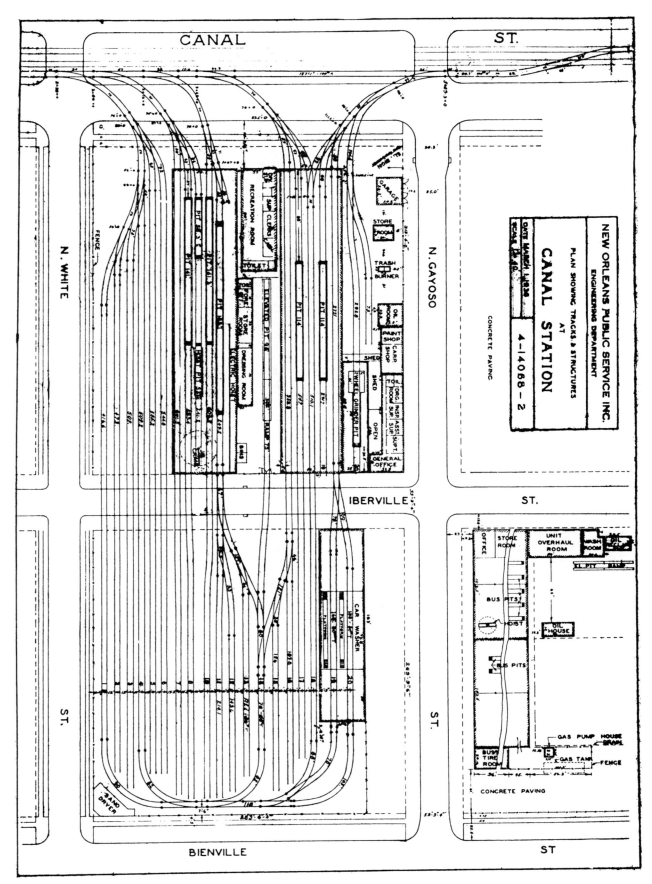

CLAIBORNE: Urquhart and Almonaster (now Franklin Avenue)—no plan available. This barn was built in 1870 by Canal & Claiborne Sts. RR. Co., last used in 1915, with cars going to Poland Barn. The Claiborne (North) cars were serviced here and light repairs performed. Major work was done at Carrollton after 1899. Gauge was 4' 8½".

EIGHTH STREET: Carondelet and 8th Streets — no plan available, only a sketch from Charlton's memory. Established about 1866 by St. Charles St. RR. Co.,

last used about 1908. Marigny took over for all three lines of the St. C. St. RR. Co. at that time. During its last few years, 8th Street housed upper end of Carondelet Line and all the Dryades Line. Gauge was 5' 2½".

ESPLANADE: Esplanade Avenue near Bayou St. John —no plan available. This barn is one of four established by New Orleans City RR. Co. in 1861 (Canal, Esplanade, Magazine, and Poland). Used for passenger cars until about 1902. Coincident with establishment of Belts, cars were sent to Canal Barn and this barn used

Canal Station, 1896.                    E. Harper Charlton Collection

Heading out of Canal Station storage yard, 1961.  Flags for local charity drive.          Courtesy Otto A. Goessl

Raised inspection track, Canal Station, about 1949.

*Courtesy Otto A. Goessl*

Canal Station yard, January 1960.

*courtesy Wilbur T. Golson*

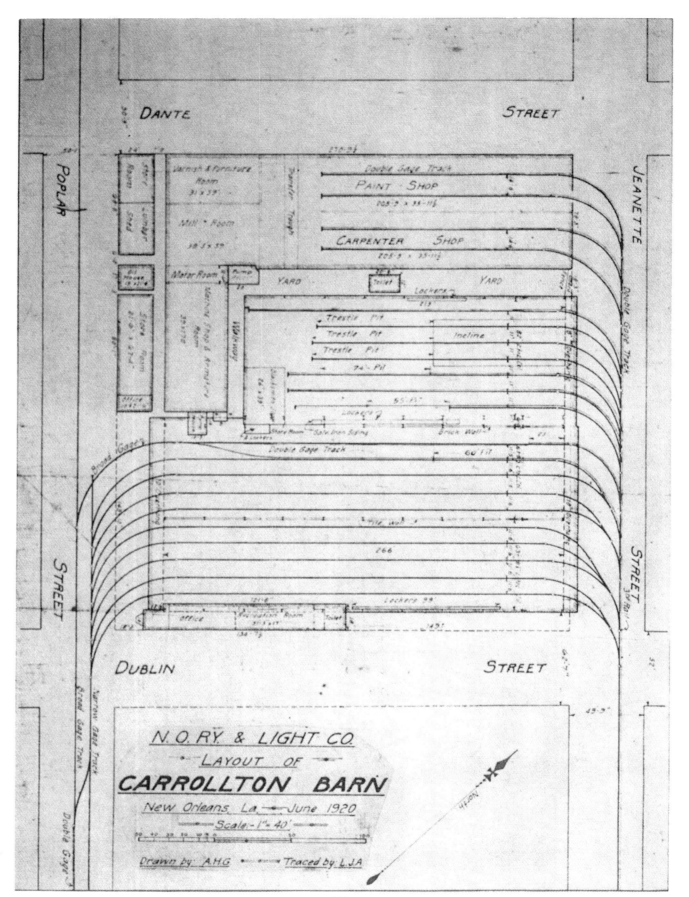

N. O. RY. & LIGHT CO.
LAYOUT OF
CARROLLTON BARN
New Orleans, La. — June 1920
Scale - 1" = 40'

Drawn by: A.H.G. — Traced by: L.J.A.

Carrollton Station, about 1925.                                        *Courtesy N.O.P.S.I.*

*Courtesy Otto A. Goessl*

September 4, 1951. Both Claiborne and St. Charles Lines were using Carrollton Station. Cars 818, 817, and 839 rest on Jeanette St. test track after morning rush hour.

Line-up of FB&D types at Carrollton Station, 1899.          *Courtesy N.O.P.S.I.*

*Courtesy N.O.P.S.I.*
Claiborne Barn of the Canal & Claiborne RR. Co., corner Urquhart and Lafayette (now Franklin).   Circa 1900.

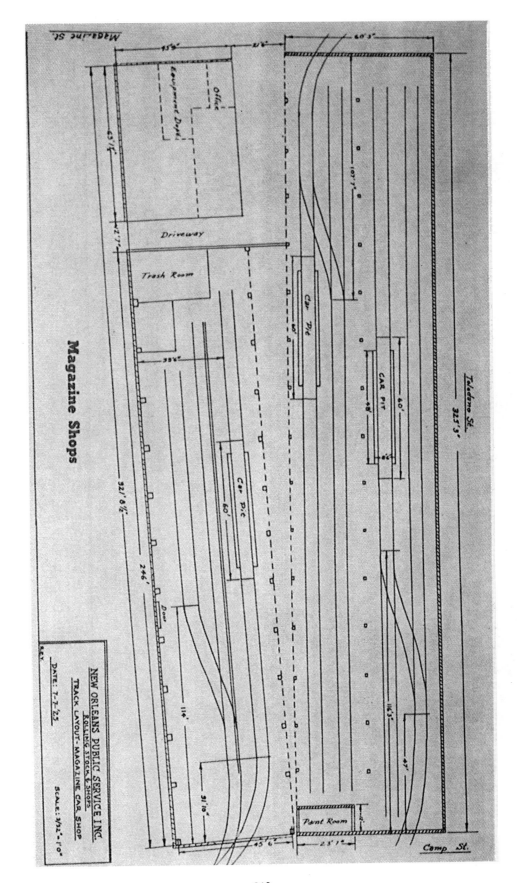

Magazine Shops

NEW ORLEANS PUBLIC SERVICE INC.
ROLLING STOCK & SHOPS
TRACK LAYOUT - MAGAZINE CAR SHOP

DATE: 7-7-'23        SCALE: 1/32"=1'-0"

213

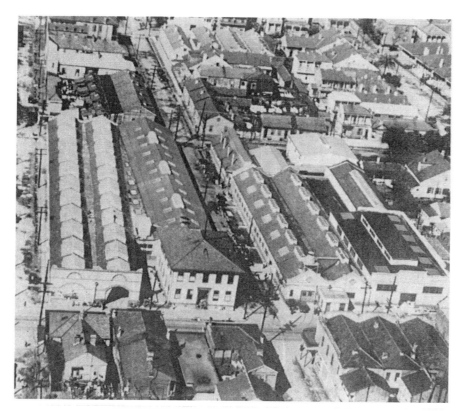

Aerial view Magazine Shops, January 1928.

St. Charles St. RR. Co. barn at Marigny and Decatur Sts., about 1902.

"Cream Cheese" Barn (Orleans RR. Co.) at Grand Route St. John, Gentilly Blvd., and Laharpe Sts., about 1900.

for work equipment and material yard. Abandoned about 1915—gauge, 5' 2½".

*JACKSON:* St. Charles and Felicity—no plan available. This old station saw most of its life as a mule car barn and was used by electric cars only a short while. Thereafter, all N. O. & C. RR. cars were housed in the Carrollton Barn. Date established unavailable, but it is known New Orleans & Carrollton RR. was using it in 1850. Gauge 4' 8½", last used in 1893.

*MAGAZINE:* Magazine and Toledano Streets (see plan, as shops). Established in 1861 by New Orleans City RR. Co. Used as car barn until 1903, when it was rebuilt into main shops for all lines. Lines using it were thereafter housed at Arabella. The Magazine SHOPS

had foundry, plating department, did truck work, made all trolley wheels and performed usual general shop work. Gauge 5' 2½"—closed 1915.

*MARIGNY:* Marigny and Decatur Streets — no plan available. Established 1896 by St. Charles St. RR. Co. when the company electrified. Housed about half of the Clio and Carondelet Lines' cars. Took over company's repair work from 8th Street. Gauge was 5' 2½", last used 1922.

*ORLEANS:* Laharpe, Gentilly Blvd. and North Dupre (no plan available). Established 1868 by Orleans RR. Housed Bayou St. John, Broad, French Market, and French Market-City Park (later City Park) cars. Did general servicing and repair work until about 1904

Prytania Barn, about 1930. Shed once covered four tracks at left.

when Magazine Shop took over. Gauge 5′ 2½″, closed down Jan. 2, 1922 (cars transferred to Canal Barn).

*POLAND:* St. Claude and Poland Avenues (see plan). New Orleans City RR. Co. opened this barn in 1861, one of the three largest barns in the city. Housed many of the downtown lines at one time or another, among which were: Dauphine, Levee-Barracks, France, Desire, Claiborne, Gentilly, and St. Claude (and for a time, Villere).

Gauge 5′ 2½″ originally, double gauged 1915 to accomodate Claiborne cars. Changed to wide gauge in 1926 and discontinued November 25, 1934. Cars were transferred to Canal Barn.

*PRYTANIA:* Prytania and Robert Streets (see plan). Established in 1884 by New Orleans City & Lake RR. Co. and used exclusively for Prytania Line until 1922, when Clio, and Carondelet cars were housed there. This was strictly a "station"—no car repairing, only storing and servicing. Gauge 5′ 2½″, closed down 1932.

*NAPOLEON SERVICE AND MATERIAL YARD:* Located at foot of Napoleon at Tchoupitoulas Street. Dates from 1893 when New Orleans & Carrollton RR. Co. built a power house on the site. In 1915, coincident

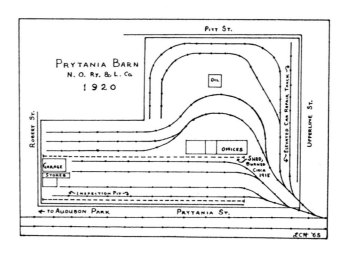

with abandonment of Esplanade Yard, Napoleon became chief yard of system. Gauge was 5′ 2½″.

In the last months of the Napoleon Line, this yard housed that line's cars. Afterwards, the Brown hoist was stored there without any physical connection with other rails. Today, a few rails remain, but even the Brown hoist is gone. The yard is used to train bus drivers today. Also, Car 453 is located there and is used to train motormen.

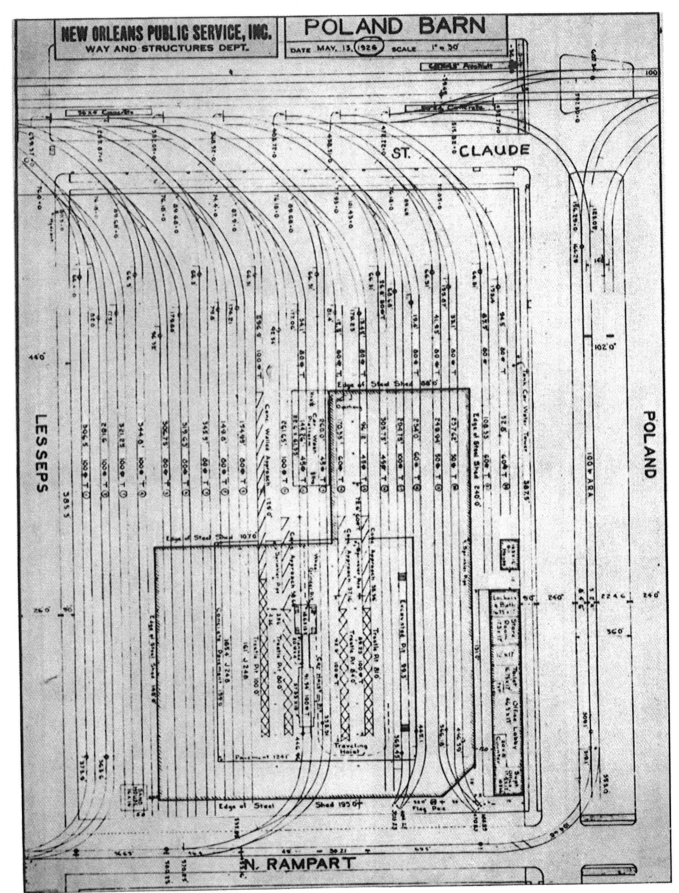

N.O.Ry. & L. Co. Poland Barn in 1917, reconstructed after 1916 hurricane.    *Courtesy N.O.P.S.I.*

Poland barn of N.O.C.RR.Co. before 1916 Hurricane, circa 1902.    *Courtesy N.O.P.S.I.*

GE motor at work, April 18, 1955.                    *William B. Harry Photo*

## CHAPTER 8

# SEWERAGE AND WATER BOARD

A little known New Orleans electric railway was the Sewerage & Water Board's trolley freight line. When the city built its water purification plant in 1908 on Eagle Street between Spruce Street and Claiborne Avenue, it built its own standard gauge electric railway down Eagle Street to the steam railroad tracks alongside the river. Original electric and compressed air locomotives remained in service on the S. & W.B. until diesel engines entered the scene in 1959.

Mr. Frank Haas, Superintendent of the Water Purification Plant for many years, kindly supplied a detailed description of the S. & W.B. operation and equipment. Mr. Haas is an old New Orleans hand, having graduated from the Boys' High School in 1901, and from Tulane in 1905.

Electric operation began with the completion and opening of the Water Purification plant in 1908. The Board's first freight engine was No. 50, built by Westinghouse and Baldwin in July, 1907, bearing Baldwin plate No. 31285. In the 1920's, a Porter compressed air four wheel locomotive was purchased second hand. The engine was built in 1915, came to the Board with a three stage air compressor for filling the locomotive's three tanks to a maximum pressure of 1,000 pounds

per square inch. The compressed air engine shunted cars on plant trackage not under trolley wire, also relieved No. 50 when the electric engine was under repair.

A 1910 GE electric engine was purchased second hand from the Gulfport & Mississippi Coast Traction Co. in the late 1920's. This was the Board's second and last electric freight engine, No. 65.

The Sewerage & Water Board has some special service rail equipment, also. There is No. 25, a 1920 model Industrial Works (Bay City, Mich.) eight-wheel crane, electric powered, but originally steam. S. & W.B. converted the crane to electric trolley operation, yet the old steam boiler is still in place, but unusable. There is one additional crane on rails on top of the boiler roof, sixty feet up. The crane was placed there in 1928 to help install new boilers that had to be raised and lowered through the boiler room roof. Mr. Haas reminds us the crane is now used to raise heaters for cleaning, and that the crane will probably remain in use forever.

Other equipment includes: one eight-wheel flat car, originally an oil car (oil tank removed, buried for use

219

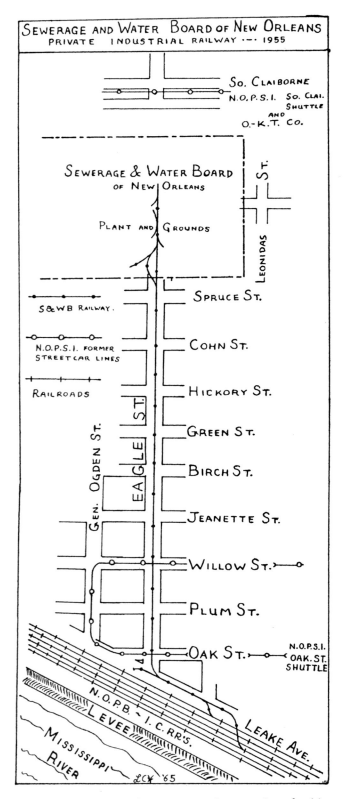

So. CLAIBORNE
N.O.P.S.I. So. CLAI.
SHUTTLE
AND
O.-K.T. CO.

SEWERAGE & WATER BOARD
OF NEW ORLEANS

PLANT AND GROUNDS

LEONIDAS ST.

SPRUCE ST.

S & W B RAILWAY.

COHN ST.

N.O.P.S.I. FORMER
STREETCAR LINES

HICKORY ST.

RAILROADS

GREEN ST.

BIRCH ST.

GEN. OGDEN ST.

EAGLE ST.

JEANETTE ST.

WILLOW ST.

PLUM ST.

OAK ST.

N.O.P.S.I.
OAK. ST.
SHUTTLE

N.O.P.B. - I.C. RR'S.

LEVEE

LEAKE AVE.

MISSISSIPPI
RIVER

LCK '65

*Courtesy Wilbur T. Golson*

**No. 50, S&WB's Baldwin-Westinghoue motor, January 1960. Electric operation ceased June 1959.**

and, two hopper cars, Nos. 101 and 102. No. 101 is kept full of coal in case emergency fuel is needed. No. 102 needs new sides and body.

Only the electric engines left the plant grounds in normal service. During the last years of electric operation, the engines could not be identified by number, as the two machines had been repaired and repainted, without numbers. Both engines were about the same size, but the heavier one (No. 65) had strengthening ribs cast on chassis ends and sides.

Additional data on crane No. 25: Capacity with jack beams, 40,000 lbs. at 13' radius; 8,600 lbs. at 45'. radius; and without the jack beams, 40,000 lbs. at 12' 3" radius; 7,100 lbs. at 45' radius.

The crane on the boiler room roof has a capacity of 15 tons at 12' radius, down to 2.7 tons at 50' radius. It has no outriggers.

The two electric locomotives bear a good resemblance to mining locomotives below the sills, while their cabs were probably home-made. In fact, No. 65 was classed as a mining locomotive in the GE Instruction Manual, which also credited the engine with serial No. 1985, rating LS-209-B2, voltage 500. Electric current on the S. & W.B. was 600 volts DC, supplied by the City of New Orleans' own generating plant.

as fuel oil service tank), with chassis strengthened with cross beams for hauling heavy machinery within the plant grounds; one cinder car, without sides, used in emergency only. Plant uses natural gas, and can use pulverized coal or fuel oil—hence, no cinder problems;

*Courtesy H. K. Vollrath*

S&WB 65, built 1910 by GE for Gulfport & Mississippi Coast Traction Co. GE instruction manual classed it as mining loco. No. 65 had serial No. 1985, rating LS-209-B2, voltage 500.

*R. J. Anderson Photo*

Industrial Works crane, built 1920. Converted to electric trolley operation by S&WB, steam boiler retained. Inactive when photographed in 1948.

Porter compressed air locomotive, stored and dead, May 1963. Builder No. 5731, acquired second hand by Sewerage & Water Board in 1915.

The OK - LR&N wreck, looking up LR&NCo tracks toward Lake, Nov. 18, 1926.  *Chas. L. Franck Photo, Taken by A. Pelle*

## Statistics and Final Compendiums

*Important Dates in Louisiana Electric Traction*

| | First Mule Car | Last Mule Car | First Electric Car | Last Electric Car |
|---|---|---|---|---|
| Alexandria | Feb 16, 1891 | 1900? | Feb. 26, 1906 | Dec. 18, 1926 |
| Algiers | 1882 | Aug. 31, 1907 | Sep. 1, 1907 | Jan. 23, 1931 |
| Baton Rouge | Oct. 16, 1890 | Apr. 4, 1893 | Apr. 5, 1893 | Apr. 23, 1936 |
| Lake Charles | 1891 | 1905/1906 | Feb. 1, 1906 | June 29, 1927 |
| Monroe | -------- | -------- | June 15, 1906 | Aug. 21, 1938 |
| New Orleans | Jan. 1835 | 1899 | Feb. 1, 1893 | (Still oper.) |
| Shreveport | Jan. 1, 1871 | July 26, 1899 | Sep. 20, 1890 | Dec. 10, 1939 |
| Burnside | 1900 | 1922 | -------- | -------- |
| Orleans-Kenner | -------- | -------- | Feb. 28, 1915 | Dec. 31, 1930 |
| St. Tammany & N. O. | -------- | -------- | June 1915 | June 1918 |
| S. W. Traction & Pwr. | -------- | -------- | May 24, 1912 | June 1918 |
| Bogalusa (Industrial) | -------- | -------- | 1928 | (Still oper.) |
| Sewerage & Water Board Purification Plant, New Orleans (freight) | -------- | -------- | 1908 | June 1959 |

*Span of Operation — Electric Lines Only*

| | | |
|---|---|---|
| Alexandria | 1906 to 1926 | 20 years |
| Algiers | 1907 to 1931 | 24 " |
| Baton Rouge | 1893 to 1936 | 43 " |
| Lake Charles | 1906 to 1927 | 21 " |
| Monroe | 1906 to 1938 | 32 " |
| New Orleans | 1893 to | (Still operating, 72 years as of 1965) |
| Shreveport | 1890 to 1939 | 49 " |
| Orleans-Kenner | 1915 to 1930 | 15 " |
| St. Tammany & N. O. | 1915 to 1918 | 3 " (started 1909 as gas-powered line) |
| Sewerage & Water Board (freight) | 1908 to 1959 | 51 " |
| S. W. Traction & Pwr. | 1912 to 1918 | 6 " |
| Bogalusa (Industrial) | 1928 to | (Still operating, 37 years as of 1965) |

## LOUISIANA STREET AND INTERURBAN RAILWAY MILEAGES

| Location (or company) | 1835 | 1850 | 1861 | 1871 | 1880 | 1890 | 1900 | 1910 | 1915 | 1920 | 1930 | 1940 | 1950 | 1964 |
|---|---|---|---|---|---|---|---|---|---|---|---|---|---|---|
| Alexandria | 0 | 0 | 0 | 0 | 0 | 1.3 | 0 | 4.5 | 5.5 | 6.1 | 0 | 0 | 0 | 0 |
| Algiers | 0 | 0 | 0 | 0 | 0 | 3.3 | 3.8 | 4.3 | 9.3 | 9.3 | 4.0 | 0 | 0 | 0 |
| Baton Rouge | 0 | 0 | 0 | 0 | 0 | 3.5 | 3.6 | 3.6 | 6.4 | 6.4 | 9.6 | 0 | 0 | 0 |
| Lake Charles | 0 | 0 | 0 | 0 | 0 | 1.3 | 2.1 | 7.6 | 8.2 | 8.2 | 0 | 0 | 0 | 0 |
| Monroe | 0 | 0 | 0 | 0 | 0 | 0 | 0 | 9.7 | 8.9 | 9.0 | 8.0 | 0 | 0 | 0 |
| New Orleans | 8.8 | 8.5 | 40.3 | 77.0 | 125.0 | 141.0 | 177.2 | 201.3 | 217.4 | 222.1 | 172.7 | 109.0 | 48.0 | 15.0 |
| Shreveport | 0 | 0 | 0 | 3.00 | 1.4 | 7.7 | 9.0 | 15.0 | 30.5 | 30.5 | 35.2 | 0 | 0 | 0 |
| Burnside | 0 | 0 | 0 | 0 | 0 | 0 | .2 | .2 | .2 | .2 | 0 | 0 | 0 | 0 |
| OrleansKenner Line | 0 | 0 | 0 | 0 | 0 | 0 | 0 | 0 | 10.5 | 11.9 | 10.5 | 0 | 0 | 0 |
| St. Tammany & N.O. | 0 | 0 | 0 | 0 | 0 | 0 | 0 | 13.6 | 13.6 | 0 | 0 | 0 | 0 | 0 |
| S. W. Traction & Pwr. | 0 | 0 | 0 | 0 | 0 | 0 | 0 | 0 | 14.2 | 0 | 0 | 0 | 0 | 0 |
| | 8.8 | 8.5 | 40.3 | 80.0 | 126.4 | 157.9 | 196.3 | 259.8 | 324.7 | 303.7 | 240.2 | 109.0 | 48.0 | 15.0 |

NOTE: New Orleans mileage does not include the following; Jefferson & Lake Pontchartrain Ry. Co. 4.1 mi. 1853-1864), Pontchartrain RR. Co. 4.96 mi. (1830-1935), New Orleans Terminal Co. (ex-New Orleans & Western RR.) passenger operation 7.25 mi. (1896-1920); New Orleans Spanish Fort & Lake (ex-Canal St. City Park & Lake) 6.7 mi. (1875-1903); and Sewerage & Water Board electric freight line. .95 mi. (1908-1959).

The electric railway (private) at Bogalusa is not listed—one mile of track, still operating.

# VITAL STATISTICS

## New Orleans — Street Railways

| Year | Population | St. Ry. Mileage | Passengers Carried | Auto Registration | Rides per Capita |
|------|-----------|-----------------|--------------------|-------------------|------------------|
| 1840 | 102,193 | 7.7 | N/A | -0- | N/A |
| 1850 | 116,375 | 8.5 | N/A | -0- | N/A |
| 1861 | 170,000 (e) | 40.3 | N/A | -0- | N/A |
| 1870 | 191,418 | 77.0 | N/A | -0- | N/A |
| 1880 | 216,090 | 125.0 | 23,716,327 | -0- | 109 |
| 1890 | 242,039 | 141.0 | 30,510,662 | -0- | 126 |
| 1900 | 287,104 | 177.2 | 53,184,273* | N/A | 185 |
| 1910 | 339,075 | 201.3 | 80,408,085 | N/A | 237 |
| 1915 | 364,000 (e) | 217.4 | 83,184,938 | N/A | 229 |
| 1920 | 387,219 | 222.1 | 109,927,440 | N/A | 206 |
| 1924 | 422,000 (e) | 221.0 | 145,156,000 | 29,200 | 344 |
| 1925 | 430,000 (e) | 219.0 | 145,676,056 | 37,300 | 338 |
| 1926 | 435,000 (e) | 209.0 | 148,488,286 | 39,100 | 340 |
| 1929 | 450,000 (e) | 174.0 | 96,898,277** | 48,000 | 211** |
| 1930 | 458,762 | 172.0 | 116,207,798 | 53,100 | 253 |
| 1935 | 474,000 (e) | 124.7 | 102,000,000 | 54,000 | 215 |
| 1940 | 494,537 | 109.0 | 124,000,000 | 68,700 | 250 |
| 1945 | 520,000 (e) | 108.0 | 246,668,635 | 70,900 | 474*** |
| 1950 | 570,445 | 48.0 | 216,817,236 | 103,300 | 380 |
| 1960 | 627,525 | 25.0 | 164,075,000 | 180,000 | 261 |

NOTES:
  * This figure is for 1902.
 ** The year 1929 witnessed a lengthy strike.  Many lines abandoned; mileage fell from 191 to 174.
*** World War II.
(e) Estimated
N/A Not available

*Courtesy N.O.P.S.I.*

Mule car barns, Algiers Gouldsboro & Gretna RR.  Only double end mule cars in New Orleans found in research.  Note front AND rear platforms, and umbrella posts (rare for mule cars).  Photo circa 1900.

## Interesting Projected Street Railways

The story of New Orleans' street railways would not be complete without mentioning other projected but never built street railways not covered in Chapter 1. Below are listed eight such bright but hapless ventures.

1. *Mr. J. Arrowsmith:* March 23, 1835, this New Orleanian secured a city ordinance to build a street railway on Orleans Street from St. Claude to the cemeteries near Bayou St. John. Transportation free, city subsidy. According to Gibson's *Guide and Directory to The State of Louisiana and The Cities of New Orleans and Lafayette,* 1838 issue, the street railway out Orleans Street was at least completed insofar as track is concerned. To quote, from page 240: "The Orleans Street (sic) Rail Road is a mile and half long and cost (sic) already $12,000.00, but owing to the supine-ness or culpability of the first municipality council, it is useless to the public, and a dead loss to the owner. It was intended as a route to the grave-yard." The New Orleans *Bee* reported on March 18, 1836 that "The Orleans Street RR. will commence with hourly service and a 12¼c fare." It is doubtful the ill-fated line lasted a year.

2. *Butchers & Drovers RR. Co. of (the City of) New Orleans:* Louisiana Legislature Act. 209, March 21, 1861, approved a mule car line from Water and Harmony Streets, down Water Street to drainage canal in rear of 4th District, thence along levee until intersection with N. O. J. & G. N. RR.

3. *Upper City RR. Co.:* Chartered November 17, 1873 to run through 4th District from River to Roman Street (N. O. City Ordinance A.S. 2519). Charter signed by Mr. Edmund H. Adams, Mr. Norman Griswold, and Mr. Wm. Bogel.

4. *Exposition Ry. & Improvement Co., The:* Chartered February 28, 1884 by Mr. Henry Shaw, Mr. Victor Meyer, Mr. Samuel P. Blanc, and Mr. Thomas L. Airey—planned a railway from downtown New Orleans to the Exposition Grounds (Audubon Park). Rights purchased by the Canal Street & Exposition Ry. Co. December 4, 1884.

5. *Canal Street & Exposition Ry. Co.:* Same plans as E. Ry. & I. Co. Chartered November 19, 1884. Officers were: Mr. Jno. A. Grant, Mr. E. B. Wheelock, and Samuel H. Kennedy.

6. *New Orleans Elevated Ry. Co.:* Chartered April 7, 1883 by same group chartering The Exposition Ry. & Improvement Co. Planned an elevated railway along Mississippi River levee from downtown to the Exposition Grounds. Company tried to sell 50,000 shares of stock to achieve a capitalization of $5,000,000.

7. *New Orleans Rapid Transit Ry. Co., The:* Chartered September 10, 1884 and authorized by city ordinance C.C. 771 of July 8, 1884—planned by Mr. Henry Shaw and associates. This was one of the four projected but never built lines contemporaneus with the New Orleans World Cotton Exposition of 1884-85.

8. *Canal & Audubon Park Street Ry. Co.:* Chartered November 15, 1892 by Mr. M. J. and Samuel J. Hart, and Mr. Emile Morlat. No other data available.

Two maps in the 1850's show a street railway in Peters Avenue from St. Charles to Tchoupitoulas. Research could discover nothing further.

Another street railway name that may creep near to confuse us is the Citizens Railroad Company. No charter could be found. This organization tried to secure a franchise for the Poydras-Magazine Line in 1834—but the C. RR. Co. failed. The New Orleans & Carrollton RR. Co., of course, got that franchise.

There possibly were other organizations and companies that secured charters, rights, ordinances, and franchises to operate street railways in the city; the above are mentioned to clarify any confusion that may arise at their mention. All such companies either died on paper or were absorbed by the operating street railway systems.

# BIBLIOGRAPHY

The most difficult material to research were car line service changes, the dates car lines began service, were electrified, then were either merged, re-routed, or discontinued. The following sources provided this type of data:

From 1831 to 1836, The Louisiana *Advertiser,* The New Orleans *Bee,* and the *Commercial Bulletin,* all three New Orleans newspapers.

From 1837 to 1872, The New Orleans *Daily Picayune.*

From 1872 to 1914, The New Orleans *Times,* later New Orleans *Times-Democrat.*

From 1893 to 1897, electrification dates from N.O.P.S.I. records, verified in New Orleans *Times-Democrat.*

After 1914, all service changes from N.O.P.S.I. records. Service changes, such as re-routings and mergers, after 1897 and before 1914, from N.O.P.S.I. verified in New Orleans *Times-Democrat.*

Equipment data and car assignments were from N.O.P.S.I. records for Charlton's 1955 work as well as for this volume.

## Other sources were, as follows:

Allison, James E. & Co., St. Louis, Mo. "Report on the Street Railway Service in New Orleans", July 16, 1919.

Bayley, G.W.R. "History of the Railroads of Louisiana", Volume 30, Louisiana Historical Quarterly, a reprint from New Orleans *Daily Picayune.*

Blain, Hugh Mercer, "A Near Century of Public Service in New Orleans", N.O.P.S.I., New Orleans, 1927.

Beeler, John A., "Report to Commissioner of Public Utilities of the City of New Orleans", New York, 1923.

Charlton, E. Harper, "Street Railways of New Orleans", Interurbans Special Number 17, Los Angeles, Cal., 1955.

Electric Railway Journal (later Street Railway Journal).

Electric Railway Review (Street Railway Review), Wilson Co., Chicago, Ill.

National Association of Manufacturers, "New Orleans Street Railway Strike 1929-30", New York, N. Y. 1930.

Supreme Court of Louisiana, 8th District, "James H. Young vs. Magazine Street Railroad Company No. 12" and "Magazine Street Railroad Company vs. James H. Young, No. 13", *Brief of the Company.*

United States Census Report, 1880.

Mass Transportations' Directory, Chicago, Ill.

McGraw Electric Railway List, McGraw-Hill Co., Inc., New York, N. Y.

Moody's Manual of Public Utilities, New York, N. Y.

Poors Manual of Public Utilities and Manual of Railroads, New York, N. Y.

The Official Guide of the Railways, National Railway Publishing Co., New York, N. Y.

# INDEX

LaVergne, TN USA
21 June 2010
186855LV00001B/3/A